JIHADI JOHN

JIHADI JOHN

ROBERT VERKAIK

ONEWORLD

A Oneworld Book

First published in Great Britain, North America and
Australia by Oneworld Publications, 2016

Copyright © Robert Verkaik 2016

ISBN 978-1-78074-943-3
eISBN 978-1-78074-944-0

Typeset by Hewer Text UK Ltd, Edinburgh
Printed and bound by Clays Ltd, St Ives plc

Oneworld Publications
10 Bloomsbury Street
London WC1B 3SR
England

Stay up to date with the latest books,
special offers, and exclusive content from
Oneworld with our monthly newsletter

Sign up on our website
www.oneworld-publications.com

CONTENTS

PROLOGUE

There is a surreal moment, quite early on in the now infamous video of the execution of American journalist James Foley, when the masked killer momentarily loses his balance and stumbles sideways towards his victim. It is a single misstep which belies the horror of what is about to follow. Yet for a second or two as the two figures stare out of the screen – the kneeling Foley dressed in an orange jumpsuit and his knife-wielding assassin all in black – this unexpected stumble raises the hope that the footage might be staged and what we are witnessing is a cartoon killing. And then Jihadi John recovers and it is all too apparent that what we are being asked to watch is not make-believe, but an act of savagery as horrifying and disturbing as it is possible to witness.

As James Foley prepares for his fate his bottom lip wobbles involuntarily and then the killer places his right hand under the victim's chin. What happens next is so merciless and lacking in humanity that with one single hack of his knife Jihadi John changes the definition of terrorism, obliterating our safe assumptions about what one human is capable of in the twenty-first century.

In early 2014 the terror group now called Islamic State (IS) began to pool its growing collection of Western journalists and aid workers, which it had abducted or purchased from other jihadists and criminal gangs in Syria. The group's leader, Abu Bakr al-Baghdadi, ordered that they should all be taken to the city of Raqqa in the north east of the country. This ancient Syrian settlement on the banks of the Euphrates had been founded by the Greeks and was once a jewel in the crown of the Byzantine Empire, but now it was the benighted capital of the Islamic State's self-declared caliphate. Raqqa was to be the home, and for some the final resting place, of twenty-three prisoners from twelve countries, each of whom was to be ransomed or executed for political and financial gain. Among their number was James Foley, who had been captured close to the Syria–Turkey border while reporting on the Middle East conflict. Foley had teamed up with a British photo-journalist for a reporting assignment in Syria in 2012. In November that year they had stopped off at an internet café in Binesh, close to the Turkish border, to file their work. As they busied themselves uploading their film and pictures a man with a long, bushy beard came into the café and sat down at one of the computers. According to witnesses he eyed the foreigners closely, then got up and left the café abruptly. The two journalists spent another hour sending material back to the Western news outlets for whom they worked. Then they went outside the café to look for a taxi to take them back across the border and a well-earned rest from their intrepid reporting. As they approached the safety of Turkey a van sped up on the left side of the taxi and cut it off. Masked fighters jumped out. They shouted at the journalists to lie on the ground beside the taxi. They handcuffed them and bundled them into the van. Both men had become prisoners of a breakaway faction of an al-Qaeda-linked terror group, Jabhat al-Nusra, who later handed them over to the Islamic State.

The prisoners were incarcerated next to an oil installation

near the river Euphrates. In charge were three British jihadis, later given the name 'the Beatles' by the hostages, on account of their British accents and because of the pleasure they took in 'beating' their prisoners.

By 2014 Foley was already a veteran, having survived a year in the hands of the jihadists. A year of captivity had left him very thin, and he sported a long, bushy beard. He had converted to Islam, taking the Islamic name of Abu Hamza. Foley had been held by Libyan militants two years earlier, while reporting on the downfall of Gaddafi. Then, his Western nationality had protected him from the vengeance of his kidnappers. Now, his American citizenship meant he was to be singled out for a special kind of brutality invented by a new brand of jihadist.

The twenty-three hostages were kept together in a block of underground rooms which they shared with their jailers. They were given the equivalent of just a teacup of food each day.[1] Their confinement was spent in almost total darkness, except in one basement room, where a finger of sunlight stretched under the locked door. After dusk, they could not see anything and often spilled their meagre rations over themselves. They had no mattresses and few blankets. Some of the prisoners used their trousers as makeshift pillows by tying one end and filling the trouser legs with rags.[2]

Under such conditions, the prisoners sometimes turned on one another. But James Foley, despite being on the receiving end of the most savage of the punishments, knew how important it was to maintain morale. He often shared his food with his colleagues. In the bitter cold of the Syrian winter, he even offered one prisoner his only blanket. He took charge of group entertainment, encouraging home-made board games and storytelling. The others relied on him to boost their flagging spirits.

Yet he was the one who also suffered the most. A Spanish journalist, Javier Espinosa, spent many months with Foley as a fellow prisoner of the Islamic State. The two men became close friends. Espinosa recalls his shock at seeing his friend after a long separation: 'His body could not hide the long months of starvation – he looked older and thinner, but he retained the unbreakable spirit which characterized him.'[3]

Foley continued to make the best of his situation and clung to dreams of release. While America had stayed out of the conflict and held back its armed forces, Foley reckoned he had every reason to hope for the best. Sadly, as time went on, an increasingly belligerent American Congress sought justification to unleash its military might against a rampant Islamic State which had swept across huge swathes of north Syria and north Iraq, meaning that the longer he was held, the poorer his chances got.

On 7 August 2014 President Obama authorized American airstrikes in Iraq to rescue the stranded Yazidi minorities and protect US personnel and facilities in Irbil and Baghdad. After a short campaign amounting to a total of sixty-eight strikes from jets, bombers and drones, Obama declared that Iraqi and Kurdish forces, with US air support, had retaken a strategic dam north of Mosul and had pushed back the frontline beyond Irbil.

Within hours of that announcement, the Islamic State posted an online message warning it would attack Americans 'in any place' in response to the airstrikes. 'We will drown all of you in blood,' it said.

Foley and the other hostages must have sensed the tension among their captors as the 'Beatles' took out their frustrations in beatings and torture. The cat-and-mouse negotiations between the Americans and the Islamic State were reaching their endgame. But Foley refused to give up on the hope of release. What he could not have known was that his captors had placed such an unrealistically high price on his head that freedom was no longer an option. The Islamic State negotiators had told the Foley family in an email that, if they ever wanted to see their son again, they would need to find $132 million. All the while, President Obama repeated his government's time-honoured mantra that America would not negotiate with terrorists.

When the jihadists came for Foley in the early hours of an August morning, there was real intent in what his jailors had planned for him. It was immediately apparent that this was not the latest round of the usual torture. Foley was dressed in an orange jumpsuit and his hands were cuffed behind his back. He was dragged onto a flatbed truck, which sped off through the back roads of Raqqa.[4]

There would have been plenty of residents on the streets to witness the convoy of vehicles as it crested the top of the hill and headed to a desert location south of the city.[5] Slumped on the back of the truck in plain sight, Foley served as a warning to the people of Raqqa that the city's new overlords would show no mercy. What happened next was played out on a video which the Islamic State released on 19 August 2014, entitled 'A Message to America'. Its message sent shockwaves around the world.

A masked man dressed in black is shown standing in an unidentified desert location beside a kneeling prisoner whose hands are tied behind his back. The masked man speaks: 'Obama authorized military operations against the Islamic State, effectively placing America upon a slippery slope towards a new war against Muslims.' The video then reprises a clip of Obama's announcement, followed by a statement from the prisoner, who addresses the camera in quivering tones: 'I call on my friends, family and loved ones to rise up against my real killers, the US government, for what will happen to me is only a result of their complacent criminality,' he says. He asks his parents not to accept 'any meagre compensation from the same people who effectively hit the last nail in my coffin with the recent aerial campaign in Iraq.'

Then Foley appeals to 'my brother John, who is a member of the US Air Force,' to 'think about what you are doing. I wish I had more time,' Foley says. 'I wish I could have the hope for freedom to see my family once again, but that ship has sailed. I guess all in all, I wish I wasn't an American.'

The masked jihadi identifies the prisoner as 'James Wright Foley, an American citizen of your country.' He then reaches down with a large, black knife and begins the beheading of the prisoner. The screen fades to black and the next image is of a body with a head placed upon its chest.

The sudden, grotesque act of Foley's beheading was shocking and mesmerizing in equal measure. It forced people to confront the stark truth that there were men alive in the world today who were capable of acts of savagery once thought consigned to the Middle Ages.

After the revulsion came the questions. Who was this hooded man who spoke with an English accent but bore such hatred for the West that he could stand in front of a camera and cut off another man's head?

In the following days, weeks and months, the search for the identity of the murderer became an obsession of the media – and especially the tabloid press. After each video of each grisly beheading, beamed around the world in horrifyingly graphic detail by the world's biggest broadcasters, my editor would wearily ask the same question. Do you know who Jihadi John is? In turn I would offer names to the police and the government in a quest to uncover the identity of the British terrorist who was now the Islamic State's executioner-in-chief and for many the very personification of evil.

In the vacuum of any identifying information, newspapers filled the void by carrying a welter of false stories declaring Jihadi

John to be one of many vocal Islamic State jihadists tweeting from inside Syria. Many of these terrorists extolled the barbarity of Jihadi John and made their own blood-curdling threats against the West directly on social media. But one by one each of these putative Jihadi Johns was met with a categorical denial by the authorities. I was sure the security services knew who he was but short of them telling me (which they had made perfectly clear they wouldn't) or heading out to Syria to find him myself, I regarded the fevered speculation as to his identity to be a waste of my journalistic time. After six months of getting nowhere I was sick of the very mention of Jihadi John, believing his identity would never be known. Then, on 26 February 2015, I received a call from a contact saying the BBC had finally uncovered his identity and was about to reveal Jihadi John to be Mohammed Emwazi – a 26-year-old Muslim from west London.

It wasn't a name I recognised. I had followed the story because I am a journalist specializing in security, increasingly thinking it unlikely that I would find anything to contribute. And now that his identity had been revealed I felt just as useless when Fleet Street news editors asked me whether I could throw any light on Mohammed Emwazi. The name of the Islamic State's executioner-in-chief meant nothing to me.

Two days later, at five o'clock on a Saturday afternoon, I was sitting in a restaurant on London's South Bank where I was filing copy about Emwazi to the *Mail on Sunday* news desk. I had based myself there all day in the hope that a contact would agree to talk to me about his knowledge of Emwazi. But he hadn't turned up so I was cobbling together a story about the Emwazi network based on an old court document. It was close to deadline and the news editor wasn't particularly impressed with my offering for Sunday's paper.

Just before I was about to send over my story a human rights group released a series of emails all written to Emwazi, under an alias he had been using when he was in London. One of these emails was written by me. It began: 'Good to see you yesterday, Mohammed . . .' and it stopped me in my tracks. This single, long-forgotten email from me to Emwazi had suddenly rendered meaningless the Jihadi John story I was about to file. And as my mind raced it quickly dawned on me that I was now the story. This email, along with several others sitting in my inbox from 2010–11, proved I already knew the person the world's media had spent the summer searching for. I started to feel anxious and excited at the same time. I desperately racked my memory for an image of the man I had met and interviewed. But as hard as I tried I just couldn't picture him. It was as if the video footage of the masked Jihadi John had obliterated all other images I had once had of Mohammed Emwazi. As I reread the email I couldn't recall writing it or sending it. Every time I tried to remember the man I had met in December 2010 all I could see was the obscured face of the IS executioner. It was only in the days that followed that I was able to use emails and snapped recollections to put a human face to Jihadi John.

The man I had known five years ago was polite and helpful. He showed empathy for me and my work as a journalist and he had trusted me by sharing very personal details about his life. He had confided in me about his relationship break-ups, his work woes and his conviction that he was an innocent citizen being unfairly persecuted. He desperately wanted his story to be told as he felt that MI5 was destroying his life. He had recently sold his laptop on the internet, and now believed it had been purchased by the security services. He was under so much stress that he often felt like a 'dead man walking' and once even emailed me to say he was thinking of taking his own life.

How could this young Muslim man, who had appeared to me as a victim, have gone on to carry out such horrific acts of butchery? How could this embodiment of evil be the same man who had sat with me complaining about his girlfriend troubles?

The police and MI5 had serious concerns about Emwazi as long ago as 2009, well before the emergence of the Islamic State. When I knew Mohammed Emwazi he was a troubled young man but I do not believe he was yet capable of murder. In many ways, he was no different from other young Muslims who had complained to me about harassment from the police and MI5. A small number of them are now locked up in foreign prisons, under tight surveillance by security services, or have been killed taking part in jihadi terrorism. When I knew them they were young men struggling to reconcile their British identities with what they perceived to be a world-wide persecution of Muslims. It would be hard to argue that none of them was interested in Islamist extremism or had contact with known terror suspects. Yet none of these men had a criminal record and all appeared genuine in their wish to lead peaceful lives in the UK.

There are hundreds, maybe thousands, of young Muslim men today wrestling with their plural identities. A tiny number may join terrorist groups, and they must be properly investigated by our security agencies. But the vast majority want to engage in an open dialogue without fear of harassment or intimidation. Official figures put the number of British Muslims who have travelled to Syria and Iraq approaching eight hundred. But the real figure is probably double this. Many of those who have gone to Syria and Iraq seem to hold a sincere belief that they can alleviate the suffering of their brother and sister Muslims. Some have no intention of returning to Britain while others have already slipped back into the UK to quietly resume their lives. A handful now pose a murderous threat to the West. But few of them will ever become the most wanted terrorist in the world.

Hundreds of secret agents and spies were tasked by a host of security agencies in an international manhunt to capture or kill the Islamic State executioner-in-chief, who the media gleefully dubbed Jihadi John. On 13 November 2015 a Pentagon spokesperson revealed that he had been targeted in a drone strike in Raqqa, Syria, the day before, with a Hellfire missile hitting a car travelling through the city. But the question remains how Mohammed Emwazi went from being a quiet teenager living in west London to the public face of the most feared and merciless terror organization in the world.

The British authorities have been accused both of playing a part in Emwazi's radicalization and of not doing enough to stop him from leaving. I too have asked myself whether I should have done more to halt Mohammed Emwazi on his path to terrorism. I met him and engaged with him in his struggles with the British security services. He regarded me as a sympathetic member of the media who had written about similar cases to his own. He had complained to the police, the Kuwaiti embassy and an advocacy group which helps victims of the war on terror. And when all that had failed, he entrusted his faith in me.

CHAPTER 1

MOHAMMED THE OUTSIDER

Mohammed Emwazi's family belonged to the Bedoon or Bidun minority, the people of Kuwait who are not recognized as full citizens. *Bedoon* means 'without' in Arabic and refers to their stateless designation. In the 1950s Emwazi's grandfather was a respected tribal leader, but he had refused to accept a Kuwaiti passport offered by the government during the country's first census, which led to the declaration of independence in 1961. He was, according to a family friend, a proud man who felt confident in his position in tribal society and regarded a passport as little more than a state handout. But his pride and, more importantly, his decision to reject Kuwaiti nationality, would have damaging repercussions for the Emwazis for many generations.[1]

In the 1980s Mohammed Emwazi's father Jassem had overcome his statelessness and found work as a policeman in Tayma'a, a town twenty miles north west of Kuwait City in the district of al-Jahra. According to a family member, Jassem was very proud of his job and had his services to law and order recognized by the Kuwaiti government.[2] The family have kept a certificate presented to Jassem by the Kuwait police force which includes a citation referring to his loyalty and good work.

Tayma'a, or Taima as it is also known, is a ghettoized, urban sprawl where the Bedoon live among corrugated buildings, set apart from the Kuwaiti population. Traditionally Bedoon migrants are taken on as soldiers in the lower ranks of the Kuwaiti army. In the 1980s, those who weren't given a military post often ended up scraping a living selling street food or begging. Jassem was one of the lucky few who escaped the hardships of a life on the fringes of society.[3]

By 1987 his prospects looked even brighter. He met Ghaneya, an immigrant from Yemen, and received her family's blessing to marry her. Friends at the time remember the Emwazis were prosperous enough to hold the ceremony in a large white tent.[4] Ghaneya conceived in the months after the wedding, and the Emwazis had everything they could have hoped for – a good job, a loving family and the unusual freedom to mix with both the Bedoon and the local Kuwaitis.

But in 1989 Kuwait's 200,000-strong Bedoon population faced a sectarian crackdown.[5] The world was in the grip of an economic downturn and Kuwait decided to put the squeeze on the Bedoon, as a sop to the country's own working class struggling under the financial hardships.[6] There was also historical suspicion that the Bedoon held no loyalty to Kuwait and that many still regarded Iraq as their natural home.[7] These long-held resentments fuelled allegations of fifth-columnist penetration linked to a spate of terrorist attacks against the Kuwait government.[8]

And so at a stroke the Bedoon were wiped from Kuwait's official census. Overnight, they were stripped of their rights to passports or other identification papers, leaving them unable to obtain birth, death or marriage certificates.[9] Because of this, the Bedoon were forbidden from holding driving licences, sending their children to school or accessing hospital care. Even housing and social security were denied to them.[10] Any Bedoon with a job had his or her employment status reviewed.[11] Officially the Emwazis, along with the rest of the Kuwaiti Bedoon population, did not exist.[12]

For the Emwazis, who had little Mohammed on the way and were planning life as a new family, the sectarian crackdown represented an extraordinary reversal of fortune. For Jassem personally it meant the real possibility of losing his job and the end of a steady income which the family had come to rely on. This, however, was just the beginning of their troubles, as events in the region were about to take a dramatic turn for the worse.

Iraq's leader, Saddam Hussein, had long harboured territorial ambitions over Kuwait and in 1990 launched a lightning assault, taking Kuwait's complacent generals by surprise. The comparatively small military forces of the oil-rich Gulf state were quickly overwhelmed by the world's fourth largest army. The country's ruler, Sheikh Jaber al-Ahmed al-Sabah, fled into exile in his armour-plated Mercedes, across the desert to neighbouring Saudi Arabia. He was soon followed by Kuwait's wealthy sheikhs, businessmen and anyone else who had the resources to escape. The Kuwaiti state was turned over to the new Iraqi rulers.

For the Bedoon, having recently been made stateless, the situation was particularly dire. Jassem Emwazi, who did not have the funds or contacts to follow the exodus, found himself at the mercy of a brutal regime that had a history of oppressing the Bedoon. The family quickly had to learn how to survive in a martial state that considered the Kuwaiti Bedoon to be traitors and enemies of Iraq.[13] At the same time they had to be equally careful of not falling under the suspicion of Kuwaitis, who suspected the Iraqi Bedoon of helping the invaders.

In February 1991 the American-led coalition forces launched a sustained air and ground assault on Iraqi forces inside Kuwait. It took just four days for Saddam's armies to be cleared from Kuwait but not before a major attack on an Iraqi armoured division stationed on the outskirts of al-Jahra. Thousands of Iraqi soldiers were burned to death in their vehicles when the leader of the coalition forces, General Norman Schwarzkopf, issued orders to blockade a hundred-mile radius of Kuwait City. The retreating Iraqi convoys, stalled on Mutla Ridge on Highway 80 just outside the town, became sitting ducks for the Apache helicopters and fighter-bombers which were launched against them.

While the Americans and their Saudi allies celebrated the vanquishing of Saddam and the alleviation of the threat to oil security, the returning Kuwaitis began the business of settling scores. The authorities acted ruthlessly against the Bedoon, sending thousands to Iraq and into the arms of Saddam. Although the Emwazis, who had no real links with Iraq, escaped deportation, they remained discriminated against and lived in constant fear of forced removal.[14]

Given their persecution by domestic authorities just as much as foreign invaders, it is easy to see how a sense of alienation and resentment may have become deeply rooted in the Emwazi family's psyche. Jassem had not entirely given up on Kuwait but over the next few years his prospects became bleaker than ever.[15]

So in 1993 when Mohammed was aged six, the Emwazis decided to take a chance on a new life in the West. They settled on Britain because they had distant relatives who had moved to London and had sent back stories of a city in which many creeds and colours mixed freely with one another.[16] Most importantly, for Jassem, this included the Bedoon, who were not regarded as a pariah people but genuine refugees.

On arrival in the UK the couple put their case for asylum to the Home Office and argued that they had been denied citizenship by Kuwait.[17] The Home Office has published guidance which shows that those who can prove they are Kuwaiti Bedoon will be usually granted refugee status in the UK. However, the guidance by no means guarantees the right to asylum. It makes clear: 'The individual circumstances of Bidoon in Kuwait vary greatly. All can be stigmatized through their lack of status, and the extra difficulty they can face in accessing government services. However some have close links with Kuwaiti families, and possess the support networks, contacts and wealth to circumvent any obstacles.'

The Home Office guidance also sets out the most likely ground for Kuwaiti Bedoon seeking asylum in the UK around the time the Emwazis were living in the Middle East. It says:

Internal instability in the mid-1980s, linked in particular to Kuwaiti support for Iraq against Iran during the Iran–Iraq war, led to a series of bombings, assassination attempts and minor civil disorder, sponsored by Iran. This led to a security clamp-down by the Kuwaiti authorities. In particular, the fact that a small number of Bidoon were implicated in terrorist offences caused the Kuwaiti government to look again at their status.

Britain was aware that some Bedoon had collaborated with Saddam's invasion of Kuwait in 1990 and may have contributed to their own statelessness. The guidance continues: 'Between the mid-1980s and the 1990 Invasion of Kuwait by Iraq, there was a further erosion of the rights of the Bedoon, including the right to free education. Some were directly affected. Others were cushioned by their positions in government service or by other personal connections.'

The government guidance meant that members of the Bedoon entering the UK were not automatically granted asylum and it explicitly authorized immigration staff to ask testing questions about their claims.

The Home Office took three years to deliberate before officials agreed to grant the Emwazi family asylum. Three years is a long time for an immigration case to be settled even factoring in Britain's often grindingly slow legal system. Certainly, three years allowed ample time for immigration case officers to fact-check the Emwazi family's story, and to trace their recent history. The Home Office would not have relied solely on the family's testimony and would have tried to secure independent evidence to prove there was a genuine and well-founded case of persecution in Kuwait. Any suggestion that the Emwazis had supported Iraqi invaders would have helped their case as this would have made it difficult for them to return to Kuwait.

Omar Emwazi, Mohammed's twenty-two year-old younger brother, insists his father was a loyal Kuwaiti citizen who was vehemently opposed to Saddam. 'When the papers tried to say that [he was pro Saddam Hussein], my mum found that certificate [presented to his father by the Kuwaiti police force] to show me what nonsense it was.'

In 1996 the application was accepted by the British immigration officials and the family was finally granted asylum.[18] The Emwazis settled in the affluent west London suburb of Maida Vale, where they had Kuwaiti relatives.[19] But they were by no means affluent themselves. With a young and growing family, the Emwazis moved home four times in the same area. Their first home was a three-bedroomed first floor flat in

Warwick Crescent. From there, they moved to a run-down terrace in nearby Desborough Close, overlooked by council blocks.

Jassem found work as a minicab and delivery van driver while Ghaneya stayed at home with Mohammed, his three younger sisters and his younger brother.[20] Local residents described the family as close and caring, with both parents arriving at the school gate each day to collect their children. They spoke Arabic around the home and attended the local mosque. As in Kuwait, Ghaneya tended to wear traditional Islamic clothes and whenever she left the house she wore a niqab.[21]

But this was not a strict Muslim household. 'They were just normal Muslims, I don't think Mohammed was particularly religious and I don't think the family forced them to be religious,' a family friend told me.[22] In fact, Mohammed went to St Mary Magdalene Church of England primary school.

Interviews with his teachers and fellow pupils show that on the outside he was no different to the other little boys. He liked S Club 7 and wanted to be a professional footballer.[23] When he was ten, Mohammed Emwazi's ambition for his thirty-year-old self was to be 'in a football team and scoring a goal' for his favourite team, Manchester United. In the school yearbook, he lists his favourite computer game as the shoot-'em-up *Duke Nukem: Time to Kill*, and his favourite book was *How to Kill a Monster* from the popular Goosebumps series.[24] His favourite colour was blue, his favourite animal a monkey. He loved eating chips and watching *The Simpsons*.[25]

Although he was usually reserved and dedicated to his religion, he got into occasional fights after school assemblies. One former classmate recalls: 'One time we had an RE lesson and he got up and talked about his religion. He wrote Arabic on the board to show us what it looked like and how it went in the other direction. He showed us a religious text and spoke about what his religion was about.' According to the classmate, who was nine at the time, Mohammed still had a poor grasp of English.[26] 'He could only say a few words at first – like his name and where he was from ... He played football every lunchtime and at the after-school football club. Through football, he learned different words and expressions. Like all the guys, he always wanted to be the striker. He wasn't so good in school, he was the bottom half of the class, but he was one of the sporty guys. He was popular.'[27]

Yet his earliest memories were formed against a backdrop of war and discrimination, an interminable asylum process, a foreign culture and a struggle for acceptance. Mohammed was the only Muslim pupil in the school, his uniform a bright red pullover with a Church of England insignia.[28]

There is a video of the children playing in the school playground. In it Mohammed can be seen playing football with the other boys. But while he is part of the game, he doesn't communicate with the other boys and when the camera pans towards him and someone shouts out 'Emwazi' he tries to cover his face.[29] Another friend has described how he developed a habit of covering his mouth when he spoke after one of the girls had embarrassed him by telling a group of classmates that he had bad breath.

In so many ways, he was a pupil that we would recognize instantly from our own school days, self-conscious and anxious to fit in. But there is one episode from his time at primary school which, if true, may hint at a turning point. A former school friend who phoned the radio station LBC in February 2015 describes the incident:

> We were in the playground and Mohammed was running away from someone, I think he was just about to get into a fight. And as he was running another guy blocked his path.

And he ran into a goal-post and hit his head on a metal goal-post and fell to the floor. This was Year 6, we didn't see him for six weeks. He was not the same ever since that brain injury. I am telling you one million per cent. He was not the same.[30]

The implication appears to be that Emwazi suffered some kind of brain damage when he collided with the goal-post, altering his personality. But I have been unable to find any other evidence to support this claim. Emwazi's family say that he was a normal, shy schoolkid who occasionally got into fights. No one has said that after the accident, or at this time, he became more aggressive or more withdrawn. And even the former school mate makes no effort to link the injury to the psychopathic violence that Emwazi exhibited in the beheading videos.

After leaving his primary school in 1999, Mohammed moved to Quintin Kynaston Community Academy, in St John's Wood, north west London, where he studied alongside former *X Factor* judge and pop star Tulisa Contostavlos. The school had consistently been awarded outstanding ratings from Ofsted, and indeed the Labour government singled it out as a model for secondary education in the capital. For a young immigrant family establishing themselves in London, the Emwazis could not have made a better choice for their son's education.

Tony Blair made two visits to Quintin Kynaston as prime minister in 2003, when he used the school as the venue for launching his children's services green paper. One can only wonder what Mohammed made of Blair's visit to the school in the year that Britain invaded Iraq. It may have been that the Emwazi family in fact sympathized with his war in Iraq. After all they would have known many Iraqi Bedoon families who had been persecuted during Saddam Hussein's reign of terror. But by the time Blair came to Emwazi's school the popular tide had turned against his misadventure in the middle east.

On that visit, Blair was met by fifty anti-war protesters, among them children from the school, who booed him and chanted 'Out, out, out'. (Three years later, he returned to the school to announce his resignation as prime minister, although not before telling staff the school was 'a wonderful inspiration'.)

Mohammed lived with his family on the run-down estate in Desborough Close for four years until 2002, the year his youngest sibling Hana was born. There were now five children to look after and so seeking more space the family moved again, this time to a larger flat in Lisson Grove, not far from Lord's cricket ground.

But Emwazi's favourite sport was football and he was an avid Manchester United fan. His father on the other hand supported Chelsea and the teams' rivalry was a source of banter between father and son. Omar recalls:

He loved playing football. He was very good at playing football. All his friends spoke about how good he was. He used to take us out for football. He supported Man United. I don't know why, I don't know about football. But him and my dad are football hooligans. My dad's a Chelsea fan. So them two were always getting into clashes. He took my dad to watch the Chelsea–Man U. and Chelsea–Liverpool match.

Omar says he remembers one occasion when his brother treated him and his friends to tickets to watch a Manchester United–Chelsea game. 'He took me and my friends to watch football too. And he always bought all the tickets. He said: "If they like they can pay, if they don't it's OK." My friends went to the mosque and tried to give him the money for the match, but my brother said "What are you doing?" and he just laughed. He called him [one of Omar's friends] back and said he doesn't need to – just a treat for me, my dad and my friends.'

One friend who became close to Mohammed Emwazi at his secondary school describes how they spent their free time together either playing football or hanging out in burger bars and chicken takeaways. He recalls: 'We became very close. I used to walk to and from school with him and later we would play football together at Paddington Rec before going to a café every Saturday morning. We were both a couple of jokers and he was a normal lad.'

However, the friend revealed that he got his first hint that Emwazi might harbour extreme views during a Year 9 lesson on Nazi genocide. He told the *Daily Mirror*:'I heard Mohammed mutter "Good. They deserved it." I thought he was joking but later he told me that he hated all Jews and blamed them for the plight of Muslims. He really meant it. He absolutely hated Jews. If we ever walked past a house in Golders Green that he knew was owned by a Jew he would shout obscenities, calling them names like "fucking pigs".'[31]

The friend, one of a number who spoke to the media but have chosen to keep their identities secret, said Emwazi's opinions hardened after the invasions of Afghanistan and Iraq: 'He fucking hated George Bush and wanted to kill him in revenge for the killing of innocent civilians. He said the same about Tony Blair. It was strange because although he was Muslim, as far as I know he never went to a mosque and he never seemed religious. I felt that because he was so young and his views so strong, that he must have picked them up from somewhere outside school.'[32]

The friend added: 'He loved rap music, particularly Jay-Z. He was actually quite small for his age but full of bravado. I only ever saw him get into a fight once and that was with an Iranian who joined us to play football one Saturday. Mohammed was punching and kicking this guy, even though he was much bigger. I had to step in to stop him being really hurt.'[33] The former friend said he last saw Emwazi at the end of the sixth form. He added: 'Our paths have gone completely different ways, I'm happily settled and have kids. He's one of the most hated figures in the world.'

Others say that Emwazi suffered from bullying at the school, which left him depressed and insular. At the age of fourteen, Mohammed was smaller than most of the other boys. A gang of older teenagers used to wait outside the school for him, the friend said. 'They would steal his lunch money and push him around a bit,' he added. 'He was very quiet and a bit scrawny back then so we used to call him Little Mo.'

The school's former head teacher, Jo Shuter, told the BBC what she remembers around this time: 'He had some issues with being bullied, which we dealt with ... but it was not seen as a huge concern.'[34] Shuter, who was head teacher for more than ten years from 2002, said there had been no indication that any pupils were being indoctrinated in extreme views: 'I am not prepared to say when the radicalization took place. All I can say is, absolutely hand on heart, we had no knowledge of it. If we had we would have done something about it.'[35] But serious concerns have been raised about the school after it emerged that two other boys went on to join terror groups: Mohammed Sakr and Choukri Ellekhlifi. Sakr, who would play a pivotal role in Emwazi's life, died while fighting for al-Shabaab in Somalia in 2012.[36] Ellekhlifi, who was two years ahead of Emwazi at the academy, was also killed while fighting in Syria in 2013.

Shortly after these revelations in March 2015, the government announced an investigation of the school.[37] But Jo Shuter insists there was no evidence of extremism when she was head teacher: 'There was never any sense that any of these young men as I knew them were radicalized when they were in school.'[38] Instead she remembers Emwazi being 'quiet and reasonably hard-working', though with the usual problems of teenage pupils. 'By the time he got into the sixth form he was to all intents and purposes a hard-working, aspirational young man who went on to the university he wanted to go to. I can't stress enough, he wasn't a huge concern to us.'

Shuter said the school had had an ethos of tolerance and created an atmosphere 'where young people could talk to adults, there was always somebody that was available to talk to if they were concerned.'[39] But when asked how she compared the boy she knew at school and the jihadist executioner that he became, Shuter was left with a sense of disbelief: 'I can't even begin to say the shock and the horror that I feel. Even now when I'm listening to the news and I hear his name I feel the skin on the back of my neck stand up because it is just so far from what I knew of him and it is so shocking and so horrendous, the things that he has done.'

Shuter's impression of Mohammed Emwazi is supported by Omar, who said that his brother had an ordinary childhood: 'He had a good upbringing, he was very shy. Initially, my sisters say that he had some trouble at school (bullies). But the way I see it was that he was very popular in school.'

In fact, Emwazi had turned his back on his religion, detached himself from his Muslim upbringing and embraced a destructive teenage lifestyle. A female friend who says she knew him well at the time describes Emwazi dressing as a gangster rapper who smoked cannabis and got into fights. The Muslim girl says she was part of a twenty-strong gang which included Mohammed Emwazi. She recalls how he took part in rowdy vodka-drinking sessions and squared up to boys who dared to challenge him. The girl, who says she knew Emwazi from when he was twelve, remembers: 'He dressed like a gangsta rapper and was very into music at that time. He was obsessed with Snoop Dogg, Eminem and Tupac Shakur. I never saw him pray or wear

Islamic dress – he would not even mention religion at all.'[40] She added: 'Being a Muslim myself I was very aware of it at the time. We had a gang and he was very much a part of it.'

In striking contrast to how he is portrayed by his former head teacher, the Muslim friend says the gang were impressed by his 'very aggressive nature' and that he 'would not be pushed around'.[41] She recalls a fight in the school sports hall when another pupil started pushing and shoving him: 'He was suspended from school for two days because of that fight, but he didn't seem to care – he was very rebellious . . . As a member of the gang, he would skip classes up to twice a week. They would smoke cannabis and cigarettes and swig cider from a bottle, outside a nearby convenience shop.'

The girl said: 'He would enjoy sitting in the corner, smoking weed. It didn't bother him that it was illegal or against his faith. We would roll joints and smoke them together. We also smoked the drug behind the school playground. Afterwards everyone – including Mohammed – would go back into class and act like nothing had happened. He was not a good Muslim.'

The gang hung together for five years until they finished school in the summer of 2006, when they went their separate ways. During a 'graduation' ceremony at a hotel in Swiss Cottage they were presented with special leavers' books. Emwazi wrote in the book that he was most likely to be 'something good'. Asked for advice to others, he put: 'Work hard and be happy.' He signed off with a smiley face.[42]

Students also named Emwazi 'gossip of the year'. One friend remembers: 'We had a very boozy night. Everyone, including Mohammed, got drunk on vodka and cranberry. There was wine and beer there as well.'[43]

Emwazi's school days present a picture of an ordinary teenager finding his place in the world. His path towards radicalization had not begun at Quintin Kynaston academy. Emwazi was not searching for an Islamic identity. His interests were secular and his friends were non-religious. Instead it would be an accidental connection within his circle of friends that would expose him to the ideas and cult of the young jihadi.

The Emwazis lived close to another family of Muslim immigrants called the Sakrs. The Sakrs had arrived in Britain from Egypt in 1978. Gamal Sakr was a small-time entrepreneur and supported his family by running a number of retail businesses, mostly newsagents and tobacconists. Mohammed Emwazi and Mohab Sakr were both Muslim boys of the same age at the same school. They had a lot in common and very soon the two boys were spending a great deal of time together, often in and out of each other's houses.[44]

Mohab's older brother Mohamed was a charismatic young man. Born in London in 1985, he grew up as a normal, sporty child. He was three school years above Mohammed Emwazi, and shortly after Emwazi arrived at the school he carved out a laddish reputation for himself. 'He was very popular amongst his friends, yet very quiet at the same time, very polite, he was just a normal child,' recalls his mother Eman.[45] But I have seen a court document which reveals another, much more worrying side to Mohamed Sakr. Shortly after Mohammed Emwazi had left school in 2006, Mohamed Sakr was at the centre of a group of young Islamist extremists who had fallen under the suspicion of the domestic security service, MI5.[46]

Gamal Sakr had wanted his sons to follow in his entrepreneurial footsteps. When Mohamed was just fourteen years old he was made a director of his father's newsagents in London's Soho. But as he hit his late teens he started getting into trouble at nightclubs and bars. 'He loved going out, he loved to dress up, to wear the best clothes, he liked everything to be top range,' recalls Mrs Sakr.[47] 'I used to tell him,

"After midnight there's no good news." So I'd say, "Make sure you are home before twelve." He said, "OK, OK, I'll try," you know.'

In July 2007 Mohamed set up in business for himself as a director running a car valeting service on the Westway in Shepherd's Bush. Companies House records show that he ran this new business, Elite Mobile Valeting Service (MVS), with two other directors, his younger brother Mohab and Amin Mohamed Ali Addala. Mohammed Emwazi was a regular visitor to MVS, where he helped out his school friend and earned extra cash washing and cleaning cars. The Sakr parents were pleased their sons had followed in their father's entrepreneurial footsteps. They were also relieved that Mohamed had appeared to have grown out of nightclubbing and the rowdy group he used to knock around with.[48]

But not all was settled in Mohamed Sakr's life. He became drawn towards the ideas of radical Islam and his wayward Westernized pursuits of nightclubs and boozy, late-night parties had been replaced by a broader interest in the Muslim world. His role model was Bilal al-Berjawi, another young British Muslim who would soon meet Mohammed Emwazi.

In 2007 Mohamed Sakr travelled to Saudi Arabia on what his parents say was a pilgrimage 'with a couple of friends and their wives', before heading to Egypt to join his family on holiday.[49] From there, the Sakrs say, Mohamed and his younger brother also visited the family of a girlfriend in Dubai.

But on his return to the UK Mohamed found himself pulled over at the airport and questioned for 'at least three hours' by 'immigration' officials. He was asked about countries he had visited and his reasons for going there. It was clear that his activities had made him a subject of interest to the security services. 'He told them, "I didn't plan to visit all these countries – it's just how my summer has happened,"' his mother recalls.

Court documents show that MI5 believed Sakr was now part of a hardcore group of Islamists living in London who the security services suspected had links to foreign jihadists.[50] They numbered no more than twelve young Muslim men who were looking to express their sense of grievance at what they believed was the persecution of Muslims in the Middle East. A central part of their worldview was an unquestioning acceptance that an alliance of powers in the East and the West were conspiring to suppress the Islamic faith and as a direct result innocent Muslims were being killed.

In Britain the security services were twitchy. It was just two years after the 7/7 bombings, when a group of bombers, a number of whom had been on MI5's radar, had caught them completely by surprise. Tony Blair had said the 'rules of the game have changed' but it wasn't just political attitudes that had hardened towards young Muslim men expressing extremist views or associating with known Islamist terror suspects. The police and MI5 were not going to be caught off guard again by a home-grown terror attack. Those who found themselves under suspicion were stamped on hard – their travel was disrupted, warnings were issued and associations were broken up.

Surveillance and intelligence gathered from a growing army of informants pointed to Sakr and his associates having strong views about overseas jihad. What MI5 and SO15, the Metropolitan Police's counter-terrorism unit, could not be sure about was in what form this network of loosely associated extremists intended to express those views. Was it a questioning phase in their lives or was their real intent to join the armed jihad?

Mohammed Emwazi was just nineteen years old when he found out that the Sakrs had come into contact with the counter-terrorism police and MI5. At this time he was only on the periphery of this group. He had a social involvement through his friendship with Mohab and his ties with the Sakr family. But whatever his own interests may have been at the time, Emwazi had decided that his immediate future lay in further education.

In 2006 he enrolled on the BSc course at the University of Westminster in information systems with business management.[51] He studied at the Cavendish campus, located between the BBC's Broadcasting House and Regent's Park in central London. The Emwazis were by no means rich and the location meant he could save money by living at home in Maida Vale while travelling into college.

A lot was expected of Mohammed. His father was a strong patriarch and had groomed his eldest son from a very early age to take his place at the head of the family. Even before he had left school, his father expected Mohammed to take on more responsible roles in the family looking after his younger siblings. As Mohammed rose to the challenge his father relied on him more and more.[52] At the same time, he was the first member of the Emwazi family to win a graduate place and this was a proud moment for all the Emwazi family.

In 2006 Westminster University had a reputation as a left-wing establishment which attracted militant students. It also had a flourishing Islamic Society. Its former president, Yassin Nassari, lived in the same part of London as the Emwazis, and was once described by the Westminster University welfare officer as 'wearing Western clothes and enjoying a drink'. But he took a break from his studies and student life after a trip to Syria, reappearing in long robes and headgear and referring to himself as 'emir' of the students' Islamic society. Then, in 2006, the year Emwazi enrolled at the college, Nassari was stopped at Luton airport after getting off an easyJet flight from Holland with his wife. Police discovered a mass of jihadi material on a laptop and a removable hard drive including blueprints for a Qassam 1.5 rocket, as used by the Palestinian terror group Hamas.

The files gave detailed measurements and information about the missile components, and showed how to make the propellant and explosive charge and the assembly of the completed rocket. Also hidden in the files were articles entitled 'Virtues of Martyrdom in the Path of Allah', 'Islamic Ruling on the Permissibility of Self-Sacrificial Operation – Suicide or Martyrdom?', 'Taking Care of the Family Left Behind by the Fighter' and 'Providing for the Families of the Martyrs'. After a short spell in prison Nassari was released back onto the streets of west London in 2008.

The university had a history of hosting extremist preachers. Speakers included Anwar al-Awlaki, an al-Qaeda leader later killed by a US drone strike in Yemen in September 2011. In April 2006, just before Emwazi began his studies, al-Awlaki gave a video speech to the university's Islamic Society annual dinner. It marked the start of a five-year period in which the society became associated with Islamist extremism, including support for the emerging terror group al-Shabaab, a movement with which Emwazi was to become closely associated.

Mohammed Emwazi's university ID card carries a portrait of a young man wearing a baseball cap and branded clothing, still looking more like a gangsta rapper than a devout Muslim.[53] His profile at this time is very similar to that of another famous jihadist called Abdel-Majed Abdel Bary.[54] Before he left for Syria, Bary was a rising rapper whose music was played on BBC radio stations. He was raised in a Maida Vale council home (now worth £1 million), not far from Mohammed Emwazi's own home. After Jihadi John first made his appearance as the knife-wielding executioner of the Islamic State, Bary was frequently named as the most likely suspect. Given his history and appearance the misidentification is understandable. Bary's father, believed to be closely linked to Osama bin Laden, was jailed in America in 2015 over a plot to blow up an embassy in Africa.

Friends have said Bary's conversion to radical Islam happened as he grew increasingly frustrated with the British authorities over the wars in Iraq and Afghanistan. And it came despite his fledgling success on the underground grime music scene, where he rapped under the names Lyricist Jinn and L Jinny. Bary appeared in dozens of videos, including one in which he posed outside the Bank of England and declared his allegiance to the global hacking group Anonymous – who in 2015 declared a cyber war against the Islamic State.

But towards the end of 2012 and the start of 2013 the aspiring rapper suddenly walked out of his west London home to go and fight in Syria. It was around the same time as Mohammed Emwazi made the same journey. Bary joined the Islamic State and has since been using Twitter and other social media to broadcast blood-curdling threats against the West. He even posted a picture of himself holding a severed head.

During the summer of 2014 Bary was widely believed to be the masked executioner of the Islamic State and for a time was investigated by the security services. His family home in London was raided by the police, which provoked another strong reaction from the rapping jihadi. He wrote: 'They have nothing to do with this, they did not even know where I am. I haven't lived at home for years you pagans.'[55] All this only served to fuel the media's conviction that Bary was indeed Jihadi John.

When Emwazi was finally identified as Jihadi John pictures of the two men looked similar. Even after the unmasking, Bary was still linked to Emwazi's group the 'Beatles', with Bary playing the part of the leader of the group, 'Jihadi George'.

In 2014 Bary claimed he was kidnapped, tortured and robbed by members of a rival Islamic terror group. The former London rapper has since fallen out with the Islamic State and fled to Turkey.[56] In November 2015 he was still being hunted by both the British security services and IS executioners, who have recently killed scores of foreign fighters for deserting. His chances of escape are dismal, as both operate inside Turkey. But he will hope that the British secret services find him first.

Mohammed Emwazi's radicalization and eventual journey to Syria and the Islamic State had only just begun. His lifestyle was to be challenged by other ideas about the world outside west London's rap scene. These ideas would bring him into contact with more serious-minded Muslims whose activities and beliefs made them of interest to the security services.

CHAPTER 2

THE JIHADI JOHN NETWORK

In the wake of the 7/7 attacks on London in 2005, Britain's counter-terrorism operatives were becoming increasingly concerned about a group of young Muslim men from London radicalized by British Islamists who had returned from training camps in Somalia. Mohammed Emwazi's friend Mohamed Sakr was of particular interest to the security services. Sakr was stopped on numerous occasions by plainclothes officers and his home in St John's Wood was frequently visited by the police.[1] After one such incident, Sakr told his mother, 'They're watching me, Momma, everywhere I go they watch me.'[2] The Sakr family were so concerned about the attention their son was receiving that they became convinced their phones were being tapped.

Mohamed Sakr kept close company with another young Muslim whom the police suspected of extremist activity. Bilal al-Berjawi, a trainee plumber, had once lived next door to the

Sakrs and the security services believed the two men were at the heart of an Islamist cell in west London. Berjawi summed up the two men's predicament when he contacted CAGE, an advocacy group which specializes in helping Muslims who are being targeted by the security services. At a meeting in their east London offices he told a CAGE director: 'Mohamed [Sakr] is very close to myself – family, friends, very close. That's when I realized myself I was starting to be followed, because I would see someone – the same person – following me, wherever I was, [in] the same car. I actually even memorized the number plate. So that's when I realized. When they came back and I interacted with them – that's when I realized that there was attention there.'[3]

Explaining the effect of the surveillance, he added: 'Me, the way I see it, obviously, I just want to be left alone – I don't want to be harassed, followed – I feel intimidated. I've got a lot of side effects, you know. I get worried, I hear noises at night because of the way they came.'[4] He explained to the CAGE director:

> I've been affected. I don't feel like I live in peace in this country. Any noise, even my wife, when the letter comes through the letterbox, she sees me jump. I think, 'What's going on?' I just want to be left alone and live my normal life. I don't want to be harassed, because I feel in this country like I'm being harassed, I'm being watched, my privacy's been interrupted – that's what it is, you see? My friends have been scared away from me because they've been approached. I feel isolated, that's what it is. So it's becoming a bit too much.[5]

Both men complained that they were only exploring their Muslim identities but court papers show that the security services had every reason to be taking an interest in their lives. Of particular concern was their determined keenness to support jihad abroad.[6]

In 2006 the focus of Islamist jihad outside Afghanistan and Pakistan was on the Horn of Africa, especially Somalia, where an organization called the Islamic Courts Union (ICU) had established control over large swathes of the country by overcoming weak Somali government resistance. The ICU was a loose formation of Islamic groups which had been able to restore some sort of civil order after years of violent anarchy in Somalia, opening Mogadishu's airport and winning support from a Somali majority. 'The Courts achieved the unthinkable, uniting Mogadishu for the first time in sixteen years, and re-establishing peace and security,' a Chatham House briefing paper concluded at the time.[7]

But in reality, the group's government of Somalia tottered from crisis to crisis, perilously close to collapse. From the moment of its birth 'there was nothing ideal about the ICU; it was holding together a coalition of interests that ranged from the best of the moderates to the worst of the militants,' claims Mukoma wa Ngugi, an assistant professor of English at Cornell University and the author of *Black Star Nairobi* (Melville House, 2013) and *Nairobi Heat* (Melville House, 2011).[8]

In time, the extremist factions emerged as the dominant force. They began to impose a strict version of shari'a law, shutting down cinemas, sports venues and co-educational events. Cigarettes, alcohol and *khat*, the popular leafy narcotic chewed by Somalis, were all banned.

In Washington military strategists started sounding alarms, summed up by President George Bush's response to a question about unrest in Somalia: '[Our] first concern, of course, would be to make sure that Somalia does not become an al-Qaeda safe haven, doesn't become a place from which terrorists plot and plan.'⁹

When the ICU threatened neighbouring Ethiopia, America backed an armed response. Ethiopian forces swept through the country before quickly taking Mogadishu. In the face of the military onslaught, the ICU splintered, with moderates going into exile and the militants forming the terror group al-Shabaab, meaning 'the youth'.

'This meant that what should have been a Somali problem, requiring a Somali solution to address militancy within the ICU, became an Ethiopian and American problem,' says Mukoma. 'The end result was more anarchy in Somalia that now had no chance at a central authority, and the birth of al-Shabaab.'¹⁰

In the long run, it is hard to say what central government could have achieved. The ICU might have united Somalia into a country that ruled in the interests of the majority – or it could have been an outpost of terror.¹¹ It fell to soldiers of al-Shabaab to carry on the fight with the explicit backing of al-Qaeda and its leader, Osama bin Laden. Al-Shabaab was the Islamic State of its day, with its avowed intention of declaring a caliphate across east Africa.

Viewed from Britain, Somalia was a natural choice for young Muslims looking to follow the call of jihad, and many British jihadists gravitated towards that part of Africa. The duty of jihad has its roots in the teachings of the Qur'an. In its most basic form *jihad* means 'struggle'. However, there is not a coherent doctrine by which jihad can be understood. It is a complex religious tenet that is explained well by academic Michael Bonner in his history of jihad: 'In all these places – involving jihad and other words derived from its root – the Qur'an calls for devotion to God, righteous conduct, utter dedication and indeed, sacrifice of oneself ... Such an attitude may, of course, involve physical combat, but in most of these cases this is not obviously what is meant.'[12]

Nevertheless it is this reference to military jihad which the more extreme Islamic scholars have used to justify violence. When extremists call upon young Muslim men to perform jihad they are asking them to take up arms against anyone who threatens Muslims anywhere in the world. To a young Muslim growing up in the West the notion of an adventure supporting a just cause to defend fellow Muslims in a foreign land can hold a very strong appeal.

This is how one member of Emwazi's network explained the attraction: 'I wanted to contribute to the Islamic society which had been established there and which was limited in terms of knowledge and resources. I thought I could give assistance and went in order to teach computer skills.'[13] Another asked: 'Why should I live in a country where I have to lower my eyes whenever I leave the house in case I pass a woman who is baring her flesh?'

But the July 2005 terror attacks on London – the devastating bombs of the 7th and the failed attempts of the 21st – were a salutary reminder of the dangers posed by young men travelling between the UK and Somalia in the name of radical Islam. Three of the failed 21 July bombers, Muktar Said Ibrahim, Ramzi Mohammed and Yassin Omar, were Somali nationals and the fourth, Ismail Abdurahman, was a British national born in Somalia. MI5 believed al-Shabaab and its satellite networks in the West now represented the greatest threat to British interests and expected a terror attack to be launched very soon. Bilal al-Berjawi and Mohamed Sakr topped MI5's growing list of 'jihadists of interest' linked to al-Shabaab.[14]

Bilal al-Berjawi was Lebanese but his parents had brought him to London when he was a small boy. As a teenager, Berjawi was part of the same west London gang culture that attracted Mohammed Emwazi. According to a community worker who knew him at the time Berjawi played a central role in a Muslim gang which was fighting Irish gangs in the area. Berjawi was not particularly religious but by the time he was nineteen he had married a Somali wife and taken a much greater interest in his faith and the politics that supported it.[15] Court papers show that Berjawi and Sakr attended the same mosques and schools and played in the same five-a-side football teams in west London.[16] A friend of Berjawi told me that he liked to use a moped to travel across London to keep in contact with the network. 'He looked like a pizza delivery rider and so he didn't attract much attention visiting the brothers.'[17]

By 2006 MI5 had followed the trail of the 21/7 bombers, charting the underground network that had supported them. Surveillance teams had found evidence that one of the group, an Ethiopian known only as J1, had been in direct contact with two of the failed bombers on the day of the attempt.[18] J1, born in 1980, had also telephoned Hussain Osman, an Ethiopian who claimed Somali heritage, on the very same day.[19] It was Osman who police were on the trail of in Stockwell Underground station on 22 July 2005, when they mistakenly shot dead the Brazilian Jean Charles de Menezes. Osman managed to escape to Italy after the bombs failed to detonate but was arrested a few days later and extradited to the UK.[20]

The surveillance teams also discovered that in 2004 some members of the J1 group had been involved in terrorist training camps in Cumbria. An off-duty policeman out on a jog in the Cumbrian countryside had noticed a group of young Asian men going through combat exercises and so he rang his superiors to tell them of his suspicions.[21] Among the camp's participants were at least two of the 21/7 plotters.[22]

In a separate operation, J1 was stopped by police in Scotland in 2004 with three other suspects. All of them were wearing white plastic gloves and were unable to offer police a plausible reason for their suspicious behaviour. MI5 believed they had joined or were about to join one of the camps in Cumbria.[23] The sum of this gathered intelligence allowed security chiefs to put pressure on the London cell by ensuring that the suspects' lives were made as uncomfortable as possible. The men's family homes were visited by police, all international travel was disrupted and the suspects found themselves being pulled over again and again to answer questions about their links to Islamist extremism.

With the 21/7 bomb plotters safely behind bars, Berjawi and Sakr were singled out for the most aggressive counter-terrorism targeting.[24] By 2006, the year Mohammed Emwazi started his course at Westminster University, life had indeed become very uncomfortable for both men, so much so that they realized they would need to look beyond Britain if they were to fulfil their religious duty of jihad. Somalia and the burgeoning al-Shabaab movement was the obvious choice.

So by the time Emwazi had embarked on his university career, Sakr and Berjawi were fully engaged with supporting the new Islamic movement emerging in east Africa.[25] The leading figures in this radicalization process had moved away from the teachings of British-based clerics like Abu Qatada or even Abu Hamza. Qatada and Hamza had dominated the extremist thinking of young British Muslim men for over a decade. But now both men were in prison and effectively out of business. In their place, the group looked to the leaders of the more dynamic al-Qaeda movement in east Africa. Here they found experienced fighters who had acquired legendary status, having established their combat credentials fighting in Afghanistan, Iraq and now Somalia. These were not armchair jihadists fighting a war of words on London streets but real-life jihadi warriors.

Among the most influential was the Kenyan fighter Fazul Mohammed, a linguist fluent in English, Arabic, Swahili and French.[26] Few al-Qaeda leaders at the time could claim to have played as central a role in the war against America as Fazul Mohammed. He was part of an al-Qaeda unit based in Mogadishu in 1993 when the American military suffered its largest loss of life since Vietnam, a battle which was immortalized in the Ridley Scott film *Black Hawk Down*.[27] He was also accused of planning the 1998 bombings of the US embassies in Kenya and Tanzania, as well as the November 2002 attacks in Mombasa, Kenya in which a car bomb struck a hotel and missiles were fired at an Israeli airliner. In November 2009, Osama bin Laden personally named Fazul Mohammed as the head of al-Qaeda in east Africa.[28]

Fazul's plans for a worldwide terror campaign had made him a marked man and the CIA had unsuccessfully targeted him in several airstrikes. In 2007 he was reported killed in a US naval strike during Ethiopia's invasion of Somalia, but he survived. Later that year, the US Navy targeted Fazul in a naval operation off the coast of Puntland. The following year, he narrowly escaped an American special forces raid in Kenya. It wasn't until 2011, just before his fortieth birthday, that his death was officially confirmed. He died not from a US drone strike but in a shoot-out with Somali government security forces just outside Mogadishu.[29] The local counter-terrorism forces recovered a document on a flash drive found on his body which included plans for an attack on targets including Eton College and the five-star Dorchester and Ritz hotels in London, similar to the 2008 Mumbai attacks that killed more than 160 people. The document proposed two months' training in Somalia for British and other Western recruits selected for the attack, including target reconnaissance, hostage taking, weapons and counter-surveillance.[30]

Court documents show that in 2006 Bilal al–Berjawi and four other Londoners left the UK to attend an al–Qaeda training camp in Somalia. MI5 told the court that the terrorism they were alleged to be engaged in might not be restricted to the Horn of Africa and neighbouring states. An MI5 report summed up security services' suspicions, saying: 'Although we are not aware of any attack in the United Kingdom having yet been perpetrated by terrorists trained in Somalia it may only be a matter of time before an attack by such a person is attempted. Cutting off a valuable source of support for those groups is necessary in the interests of national security.'[31]

The camp where the British jihadists were being trained was run by Fazul Mohamed, who instructed the British group to return to the United Kingdom as a sleeper cell 'to carry out facilitation activities and to recruit individuals to work on behalf of al–Qaeda and/or al–Shabaab', according to intelligence gathered by MI5.[32]

One terror suspect who attended the camp where the British were being trained was Abdul Malik Bajabu, a Kenyan accused of helping in the 2002 Mombasa attacks. Malik was captured at an internet café in Somalia on 13 February 2007 when security officers found him carrying a piece of paper containing contact information for associates, including those located in the UK.[33] He was later held in Guantánamo Bay where his file states: 'Attendees at Harun Fazul's training camp included eight foreigners from various countries that were to return to their home country after the training as sleeper operatives to await further orders.'[34]

Among the group of British jihadists with Berjawi at the camp was a man who for legal reasons can only be referred to as CE. He is now in his mid–thirties, a graduate of London

Metropolitan University who came to Britain from Iran as a youngster and grew up on a council estate in Ladbroke Grove, west London. He was also an associate of Mohammed Emwazi. Three of the other Britons at the training camp in Somalia were also west Londoners, named as Mohammed Ezzouek, Hamza Chentouf and Shahajan Janjua. When the Americans launched airstrikes against the terrorist camps, the jihadists simply joined the refugee convoy and fled Somalia. But as they approached the Kenyan border local security forces were waiting for them and they were picked up.

For the next three weeks they were interrogated by Kenyan intelligence officers. The men later claimed that during their detention they were tortured and that MI6 or MI5 were overseeing the questioning.[35] CE claimed he had travelled to Somalia partly for 'adventure' and also to help impoverished youths. Ezzouek, twenty-six, from Paddington, later said in an interview that he had been asked about the east African embassy bombings. He claimed he had been studying at a Qur'anic school in Egypt and moved to Somalia to experience life under shari'a law.[36]

Chentouf, twenty-five, now lives in a council flat close to Ladbroke Grove. 'He went with twelve friends,' said his mother. 'There was only one other Moroccan boy — Ezzouek. Hamza said he was going for six months to study the Qur'an.'[37]

All four Britons were captured by Kenyan security forces as they crossed the border but almost immediately sent back to a hostile Somalia in an extra-judicial move criticized by human rights charity Reprieve. It was only when Janjua — who said he had been attending a friend's wedding in Mogadishu — managed to get a message back to friends in the UK that the Foreign Office stepped in to help. Amid claims from Reprieve that the Britons faced execution, a plane was chartered to airlift them out of Somalia at an estimated cost of £50,000, while an RAF jet transported them from Nairobi to the UK.[38]

All of this links CE to Mohammed Emwazi, which later connects Emwazi to this group of west London jihadists. CE cannot be named because he is still subject to strict court orders. But at the time of his detention he told MI5 that following the invasion of Somalia he made his way along the coast in a convoy to the Kenyan border via Kismayo and Ras Kambone. But he resisted any claim that he had taken part in any fighting, saying only that he had seen jet planes overhead and did not witness any fighting at first hand. He said that he has never been armed. Nevertheless, the security services were sufficiently worried about CE's potential threat to the UK that when he returned he was placed on a control order. During his court case he said he fled across the border into Kenya where he was detained and questioned by the Kenyan authorities and by the British secret services before being rendered to Somalia.[39]

The British courts have declined to confirm or deny whether the British security services were involved in the men's capture but judges have made it clear that they believed CE had been at the terrorist training camps and had returned to the UK to begin the recruitment of others. It is worth noting, though, that MI5 did not claim he was part of a terror sleeper cell planning an attack on the UK.[40]

Whatever the British men's intention, MI5 felt confident that their alleged activities had been successfully disrupted. Yet notwithstanding the efforts of MI5, the London network, which now numbered around twenty Muslim men, remained active and operational. In terms of counter-surveillance experience the group had matured. Cell members used passwords, met surreptitiously at each other's houses and were seen to engage in deliberate surveillance evasion tactics.[41] And most worryingly of all, the network's leaders were still directing operations.

Bilal al-Berjawi had been with the other British men in Somalia but had managed to evade the attentions of both the Kenyan and British security services. He did not need 'rescuing' from Mogadishu and instead travelled back to London under his own steam.

Another member of the group also returned home separately. His name was Ibrahim Magag, a London Underground train conductor who had arrived in Britain as a refugee in 1992 and married a British woman in 2009. Together with Berjawi and Sakr, Magag was the third leading member of the network in west London. He lived in his wife's council flat with her young son from another relationship. Magag was a key terror fundraiser and organizer, operating not just in Britain but across east Africa, having already made several visits to Somalia.[42] MI5 firmly believed Magag had travelled to Somalia specifically for the purpose of engaging in terrorism-related activities.[43]

Documents from his court case show that he was involved in 'arranging financial and other support for al-Qaeda associates in East Africa'. The document, which is based on MI5 intelligence, adds: 'This support includes enabling associates to travel to Somalia to pursue terrorism related activities there.'[44]

While everyone else was scrambling to get out of Somalia as the country spiralled into civil war, Magag coolly took a plane in January 2007 from London to Hargeisa, the capital of Somaliland, via Dubai and Nairobi. A month later he was back at Nairobi airport, where he was detained and deported to Dubai. There he was held and questioned by security officials.[45] During his detention he tried to swallow a piece of paper containing a series of telephone numbers. He was also found to be in possession of three brand new mobile phones and $4,600 in cash for which he had no sensible explanation. He was deported to the UK where he was released.[46]

In April 2008, Magag, was stopped by police in London when he was carrying £1,000 in cash which MI5 strongly suspected was earmarked for terror funding. The security services report not only makes it clear that Berjawi, Magag and Sakr were leading members of a terrorist network but suggests that all three were involved in the financial support of international terrorism.

The jihadi escapades of Sakr and Berjawi, the two charismatic leaders of the group, must have left an impression on the younger Mohammed Emwazi. In 2007 Emwazi was closely connected to Sakr and Berjawi. They lived nearby, shared cultural reference points and encouraged Emwazi to take an interest in their political and ideological interpretation of the unfolding events in east Africa. Stories would have been passed from friend to friend about how the London jihadists had slipped out of the UK and joined a brotherhood of fighters in war-torn Somalia. Pictures circulated among the group included photographs of London Muslims brandishing weapons like AK-47s and rocket-propelled grenade launchers.

This may have influenced Emwazi's view of the world as he spent more and more time socializing with Muslim men outside university. But it was the exploits of his older mentors, Mohamed Sakr and Bilal al-Berjawi, who like him had started off in street gangs, which offered Emwazi role models whose Islamic destiny could be emulated. Their bravado about run-ins with MI5 and how they had outfoxed the 'feds' by playing clever during questioning gave jihad a 'gangsta' context which made it feel both exciting and worthwhile.

The CAGE director Asim Qureshi, who had known both Berjawi and Emwazi, said: 'Emwazi certainly looked up to Bilal. I really see Emwazi as the younger guy trying to get into the group. He doesn't have a long history of practising his religion. He is very much a street lad and he kind of looks up to these guys in many ways.'[47] Emwazi's fascination with Berjawi's jihad in Somalia is confirmed five years later by the accounts of his hostages in Syria, who said he forced them to watch videos of al-Shabaab.[48]

A former Islamic State collaborator has also described how Emwazi was 'obsessed' with the situation in Somalia. 'He told me that if he had gone to Somalia he himself could well have been killed ... It was strange: we were in the middle of a war and he wanted to talk about another war. Mohammed was obsessed with al-Shabaab, he was angry about what had happened in Africa. Some of his friends have been killed, some sent to prison and he thought they had been betrayed.'[49]

In early 2009 Berjawi and Sakr were planning another foreign adventure. This time they decided to travel to Kenya as tourists interested in going on 'safari'. This is what Berjawi told CAGE: 'I decided to go on a safari trip in Kenya. As myself, I'm very interested in animals and that, so I decided to go there with my friend Mohamed [Sakr] – we planned it out, you know – when we had time off work we said we'd go there. Our original plan was to stay for a couple of weeks. We extended it over there.'[50]

But British security services believed the real intention was terrorism. In Mombasa, Kenya's second city, Sakr and Berjawi aroused the suspicions of the manager of the hotel where they were staying.[51] A local intelligence report notes that they had been joined by a third man called Najid Mansour. Police raided the hotel and Berjawi and Sakr were deported via Nairobi. A laptop belonging to Mansour was found at the premises which contained extremist material including encouragement of violent jihad and instructions on making car bombs.[52]

An MI5 report later concluded: 'When interviewed on return to this country, Berjawi and Sakr did not tell entirely the same story.'[53] Both men claimed they were also interrogated by British intelligence officials in Nairobi. While the two were still being detained in Kenya, police arrived at the Sakr family home with a search warrant.[54] Cards left behind by officers identify them as members of SO15, the Met's counter-terrorism squad. Sakr's father says he was shocked to be told that the family might have to vacate their home for up to two weeks while officers searched the premises, although the family's anger may have been slightly ameliorated when they found themselves put up in the nearby Hilton hotel.[55]

Two days later the family was allowed home. And shortly afterwards Mohamed Sakr and Bilal al-Berjawi were deported back to Britain. Upon Mohamed's return Gamal Sakr challenged his son: 'I was asking questions, "Why has this happened?" and Mohamed said: "Daddy, it's finished, it will never happen again. It's all done and dusted." So I just put a cap on it and continued with a normal life.'[56] Nevertheless, Mohamed's mother insisted on accompanying him to the mosque so she could hear the sermons he was listening to. 'I wanted to hear what they're saying, I was always on top of this, always. I wanted to know why the police were after him, why?' Mrs Sakr said. 'So he used to take me to different mosques, and the sermons were normal, nothing unusual.'[57]

At the beginning of 2009 Mohammed Emwazi was busy preparing for his final exams. In just five months, however, he too would be heading to Africa on 'safari' with two friends. Even before he had graduated from Westminster University, he seems to have been well on the road to radicalization. I spoke to a family friend, who is ten years older than Emwazi and greatly respected among the Muslim youth for his time spent in Afghanistan, but he did not want to be identified. 'We met in Regent's Park Mosque. He was a quiet guy and we used to greet each other. He had a beard and was practising. He was well mannered and he was known for his good manners. We became very good friends.'

Regent's Park Mosque was popular with young Muslims from all over London who wanted to take a more dynamic interest in the conflicts afflicting Muslim populations. Outside the mosque the Islamic faithful were greeted by groups of young men with beards urging support for their 'brothers' fighting in Iraq and Afghanistan. They shook collection boxes with which they ostensibly solicited cash for humanitarian projects but few people asked questions about where or who would directly benefit from these donations.

'He [Emwazi] was looking for marriage and really wanted to live abroad,' the friend said. 'But he had a fiancée in London and I think had "sat down" with her family. I told him he should marry her.'[58] A family member has confirmed that Emwazi, like his mentor Bilal al-Berjawi, had chosen a Somali woman living in London as his fiancée.

By now Emwazi was praying four or five times a day according to Islamic custom. But because he had come to Islam late he had a lot of catching up to do. A central part of his study of Islam was memorizing the Qur'an so he could be called a *hafiz*. The Qur'an is divided into 114 *surahs* or chapters, containing 6,236 verses, comprising some 80,000 words. Most Muslims who complete the difficult task of becoming a *hafiz* study as children in Islamic schools so that they can be instructed in the *tajwid* or the rules of recitation. This process generally takes between three and six years of intensive learning. Doing this demonstrates total commitment to Islam.

To achieve this, Emwazi approached a teacher known to his group. By all accounts he was diligent in his studies and made good progress. His teacher recounts a story of how, during one of his lessons, Emwazi was reciting an easier section of the

Qur'an. The teacher said to Emwazi: 'Let's start with the chapter of sincerity.' But almost as soon as he started to recite it he broke down in tears. The teacher said he was crying for hours and simply inconsolable. When they finally managed to calm him down, he explained that he had recently been to hospital where a respected member of the Islamic community he knew well was dying from cancer. Emwazi went every day to the hospital to see the man and they had become very close. One day, while visiting, he told the man he was going to the canteen to get some food. Before he went he promised when he came back he would read the chapter of sincerity to him as it is a part of spiritual healing called *rukya*. Sadly, when he came back from the canteen the man had died.[59] Asim Qureshi, who was told this story, says: 'What this shows was just how much of a heightened sense of emotion Emwazi possessed. Now, to many people this guy is worse than Osama bin Laden or Khaled Sheikh Mohamed but here is a young man crying because of a memory about the Qur'an and a man dying of cancer.'

His interest in religion had taken over from his academic endeavours and his final university results reflect this, as he failed one of his modules and scraped through his other courses with low marks. The family friend I spoke to says Emwazi had come to embrace Islam as a worldview. He was opposed to the West's invasion of Iraq and the continued occupation of a Muslim country. 'If you listen to Mohammed's words in the [Islamic State] videos and take away the beheadings you'll see that those really are his politics. He did blame America for the deaths of millions of Muslims.'[60]

But whether in 2009 Emwazi was ready to mobilize his politics violently is open to question. Certainly al-Qaeda's extremist view of the world required religious interpretation. The ideological struggles going on among the *ummah* (the worldwide Muslim community) needed interpretation for the uninitiated. Potential recruits needed to know that victims of the fighting and repression in Somalia were Muslims. Just as the *mujahideen*, those engaged in military jihad, had come to the rescue of Muslims in Bosnia, Afghanistan and Iraq, they were needed now in Somalia. The proliferation of Islamist propaganda on the internet rallied Muslims all over the world to this cause.

But foreign al-Qaeda leaders were too remote to be able carry their messages to the heart of Muslim communities in the West. This was work for British-based clerics who could bend the teachings of the Qur'an into a blueprint for terror. Abu Hamza, the Egyptian firebrand imam of Finsbury Park Mosque, had begun the job but since his arrest and detention in 2003 his influence had waned. Another cleric who lived much closer to Emwazi and the rest of the network was Hani al-Sibai, a former lawyer who fled Egypt for Britain after he was accused of plotting terrorism.

Sibai arrived in the UK in 1994 and set up home in the leafy suburb of Hammersmith, a few miles from where the Emwazis had settled the year before. In a series of court rulings, he is portrayed as having 'provided material support to al-Qaeda and conspired to commit terrorist acts', an allegation he denies. Sibai, citing his human rights, has thwarted government attempts to deport him for more than six years.[61]

It is not clear what contact, if any, Sibai had with Emwazi but when Emwazi was a young man growing up in west London Sibai's extremist message and the material on his home-made websites seems to have been highly influential on other young jihadists.[62] Certainly, in the dark days following 7/7, Sibai offered young Muslims an alternative narrative for the terrorist bombings.

The day after fifty-two people were slaughtered on the London transport system Sibai went on Al Jazeera television to declare the attacks as a 'great victory' for al-Qaeda, which undoubtedly they were. Sibai added: 'There are no real men except for the people of Islam. Look at the people who give reason to hold the head of Islam high ... In politics they are the masters. In the battlefield they are the masters. They are the ones who rub in the mud the nose of the occupation forces in Afghanistan, in Iraq, in Palestine, throughout the world.'[63]

He also contrasted Islamic extremists with pro-Western secular leaders in the Middle East, who, he said, 'should be placed in public squares so that people can hit them with their shoes and spit on them'. And he even disparaged the moderate position of the Muslim Association of Britain, which at the time had come out in strong condemnation of the bombers: 'These groups do not represent the Muslim public,' he said. 'They collaborate with the British police for certain interests. They want an "English Islam", and not the Islam that was sent to the Prophet Mohammed.'[64]

It is claimed that Sibai, a charismatic preacher, had 'captivated' a number of young Muslim men who subsequently went abroad to fight jihad.[65] From his home Sibai, also known as Hani Youssef, ran an effective Islamist propaganda machine that included the al-Maqreze Centre for Historical Studies. He was also described as a 'long-time ally' of Ayman al-Zawahiri, who took over control of al-Qaeda following Osama bin Laden's death.[66]

Sibai has denied the links to al-Qaeda. When the cleric first claimed asylum in the UK in 1994, he told officials he had been tortured in Egypt because he had acted as a lawyer for Islamist groups and was linked to the opposition Muslim Brotherhood. He was refused asylum on national security grounds, and was jailed in 1998 pending deportation. However, Britain was unable to obtain from Egypt the necessary assurances as to his treatment and so he was allowed to stay in the UK.

But in 2004 his case was taken up as a *cause célèbre* among the Islamist extremist community. And his presence here even came to the attention of then prime minister Tony Blair, who urged officials to do more to remove him from the UK. On one occasion Blair intervened personally to try to deport him, scrawling on a letter warning that he might have to remain in the country: 'I don't believe we shld be doing this. Speak to me.' Nevertheless, Sibai was freed after spending nine months behind bars and to this day remains in Britain.[67] His alleged links to al-Qaeda have led to his bank accounts and assets being subjected to freezing orders by the United Nations, the UK Treasury and US Treasury.

In 2014, in a publicly funded court case, Sibai went to the European Court of Justice in Luxembourg to try to get his status as an al-Qaeda affiliate overturned and allow him access to bank accounts and other financial assets.[68] In court documents the European Commission's sanctions committee alleged that Sibai 'has provided material support to al-Qaeda and has conspired to commit terrorist acts. It went on:

He has travelled internationally using forged documents, he has received military training and has belonged to cells and groups carrying out terrorist operations using force and violence involving intimidation, threats and damage to public and private property, as well as obstructing the activities of the public authorities.

[The applicant] instructed others to go to Afghanistan to take part in the fighting there. He has used an internet site to support terrorist acts undertaken by al-Qaeda as well as to maintain contact with a number of supporters around the world.[69]

It concluded: '[The applicant] is wanted by the Egyptian authorities for involvement in terrorist crimes committed inside and outside Egypt, including criminal collusion with intent to commit acts of premeditated killing, destruction of property, unlicensed possession of firearms, ammunition and explosives, membership of a terrorist group, forgery of official and other documents, and theft.'[70]

Today Sibai is an outspoken critic of the Islamic State and its leader, Abu Bakr al-Baghdadi. He made a speech strongly criticizing the killing of innocent people after the November 2015 attacks in Paris. He also denies being a radicalizing influence on Emwazi. His lawyer told me: 'To the best of his knowledge, he never met him, and does not understand how this suggestion can ever have arisen. It appears to have been conjured up by an exercise in lazy journalism, stitching names together which have never had any connection in reality. Mr al-Sibai has already previously set out in detail his reasons for considering that the actions of Emwazi and Islamic State are not consistent with Islamic teaching.'

But Sibai was by no means the only cleric with alleged links to al-Qaeda preaching in west London when Emwazi was growing up. One of his associates, Adel Abdel Bari, an alleged senior al-Qaeda operative, was in 2015 jailed for twenty-five years in the US for a series of terror plots. Both men were living in London when they were said to be part of the ruling *shura* (council) of Islamic Jihad.[71] Bari's son is Abdel-Majed Abdel Bary, the one-time rapper whose life, as we have already seen, has strong parallels with Emwazi's.

Bari senior fled to the UK in 1991 and was granted political asylum from his native Egypt in 1993, the same year the Emwazis arrived in the UK. Like the Emwazis, the Baris also chose Maida Vale for their London home. Two years later, he was sentenced to death in absentia for a 1995 plot to blow up a market in Cairo's bazaar district. In a separate Egyptian trial in 1999 he was also sentenced to life in prison.

For the last fourteen years of his time in the UK he was held in custody at the request of the Americans before his extradition on terror charges in October 2012 with Abu Hamza.[72] But despite his incarceration, he remained an influence on radical Islamists who viewed his detention on the orders of the Americans as unjust and a source of further grievance against the West. His supporters maintained that he was only ever interested in politics in Egypt and did not support violence.

Bari had been imprisoned and tortured in Egypt following the murder of President Anwar Sadat in 1981. After years of detention in Egypt, during which he gained a degree and became a respected human rights lawyer with ties to Amnesty International, Bari left the country and in 1991, the year Bary junior was born, applied for political asylum in Britain. His family joined him after it was granted, two years later.

In 1998 Bari senior advised another Egyptian terror suspect to request asylum in the UK so he could help convince Hani al-Sibai to support the Algerian GIA, a terrorist organization which based itself in London and Paris in the 1990s.[73] But Bari was arrested in London soon after the 7 August 1998 US embassy bombings.

The journalist Victoria Brittain interviewed Bari's wife Ragaa after police swooped on their home:

There was a dawn raid by British police in white contamination suits, brandishing truncheons and breaking down the front door. Ragaa and the children [including Bary junior] were traumatised. A dozen or so men were suddenly in their bedrooms, shouting for her husband, searching the children's clothes, tearing out pages from any books with telephone numbers. Adel was led away, and Ragaa, hurriedly putting on her black hijab and abaya, was told to get into a bus with her five children, one of whom was a small baby.[74]

But the British authorities found nothing to tie Bari to the embassy bombings and he was soon released. He was charged with having unlawful gas canisters but was acquitted at trial. Victoria Brittain says: 'An official letter from the anti-terrorism police at the time stated that after nine months of exhaustive investigation, they found that he and the other Egyptian men arrested with him had no connection with al-Qaeda, nor any connection with terrorism in Britain.'[75]

Yet Bari was arrested again when the United States applied for his extradition on the very charges that the British had dismissed. This time he was held at Long Lartin and Manchester prisons, at one time going on hunger strike to protest against what he considered racist treatment by guards and orders that all phone calls had to be made in English not Arabic.[76]

But the American investigators were convinced they had found a senior al-Qaeda player and refused to withdraw their request to prosecute him in America. According to Bari's indictment, the current al-Qaeda leader, Ayman al-Zawahiri, appointed him head of the London cell of Egyptian Islamic Jihad in May 1996. The next year he leased an office in Beethoven Street, in Queen's Park, west London. That office became bin Laden's 'media information office', the indictment says.[77] It was also set up

to provide a cover for activity in support of al-Qaeda's 'military' activities, including the recruitment of military trainees, the disbursement of funds and the procurement of necessary equipment (including satellite telephones) and necessary services.

In addition, the London office served as a conduit for messages, including reports on military and security matters from various al-Qaeda cells, including the Kenyan cell, to al-Qaeda's headquarters.[78]

On 19 September 2014 Bari pleaded guilty to three counts of the indictment before a federal court. These included conspiring to kill US nationals, conspiring to make a threat to kill, injure, intimidate, and damage and destroy property by means of an explosive, and making such a threat. According to the indictment, Bari transmitted, via international telephone calls to the media, the contents of al-Qaeda's claims of responsibility for the 7 August 1998 bombings of the United States embassies in Nairobi and Dar es Salaam, which killed 224 people. The next day, he transmitted threats of future attacks by the same terrorists to media organizations in France, Qatar and the United Arab Emirates. Bari additionally arranged for messages to be transmitted to and from members of the media to his co-conspirators, including Osama bin Laden and Ayman al-Zawahiri. On 6 February 2015, Bari was sentenced to twenty-five years in prison as a result of a plea bargain.

These three Egyptian clerics, Sibai, Bari and Hamza, all living in London post 9/11, helped to set the political Islamic weather. Emwazi and his network would have been aware of their statements and the hostile treatment they had received from the authorities and the media.

But an intriguing court document from a case involving a British-born terror suspect hints at another more obvious radicalizer. His name is Mohammed Hamid, a veteran extremist who liked to call himself 'Osama bin London'. Crucially, his terrorist propaganda included videos of beheadings.

Hamid, an older radical figure with links to the (now dead) al-Qaeda leader Anwar al-Awlaki, took over responsibilities for the community around Finsbury Park after Abu Hamza was arrested and imprisoned in 2003.[79]

A former crack cocaine addict who had founded the al-Qur'an bookshop in Clapton, east London, Hamid will shortly be released after being convicted of soliciting murder and providing terrorist training. But in 2004 he was the jihadi who had been running the camps in Cumbria.[80] Hamid organized Friday prayer groups at his home in east London and went on a camp in the Lake District with all four of the men convicted of the attempted 21 July bombings, Woolwich Crown Court was told. He also ran an Islamic bookstall on Oxford Street with Muktar Ibrahim, one of the guilty bombers, where he was arrested for being aggressive to members of the public and making a racist comment to a policeman.

He revelled in calling himself 'Osama bin London' and once told a police officer: 'I've got a bomb and I'm going to blow you all up.' Although he lived in north east London he travelled across the capital to attend meetings in west London where he tried to convince young Muslims to follow his terrorist ideals.

At his trial prosecution barrister, David Farrell QC, told the jury: 'His purpose was to convert such men to his own fanatical and extreme beliefs and having given them such a foundation, thereby enabling them to move on to join others in the pursuit of jihad by acts of terrorism ... The fact that some did exactly as he desired is, we suggest, highly relevant to his real purpose and his continued purpose after 21 July 2005.'

The court was told that terrorist training took the form of camping and paintballing trips. Farrell said the trips were designed to 'foster within the participants that they were training for jihad against the *kuffir*, or non-believer'. The court was shown police surveillance pictures of a training camp at a farm in Great Langdale in the Lake District in May 2004 when Hamid was caught on camera wearing a woollen hat and walking boots, alongside the four 21 July bombers.

Three months later, MI5 surveillance officers saw Muktar Ibrahim, one of the July bombers, on a camp at the same farm with fourteen others, firing imaginary weapons, performing 'leopard crawling' through streams and up hills and practising silent 'ghost walking'.

The court also heard how Hamid and two of his co-defendants, Mousa Brown and Mohammed al-Figari, were filmed paintballing in February 2005 by a BBC crew in Tonbridge, Kent, for a documentary called *Don't Panic, I'm Islamic*.

Two other July 21 bombers, Ramzi Mohammed and Hussain Osman, were at the same centre just four days before the July 7 suicide attacks in London. MI5 became so concerned about Hamid's activities that they bugged his home in September 2005 and, in April 2006, an undercover officer approached his stall in Oxford Street and was invited to join the Friday prayer meetings and to go on camping weekends in the New Forest and at an Islamic school in Sussex.

At the school in Sussex on 22 July 2006, the undercover officer recorded Hamid's comments about the 7 July deaths just over a year earlier.

> HAMID: You have the bottle, we know you have the bottle ...
> You know what happened on the tubes, four people got *shaheed* [martyred]. How many people did they take out?
> ANSWER: Fifty-two.
> HAMID: That's not even a breakfast for me. I would take my breakfast and I'll still be with my wife and children. Remember Jack the Ripper? Remember those people that never got caught? Use your intelligence, use your *hikma* [wisdom] and be effective. See how many people you can take and how long it will last.

When Hamid was arrested with two other men in September 2006 he was found to be in possession of CDs and DVDs which showed murders, beheadings and suicide bombings. Hamid was at the centre of the group which MI5 claimed included

Mohamed Sakr, Bilal al-Berjawi, Ibrahim Magag and Mohammed Emwazi.[81] Hamid also has close family ties to the part of Tanzania where Emwazi later chose to go on 'safari'.

A court document relating to a hearing involving the anonymous CE, concerning the terms of his control order, provides a tantalizing glimpse of how Emwazi had bedded in with the extremists perhaps as early as his second year of university.[82] A former senior Scotland Yard officer who helped lead the hunt for the 21/7 bombers believes Emwazi may have been known to the security services as early as 2007. 'There were about 150 Islamist militants who were being watched in London. To monitor the threat level they posed we graded them using a traffic light system with red as the most dangerous.' CE is the Iranian member of the group who had travelled to the same al-Shabaab training camp as Berjawi and Sakr. He still lives in Ladbroke Grove, under virtual house arrest, because the security services have strong concerns about his terrorist links.

The document also suggests that the security service and the Metropolitan Police's counter-terrorism unit had considered that the network to which Emwazi belonged was of real interest two years before he first tried to travel to Somalia to join al-Shabaab in 2009.[83] And this begs the question: if the authorities knew this much about his links to the London extremist network, why hadn't they made Emwazi the subject of a control order as other members of the group had been? The group of men numbered twelve core members. They all knew each other and all knew they were being watched. At least two of them were on control orders. CE was required to reside in his property in Ladbroke Grove and subject to a fourteen-hour curfew.[84] Some of those who were given control orders treated them as a badge of honour and proudly lifted up their jeans to show the others the electronic tag strapped to their leg, which they were forced to wear twenty-four hours a day. Under the terms of the order, Emwazi and the other members of the network were banned from having any contact with CE. This would have had a serious impact on the lives of the men as any breach of the contact rules could have ended in the suspect on the order being sent to prison.

The group had learned to meet secretly and use sophisticated counter-surveillance tactics. They took circuitous routes to meetings and left their mobile phones at home believing the security services could use them to track their meetings.[85] MI5 believed the network now comprised London-based and east Africa-based extremists involved in the 'provision of funds and equipment to Somalia for terrorism-related purposes and the facilitation of individuals' travel from the United Kingdom to Somalia to undertake terrorism-related activity'.[86]

The west London network which had sucked Mohammed Emwazi into its orbit was more than simply a group of like-minded radicals who dreamt of one day joining a caliphate in a foreign country. The membership was active and self-funding. The culture shared a lot with the gangs to which many of Ladbroke Grove's Muslim youths had belonged. But it had a much broader geographical reach, stretching from the tenement blocks of Maida Vale through the suburban council estates of Southall and Hounslow into the county of Surrey.

Emwazi had at last found a gang which accepted him for who he was. In fact it accepted him because of who he was – a twenty-something Arab born in a foreign land who was struggling with his identity. Some of the group, like Mohamed Sakr and Bilal al-Berjawi, shared Emwazi's Westernized past of clubs, drinking and in Emwazi's case failure with girls. Others had come to religion earlier. Now they all shared a single goal – a desire to use their energies and talents in the protection of their

Muslim brothers and sisters who were fighting against the odds and against infidel forces.

A denial of the legitimacy of the state made it easy to justify the violence and robbery which many of the men had grown up with. Encouraged by Berjawi, the group's leader and mentor, they regarded crime as the best way of funding and supporting their group activities. The money was supposed to be used to send members abroad to broaden links with al-Shabaab and al-Qaeda around the world. But a lot of the crime was carried out for crime's sake or in order to fund their own personal recreational activities.

Emwazi himself was accused and later acquitted of handling stolen bikes. But there were others in the group who had made a career out of crime. Emwazi's school friend Choukri Ellekhlifi, twenty-four, used a Taser-style high-voltage stun gun to force victims to hand over valuables including designer watches and mobile phones.[87] Originally from Morocco, he lived in Paddington until he skipped bail in 2012 and travelled to Syria to join a group of Islamist extremists waging war on President Assad's regime. He would later be killed in the fighting.

Aine Davis became the group's criminal mentor. A former Tube driver with drug-dealing convictions to his name, he converted to Islam while in prison. He had been sentenced to two years in a young offenders' institution in 2004 after he was caught with a firearm in a taxi. It is in jail that he is thought to have been radicalized. It was said that after leaving for Syria he linked up with Emwazi and they joined Islamist militias in the north of the country. But in November 2015 he was arrested by the Turkish authorities as he tried to make his way back to the UK. One paper claimed he was part of a terror cell planning attacks in Europe like those witnessed in Paris the same month.

Tam Hussein is a former youth worker who went to Holland Park School and grew up with some of these young men. He now works as a journalist who has bravely reported from inside Syria on a number of occasions. He says the radicalization of each member of the group was a complex and different experience:

> Drugs and criminality had always been a facet of Ladbroke Grove since the nineties. Golborne Road was the best place to pick up skunk and hash in west London. Anyone who grew up in the area knew that Ladbroke Grove had cornered the market. You could drive up in a car and some dealer would shake your hands, drop the punk and walk off in his joggers. Any undercover would have a hard time finding this ghost once he'd disappeared into the estates. But as time passed these men, coming mostly from the close-knit Moroccan community, felt the impact of religion in their lives. Their parents were getting old and becoming increasingly devout.
>
> They started their own families in the area and with the profundity of having one's own family they too began to consider the deeper meanings of life. 'Once a man holds his own kids in his arms,' said one, 'he starts thinking about their future, you can't help it. That's just God's way.' A few decades on and these same dealers who had shot the stuff to willing punters were sporting beards and praying five times a day looking for ways to atone themselves. These men raised in the school of hard knocks found that Salafi-jihadism fitted their temperament just like perhaps a creative temperament might prefer a Sufi understanding of Islam.[88]

Of the Ladbroke Grove group he adds:

> There was always talk of ex-Ladbroke Grove criminals suspected of a string of crimes in and around west London

51

to fund their jihadi activities. These criminal acts, it was said, were justified by the legal fiction that they were living in Dar al-Harb or 'House of War', a classical Islamic term developed by Islamic jurisprudence during the medieval period to denote the lands that the Muslim world was at war with.[89]

CHAPTER 3

MI5 AND THE
HORN OF AFRICA

After the withdrawal of the Ethiopian military in January 2009, al-Shabaab crept back into Mogadishu and began firmly establishing control over large parts of the city. From there, they extended their influence across the rest of the country. Having secured their power bases, the group's leaders looked to strengthen ties with al-Qaeda and help bring about the advancement of some kind of African jihad. Attacks against Western targets inside Somalia had made the West aware of the group's ability to wage an aggressive terrorist war against Ethiopian, Kenyan, Ugandan, American and United Nations targets.

In October 2008 al-Shabaab co-ordinated five suicide bomb attacks that hit the UN Development Programme compound, the Ethiopian consulate and various government offices, killing several dozen. The following year, al-Shabaab bombed the African Union peacekeeping mission in Mogadishu, killing more than twenty people and damaging the offices of a US firm that was purportedly providing support to peacekeepers.[1]

Their military successes combined with a slick media operation, led by mostly English-speaking Western-educated commanders, made the country attractive to European Ethiopian families looking to return home as well as extremists in search of the next jihad. This influx of foreign fighters to al-Shabaab's military camps greatly broadened the threat to the West. Some of the foreign fighters had trained in Afghanistan and Pakistan, acquiring the capacity to carry out more complex bombing operations. These fighters now held senior positions of influence inside the movement. A number of suicide bombers, including foreigners of Somali descent, were behind a wave of attacks in Mogadishu throughout 2009. The group also began exchanging fighters with al-Qaeda's branch in Yemen (al-Qaeda in the Arabian Peninsula).

Security chiefs in London and Washington regarded this as the greatest danger to Western interests. These fears were graphically realized later that year by the so-called 'underwear bomb plot' on a Detroit-bound jetliner. In that operation al-Qaeda sent Nigerian Umar Farouk Abdulmutallab, twenty-five, on a suicide mission to detonate a bomb in his underpants as the plane, en route from Amsterdam, approached Detroit. But mercifully the bomb failed to detonate, burning only Abdulmutallab's trousers and genitals.

Not long after, a Somali man with direct links to al-Shabaab attempted the assassination of Kurt Westergaard, the Danish artist whose drawing of the Prophet Muhammad had sparked riots around the world. The would-be assassin was shot by police outside Westergaard's home in the city of Aarhus on 1 January 2010, just a few days after the Detroit airliner plot. Al-Shabaab later claimed full responsibility.

But in Britain al-Shabaab remained a lawful organization, although there were plans afoot in Whitehall to proscribe the group. And as the terror threat posed by Somalia-based militants became more pressing British security chiefs urged action against al-Shabaab.

This is how Jonathan Evans, then head of MI5, summed up the threat in a speech on terrorism to the Worshipful Company of Security Professionals on 17 September 2010:

> In Somalia . . . there are a significant number of UK residents training in al-Shabaab camps to fight in the insurgency there. Al-Shabaab, an Islamist militia in Somalia, is closely aligned with al-Qaeda and Somalia shows many of the characteristics that made Afghanistan so dangerous as a seedbed for terrorism in the period before the fall of the Taliban. There is no effective government, there is a strong extremist presence and there are training camps attracting would-be jihadists from across the world. We need to do whatever we can to stop people from this country becoming involved in terrorism and murder in Somalia, but beyond that I am concerned that it is only a matter of time before we see terrorism on our streets inspired by those who are today fighting alongside al-Shabaab.

It wasn't until March, 2010 that Labour Home Secretary Alan Johnson finally made membership of or support for al-Shabaab an offence, attracting a maximum ten-year prison sentence. The new law gave MI5 and SO15 the powers to step up surveillance and disruption operations targeting suspects linked to the Horn of Africa. Anyone caught in the matrix of suspicion could expect to be stopped and questioned whenever they left British airports, regardless of their end destination. Their daily lives were interrupted by 'home visits', street stop-and-searches or intimidating telephone calls to their personal numbers. The strategy was clumsy but it let the suspect know that they were visible to the security services. Key to the new approach would be deeper penetration of Muslim communities. The police worked to gain the confidence of Muslim leaders; the security service stepped up its recruitment of informers.

The intelligence failures exposed in the wake of the 7/7 bombings showed that MI5 was woefully short of surveillance manpower. Particularly the service badly lacked experienced Asian officers who could operate in this difficult field. In fact, things were so dire in G Branch (counter-Islamic terrorism) that one former officer claimed the unit only had one Asian officer and so the suggestion was made to 'black up'.[2]

While some of the intelligence obtained was put to good purpose to foil major terrorist attacks, inevitably mistakes were made. One of the most high-profile counter-terrorism blunders was a raid on the home of two brothers in Forest Gate, east London, which resulted in one of them being shot and both being exonerated. A few months later the arrests of eleven Pakistani students and one British student ended in embarrassment when the raids had to be brought forward because of a security blunder and the men were all released without charge.

Undaunted by the negative publicity and the harm being done to Muslim community relations, MI5 pressed on with its recruitment drive. Spy chiefs believed these 'interventions' against suspects were providing valuable opportunities to recruit field agents to 'spy' on Muslim communities or, as MI5 and the police expressed it, to bring in valuable intelligence about the activities of the extremist networks, like that of Mohammed Emwazi. The security services were gambling that the risk of ruffling some Islamist feathers was justified. They anticipated that any complaints about heavy-handedness or harassment would be made to Muslim community leaders who would want to settle the issues confidentially without making a public fuss. This calculation proved to be correct until a group of north London Muslims decided to speak out.

This group comprised six young men ranging in age from nineteen to twenty-six. They were all volunteer youth workers based at a Kentish Town community centre. All were either born in Somalia or had Somali parents and they had all had their collars felt by MI5.[3] The security services had had the group in their sights for more than a year in the belief that they were linked to Islamist extremism. Most of them had made trips to Somalia. At least one was later linked to the Emwazi network. Each individual member of the group had chosen to remain silent in the hope that MI5 would eventually leave him alone. It wasn't until one of them reported his dealings with MI5 to his community leader and a meeting was called that they discovered they all had strikingly similar stories to tell.

As more young Muslims were hauled in for questioning by the police, Muslim communities became breeding grounds for mutual distrust. None of the Kentish Town men had wanted to come forward in case their friends suspected them of being MI5 spies (on the basis that there is no smoke without fire). They feared the condemnation of their own community far more than the stigma of being branded terrorists by the police. Before they went public they decided first to make official complaints to the local police commander and their MP about what they felt to be serious harassment. But it had made no difference. The harassment would stop for a couple of weeks and then one of the men would suddenly find himself back in the firing line. So in an act of desperation they decided to go the media and make their grievances public.

I was working at *The Independent* as the home affairs editor when I was contacted by the community centre chairman, Sharhabeel Lone. He invited me to a meeting with the men, all of whom he promised had interesting stories to tell. He warned me in advance that they were very nervous about talking to journalists.

It was a lovely early spring evening in 2009 when I arrived at the Kentish Town Community Centre. The door was closed but I gently rapped on it and a young male member of the group let me in. The main area was a sports hall with a door leading off to a recreation area and a meeting room. Lone, an international business consultant who spends many months of the year travelling, greeted me and ushered me into the meeting room. I was offered a place at the head of the table around which six young men had already assembled. Lone said that what I was about to hear would astound me as it involved the corroborated stories of six young men, all of Somali descent, who had decided to speak about their encounters with MI5 and SO15. He said what they were going to tell me went to the very heart of Britain's war on terror.

For many months the men had kept their contact with MI5 secret and had not even confided in their families. Only when one of them, Abshir Mohamed, a youth worker, decided to tell Lone about his MI5 encounters did the scale of the alleged intimidation and harassment emerge. Abshir Mohamed had been stopped at Heathrow airport after a family visit to Saudi Arabia and he and his family had found the experience harrowing. After the airport stop, MI5 had started to call him at home, putting him under enormous pressure to become an informant.

Lone said: 'Abshir called me when he reached home [from Heathrow, where he was quizzed], extremely worried and very anxious. His mother and wife, who has just had heart surgery, had been travelling with him and had to wait throughout his ordeal. Abshir is a senior youth leader who works hard to stop young Muslims getting involved in crime.'[4]

Lone called a youth leader meeting to see if others had similar experiences. What he heard appalled him. Two of the young men said they had been detained abroad and interviewed by MI5 upon their return to the UK. Another was questioned when he returned from his honeymoon to Saudi Arabia. Two more were visited by MI5 officers at home.

It was now clear to both Lone and his Kentish Town group that MI5 had deliberately targeted the men as a group. Allegations were made about the reasons for their travel, they were warned about what could happen to them if they continued with their extremist activities and then they were offered inducements to work as spies. Those who refused to co-operate received menacing phone calls and home visits.

Born in Somalia, most of the men had all come to Britain as children. Growing up in north London, they had overcome troubled backgrounds, which had occasionally brought some of them to the attention of the police. To escape these influences, their families sent them to study Arabic in Middle East countries. But none of them, claimed Lone, who has known them for many years, held extremist views or had links to terrorism.

As I glanced around the table at these young men I could see that some of them looked very nervous indeed. I explained that if they had done nothing wrong they had nothing to fear. The first to speak was Mohamed Nur, one of the oldest of the group at twenty-five. He identified himself as a community youth worker from Camden, north London. His first encounter with MI5 was early one morning in August 2008 when his doorbell rang. Looking through his spyhole, he saw a man with a red bag who was wearing a postman's uniform. But when Nur opened the door the postman told him that he was in fact a policeman and that he and his colleague wanted to talk to him. After sitting down in Nur's front room the second man produced ID and said that he worked for MI5.

The officer told Nur that they suspected him of being an 'Islamic extremist'. 'I immediately said: "And where did you get such an idea?" The officer replied: "I am not permitted to discuss our sources." But I said that I have never done anything extreme.' The officer responded that he believed Nur was interested in ideas that might harm Britain. He said that if that was the case then that was a problem. But he knew a way Nur could instead help Britain. He asked Nur to work with him by spying on others who held even more 'extreme' ideas, although he didn't explain what kind of behaviour he was expected to report on. Nur rejected the offer.

Nur then told me he felt threatened by the officer: 'The MI5 agent said: "Mohamed, if you do not work for us we will tell any foreign country you try to travel to that you are a suspected terrorist."' They asked him what travel plans he had. Nur, a keen footballer, said he might visit Sweden next year for a football tournament. The officer told him he would contact him within the next three days. But Nur told them he wasn't interested in having any further contact with the police or MI5. 'As they left my house they told me to at least consider the approach, as it was in my best interests.'

Mohamed Aden, also twenty-five, had a similar story. He said he was approached by someone disguised as a postman in the same month and that his phone was also bombarded with calls from the security service. He explained:

One morning there was a knock on the door by the postman. My wife was awake and she told me to answer the door. Half asleep I went to open it, not thinking about what had happened to Mohammed Nur. I opened the door slightly and the man said he was a postman, but as soon as he said this he moved to the side and a man and woman from MI5 were standing in front of me. They said: 'Hi, Mr Aden, we are from MI5. Can we have a moment of your time?' I was totally shocked and stopped there, I was completely angered at the fact that they had lied to me in order to get my door open. Before they could say anything else, I angrily told them that how dare they come to my home first thing in the morning and lie to me in order to get me to open the door when I had respectfully opened it for who I thought was a postman.

The men immediately accused Aden of being involved in terrorist activities.

When I told them they had got the wrong man one of the agents called me by a different name. In the middle of the conversation he said: 'OK, Mr Yusuf.' I told him: 'What the hell are you talking about, who is Mr Yusuf?' I literally ran back to my bedroom and grabbed my passport, I then showed them that it said Mohamed Aden, not Mr Yusuf. The agent didn't even move and the lady began to smile. I began to get very angry, I asked her what was so funny, but she didn't respond.

The male officer told Aden that he should co-operate with them otherwise they would make his life very difficult. 'They wouldn't allow me to travel or do anything.' But Aden told officers he wasn't going to help. He told them: 'Fine, do whatever it is you want to do, just get out of my face.' Aden says before they left he made the police officer show him his identification and then argued with the MI5 officers until the female officer produced some ID.

Aden said he was very worried. Of all the group he was the most vulnerable and least willing to have his photograph taken. He said he was worried about how the community would respond to the publicity.

In July 2008 Abshir Mohamed travelled to Egypt for his brother's wedding. But at the airport in Cairo he was detained for sixteen hours and interrogated about previous visits to the country. When he returned to the UK he was stopped at immigration by UK security officials. In familiar circumstances, Abshir Ahmed was stopped at UK immigration, this time after travelling to Saudi Arabia in order to perform a small pilgrimage or *umrah*. He was the last of the group to be approached. Both Abshirs were quizzed about where they prayed, their religious beliefs and the war in Somalia.

The youngest member of the group to be approached was nineteen-year-old Mahdi Hashi, a care worker from Camden. He had been born in Somalia in 1989. Two years later the country was gripped in civil war and his family fled for Britain. On 16 April 2004 the family received news that their son's British citizenship had been granted. Somali law at the time required that as he had taken a foreign nationality, he was no longer a Somali citizen and his east African nationality had been rescinded. In 2005 he completed his GCSEs but rather than continuing his education in the UK, he chose to leave with his family for Egypt in order to study Arabic.[5]

But the following year Hashi, who was just sixteen years old, was detained by Egypt's feared security police, who claimed his visa had expired. He spent a day being interrogated but was released with no further action being taken. A few weeks later he was arrested and questioned for a total of eleven days in a police cell no bigger than ten feet square. He claims he was never told the reason for his detention but it was later asserted that the Egyptians suspected him of having links to al-Qaeda – something he denied. He was released and deported to the UK where he was quizzed by British police and had his DNA and fingerprints taken.

In 2008 he left Britain once again, this time choosing to resume his Arabic studies in Damascus. When he returned to the UK a year later he was stopped by counter-terrorism police. 'I came back at Heathrow airport. I was stopped by two police officers. They were asking questions like "Why did you go there?" "Did you want to go to Iraq?" and "What do you think about ...?" They asked me scholarly questions about religion and jihad and suicide bombing; for example, they would ask me about the Palestinians.'[6]

Back in London Hashi started working with the Kentish Town Community Centre, helping young people who were having difficulties in their personal lives. He also started an engineering course at the College of Haringey, Enfield and North East London, and in 2009 he took up a post as a care worker for a disabled man living in north west London.[7]

In April 2009 he had arrived at Gatwick airport to take a plane to visit his sick grandmother in Djibouti, but as he was checking in he says he was stopped by two plainclothes officers. One of the officers identified himself as Richard and said he was working for MI5.

Hashi said: 'He warned me not to get on the flight. He said: "Whatever happens to you outside the UK is not our responsibility." I was absolutely shocked.'

The officer handed Hashi a piece of paper with his name and telephone contact details and asked him to call him. 'The whole time he tried to make it seem like he was looking after me. And just before I left them at my boarding gate I remember "Richard" telling me: "It's your choice, mate, to get on that flight but I advise you not to," and then he winked at me.'

When Hashi arrived at Djibouti airport he was stopped at passport control. He was then held in a room for sixteen hours before being deported back to the UK. He claims the Somali security officers told him that their orders came from London.

More than twenty-four hours after he first left the UK he arrived back at Heathrow and was detained again. 'I was taken to pick up my luggage and then into a very discreet room. "Richard" walked in with a Costa bag with food which he said was for me, my breakfast. He said it was them who sent me back because I was a terror suspect.'

Hashi alleges that the officer made it clear that his suspect status and travel restrictions would only be lifted if he agreed to co-operate with MI5.

I told him: 'This is blatant blackmail.'

He said: 'No, it's just proving your innocence. By co-oper-ating with us we know you're not guilty.'

He said I could go and that he'd like to meet me another time, preferably after [May] Monday Bank Holiday. I looked at him and said: 'I don't ever want to see you or hear from you again. You've ruined my holiday, upset my family, and you nearly gave my sick grandmother in Somalia a heart attack.'

Aydarus Elmi, twenty-three, worked as an usher and reception-ist at a cinema in London. In May 2007 he married an American citizen and in November the young couple, with a child on the way, returned to the US for a holiday. But when Elmi arrived at Chicago's O'Hare airport with his pregnant wife they were separated, questioned and deported back to Britain.

Three days later Elmi was contacted on his mobile phone and asked to attend Charing Cross police station to discuss problems he was having with his travel documents. 'I met a man and a woman,' he said. 'She said her name was Katherine and that she worked for MI5. I didn't know what MI5 was.'

The approach followed a similar pattern. For two-and-a-half hours Elmi faced questions. 'I felt I was being lured into working for MI5.' The contact did not stop there. Over the following weeks he claims 'Katherine' harassed him with dozens of phone calls. 'She would regularly call my mother's home asking to speak to me,' he said. 'And she would constantly call my mobile.'

In one disturbing call the officer telephoned Elmi's home at 7 a.m. to congratulate him on the birth of his baby girl. His wife was still seven months pregnant and the couple had expressly told the hospital that they did not want to know the sex of their child.

'Katherine tried to threaten me by saying – and it still runs through my mind now – "Remember, this won't be the last time we ever meet," and then during our last conversation explained: "If you do not want anything to happen to your family you will co-operate."'

I listened carefully to these young Muslim men's stories and as I did I was struck by their openness and sense of bewilderment at what was happening to them. All of them were courteous and friendly. Not all of them spoke perfect English while some had picked up street slang from north London. They had arguments with their parents about what was British and what was Islamic and how their lives often involved choosing between the two. Their families fed them stories about the horrors of relatives suffering in Somalia but their parents' generation weren't interested in going back to help, only counting their blessings that they were safe in the UK. Their children's generation were made to understand the plight of Muslims in their countries of origin but not expected to do anything about it. For some of them life was very tough on the streets as they had to negotiate poverty and racism. 'We liked to play football,' said one of them, 'but as soon as we found a place to play it we either got kicked out or the rich families from other districts turned up and all of a sudden we had to pay money just to kick a ball.'

Some of them, like Mohamed Nur, had been part of a Somali gang culture where they had learned to fight in order to survive on the streets and although they had run-ins with the police not one of them had been convicted of a criminal offence. Some of them had turned their lives around. All had been recruited by the Kentish Town Community Centre to work with other British Somali youths in the area who were members of gangs and were heading for trouble. In the north London community the six men I faced across the table were role models.

Nevertheless, they were young Muslim men who could not hide their religious identity. They had grown up in the aftermath of 9/11. They witnessed the wrath of America as it wreaked its revenge first on Afghanistan and then on Iraq. And as they emerged into full adulthood they found themselves Muslims in a city chosen as the location for the atrocity of 7/7. They shared the horror of that attack with millions of other Londoners. Like other Londoners, they were appalled by the killing of innocents and said so in conversation with family and friends. But now Britain was engaged in a 'war on terror' and British Muslims were expected to speak out against terrorism to show they did not support it.

'Why was it their business to condemn something which they had nothing to do with?' says Sharhabeel Lone. 'It's like a white teenager being asked to condemn one of the school massacres in America that unfortunately happen from time to time. There is simply no connection.'

But in the aftermath of 9/11 and 7/7 Muslim communities were repeatedly being asked to answer for the crimes of the terrorist. Wherever you looked Muslims were asked to declare what they were doing to prevent another 7/7. Following the atrocity a group of Muslim organizations felt compelled to pay for advertising in national newspapers offering support to

Londoners and effectively saying what had happened had absolutely nothing to do with them. Ten years later after the Islamic State attacks on Paris British Muslims repeated the exercise.

The knock-on effect was that Somali-born young Muslim men who were already struggling to find their place in a multicultural Britain were being stigmatized as a threat to society. The syllogism was that, since the people who are trying to kill us are Muslims, and these young men are Muslim, they might want to do the same. When these young men didn't understand why they needed to demonstrate to society that they weren't a threat they encountered hostile reactions. So it was hardly any wonder that they found it easier to simply disengage from mainstream society and seek refuge within their own communities. They had become unintended victims of the war on terror.

By the time I met them their views were already fixed. They wanted to know if I thought the 9/11 attack was an inside job carried out by the Americans as an excuse to attack Muslim countries. When I laughed they didn't laugh back. Mohamed Nur was surprised at my reaction. 'Haven't you seen the films on the internet about this?'

The war on terror had forced them to confront extremism while they grappled with their own Islamic identities. They wanted to explore reasons behind the conflict that was now engulfing the world but they had been forced on the defensive. Within the confines of a small, isolated peer group whose membership shared similar experiences it was inevitable that the results of their discussions would be wrapped up in self-justification or conspiracy. Their crazy ideas might sound ludicrous but when everyone is saying the same thing and no one is challenging that mindset it becomes very easy to believe. The government has diagnosed this problem but its policies for tackling it are too simplistic. You can't shake communities out of isolation overnight. Nor can you start walking into closed communities and tell them they have got it all wrong and need to start thinking like the rest of us. I think I might have been the first person from outside their community to tell the Kentish Town members that the conventional explanations about 9/11 and 7/7 are more or less true.

When I reached them they were angry about what was happening to them. They wanted to lead what they believed were peaceful lives, travelling to and from Somalia, helping fellow Muslims. And most important of all they wanted to practise their religion. The actions of the security service and the police only confirmed what they had already concluded among themselves – that Western governments didn't like Muslims.

One or two had been to Mogadishu and they said it wasn't how it was being portrayed on the television. One of the group recalled a recent visit: 'There was a lot of shooting and it got a bit crazy but life is interesting and everyone talks to you ... you've just got to be a bit careful.'

Another said that he had been in Mogadishu to visit his father and that he had been able to cross freely between government and al-Shabaab borders:

I was a foreigner and had a beard and the government soldiers always pointed their guns at me and were suspicious of me. But when I went to the [al-Shabaab] checkpoint they all looked laid back and cool. They said: 'Hey man, come over and join us.' But after a few days with them you could see what they were really like. There was only one law and that was Shabaab law. If you did anything or said anything against them they punished you. I once saw them beat up a young guy who had mental problems just because he couldn't answer some question about shari'a. It was sick and nasty.

I spent several weeks trying to get MI5 to engage with the men's stories – to answer their claims or justify their own actions and policies. But the message came back that although they had thought long and hard about the issues and the need to offer a context to what was being alleged they would not say anything on the record. A key problem facing the service is that they can never talk about individuals they have had contact with, as confirmation of working for MI5 can expose the agent to serious danger. It also makes it much harder for them to recruit once it is publicly known that they will give away the identities of agents. But behind closed doors the security service also makes no apologies for the tactics they employ. One security source has since told me: 'Those people who are on the margins of extremist networks are exactly the sort of people we should be speaking to.'

The Independent put the stories and pictures of the Kentish Town youths on the front page of the newspaper. At the time the paper was edited by Roger Alton, who was in charge of *The Observer* when it had controversially supported the Iraq war. To his credit, Alton could see that there was public interest in debating security policies and tactics in tackling terrorism, especially if one community was being singled out for special treatment and it was affecting the lives of thousands of young men and women up and down the country. He judged that if counter-terrorism policy wasn't properly scrutinized we would be storing up trouble in the future. After the article appeared word got back to me that the coverage had made the job of SO15 and MI5 more difficult. One officer told one of my colleagues that 'having claims of police harassment plastered over the papers makes it even harder to speak to these people'.

In August 2015 I called Sharhabeel Lone to try to arrange another meeting to see how the Kentish Town youth workers I had met had fared. It would be the first time we had met since 2009. Of the six, only two were prepared or able to meet me again. It seemed the intervening years had taken a heavy toll on these young men's lives.

The two who arrived at the restaurant had managed to overcome their difficulties with the security services. Mohamed Nur returned to Somalia in 2010 but not with al-Shabaab. He went back with his father, who was elected mayor of Mogadishu, to help rebuild the country. Abshir Mohamed and Mohamed Nur, now happily back in London, are each married with four children. They are studying at university and continue to provide help to disenfranchised young Muslims in their communities. Abshir Ahmed is also studying at university. Aydarus Elmi, was named by MI5 as part of the same terror network as Mohammed Emwazi. I have since been told that he has put these associations behind him. He has found steady work as a refrigeration engineer and is clear of any trouble. Mahdi Hashi, as we shall later see, returned to Somalia and was picked up fighting for al-Shabaab.

But for Mohamed Aden the problems didn't go away. Friends say MI5 continued to harass him and so he moved his family to Slough. Among the group Aden was the most withdrawn. He had had a difficult childhood after his father left the family home and he found it hard to integrate and earn money. A friend told me that he is now in Syria, possibly fighting with one of the militant groups.

The security services make no apologies for getting involved in any of these men's lives. What the suspects describe as harassment the security services dismiss as anger at being asked legitimate questions about potential links to terrorism. One Whitehall security source put it like this: 'If we accept there is a terror threat to this country, then you would expect us to want to speak to people who, for whatever reason, we believe might be involved and pose a threat to the UK. If we didn't test people's stories when they cross our radar, the public would rightly want to know why not.'

In the week that I interviewed the Kentish Town group, Bilal al-Berjawi and Mohamed Sakr slipped out of Britain for their ill-fated 'safari' to Kenya. Mohammed Emwazi was busy preparing for his finals but must have known what had happened. Once he had got his exams behind him and had graduated from Westminster with a modest 2.2 he decided to follow his friends to Africa.

Emwazi, now twenty-one, had met Marcel Schrödl, twenty-three, and an older man called Ali Adorus, twenty-seven, in Regent's Park Mosque. They appeared to have little in common other than their religion and an interest in foreign travel. Adorus, a security guard, was born in Ethiopia and came to London as a small boy while Schrödl is from Dusseldorf in Germany and was studying in the UK.

The wide spread of ages and the fact they were all at different colleges does not help support Emwazi's claim that they were going on a summer safari together to celebrate finishing their degrees. Adorus is now in a prison in Ethiopia after being convicted of trying to overthrow the government and establish an Islamic state while Schrödl is back home in Germany trying to put his extremism behind him. Later, media reports claimed that the three men were arrested by the Tanzanian authorities for being drunk and disruptive on the plane.[8] They may have been celebrating the first day of their holiday or enjoying one last fling before they joined the strict regime of al-Shabaab. (And there is plenty of evidence that terrorists enjoy a drink – the 9/11 attackers were reported to have frequented nightclubs and drunk alcohol while they were preparing for their suicide operation.)

What we do know is that in late May 2009 the trio arrived at Heathrow airport with their bags packed. Inside the suitcases they had clothes for all kinds of weather, including green combat jackets, which Emwazi said were for the safari but which MI5 argued would be useful at a military training camp.

They had decided to avoid flying directly to Dar es Salaam by taking a flight via Amsterdam, but the Tanzanian security services were expecting them and the three didn't get out of the airport.[9] As they approached passport control they were confronted by a group of armed men in military uniform who began shouting at them. While they were physically restrained an officer who introduced himself as Emmanuel told them that they were being refused entry to Tanzania. Before the three could offer any protest they were hauled out of the airport and bundled into a waiting car which took them to a nearby detention centre. They were placed in separate cells and held for twenty-four hours without food or water. Throughout the night they were threatened with beatings. On one occasion when Emwazi protested his innocence from behind the bars of the cell a guard drew his gun and pointed it at him, threatening to shoot.[10]

The next day the men were visited by British consular officials who told them the Tanzanian government had the absolute right to refuse any foreigner entry to the country.[11] Emwazi, who later said he suspected the British were behind his detention, sought an explanation from the British official but none was forthcoming.[12]

As he was marched to the departing plane Emwazi pressed Emmanuel for some sort of justification. 'This is not the Tanzanian government,' Emmanuel told him.[13] He then produced a piece of paper with his name, flight details and at the bottom the phrase 'Refuse entry and send back to the UK with the same flight'. The Tanzanian security official then added these parting words: 'You know it could be the British, your government, who were the reason for your rejection.'[14]

The three men were taken to a flight bound for Amsterdam,

the same route they had used to travel to Tanzania. But this was not the end of their ordeal. As soon as the plane landed the men were met by armed Dutch security officers who escorted them to an interrogation centre. Emwazi says an immigration officer took him to a cell where two plainclothes officers were waiting. They introduced themselves as 'Fernando, from Dutch intelligence' and 'Nick, from MI5'.[15] Emwazi later admitted to CAGE that he was flattered by the attention and thought to himself: 'I can't believe it. Am I so special?'

The two officers cut to the chase and demanded to know what Emwazi's intentions were during his stay in Tanzania. When he told them that he was planning a safari after his exams 'Nick' jumped in and accused him of lying, saying that he knew his real reason for the trip was to get to Somalia and join al-Shabaab.[16] This instantly confirmed Emwazi's suspicions about what lay behind the reason for their interest in him. Nevertheless he maintained his cool, calmly pointing out that he had a return ticket and that Tanzania was far from Somalia. Most importantly, he said there was a civil war there and he had no intention to be part of it.

'He ['Nick'] said that at the end of the day they had been following us and watching us closely. I told him that it was news to me and I had no idea about it. He knew everything about me; where I lived, what I did, the people I hanged around with,' Emwazi later recalled.[17] Such sangfroid in the face of this interrogation was bound to antagonize the British officers. The atmosphere changed and 'Nick' became more threatening. Pointing his finger at Emwazi he shouted: 'Don't try to play smart and lie to my face. Don't try to fool me. You wanted to go to Somalia.'[18] 'Nick' told Emwazi that life could get very unpleasant for him if he continued on the extremist path he had chosen. He warned Emwazi to expect further visits and knocks on the door.

And then 'Nick's' mood changed. Instead of hectoring him about the dangers of extremism and threatening him with harassment he started to offer him an alternative, a way out of his predicament. According to Emwazi's account 'Nick's' tone was conversational and more understanding of a young man taking an interest in his religion and what the officer described as the duty of jihad. The officer beseeched him: 'Listen, Mohammed. You've got the whole world in front of you; you're twenty-one years old; you just finished uni – why don't you work for us?'

The offer of working for MI5 was not a surprise to Emwazi. He knew that Berjawi, Sakr and Magag had been made similar offers and had expected MI5 to come calling. He had had plenty of time to discuss with his peers how to respond to such an approach.

In this context it is very easy to believe that Emwazi regarded his encounter with MI5 as a rite of passage in the jihadi's path to war. Perhaps he privately imagined how proud he would feel when he got back to London and shared his own personal experiences of '5-0' (the term young Islamists used to refer to MI5) with the older men in his group whom he looked up to and respected. Whatever his reasoning, Emwazi took great pleasure in rebuffing the officer. The MI5 officer responded in kind: 'You're going to have a lot of trouble . . . You're going to be known . . . you're going to be followed . . . life will be harder for you.'[19]

'Nick' left his number on a piece of paper, adding, 'We'll see you in London, mate.'

After the men were released they made their way to England by ferry and were soon in sight of the famous white cliffs of Dover.[20] But for Emwazi this was not a happy homecoming. True to 'Nick's' word, life was about to become very uncomfortable for Emwazi.

Upon reaching Dover, Emwazi was stopped again. This time two suited men claiming to be from the police 'Anti-Terror Unit' were waiting at the port building's entrance.[21] Once again the trio were escorted to an interrogation suite, where their bags were searched and they faced another two hours of questioning.[22]

Ali Adorus said this time the focus of the questioning had changed and he was asked about his religious beliefs and political views. 'They wanted to put words into our mouths and wanted to force us to say that we wanted to go to Somalia,' he said.[23]

Emwazi was questioned by two anti-terror officers who repeated questions asked by the MI5 officer in Holland but now widened the interrogation to ask him about his thoughts on 7/7 and 9/11, where he prayed and who his friends were. They also claimed that they had good intelligence that he wanted to go to Somalia.

In the next few weeks, Emwazi decided to make his first approach to CAGE to see if they could rid his life of MI5 and the police. He met Asim Qureshi at the group's east London office and told him about his experience. Qureshi decided to record the conversations to help with his note taking. In the recordings, Emwazi has a distinct and confident London street accent, associated with the west London rap scene. It is far removed from the mocking tone of 'Jihadi John', the masked man who was filmed killing at least seven people.[24] In the beheading films he came across as overblown and puffed up with his own importance. And his voice was over-strained, maybe even digitally enhanced to make him sound more threatening than he himself was capable of sounding.

In the CAGE tapes in 2009 when Emwazi was asked by the security services about his views on the attacks, he replied: 'Innocent people have ... died. What do you think? I think this is extremism ... I told him: "This is a wrong thing. It was wrong.

What do you want me to say? If I had the opportunity, would I make those lives come back? I would make those lives come back." '[25]

In another exchange, Emwazi is asked about the war in Afghanistan and here he said he watched the news and saw 'innocent people getting killed'. The security services also pressed him on his views 'of the Jews'.[26] 'I told him . . . they're a religion . . . everyone has got his right to his own beliefs . . . [he] wants to know about my background . . . about my creed . . . Islam. I told him we don't force anyone to come into religion, you know, everyone has got their own right.'[27]

Emwazi says that during the search, an officer pulled out a safari-style jacket and said: 'This jacket looks like a bit military, Mohammed.'[28] Emwazi said: 'I started laughing and asked how he could even suggest that it was military, what he was trying to prove. I had another jumper, a stylish jumper, so I asked him, what about this jumper? Was he not going to make any comment about that? He fell silent then.'[29]

Emwazi said he then requested the officer's badge number: 'I told him that when I go back to London and I will speak to my solicitors, then he would want to know who on earth was he. But he said that he could not show me his badge. I felt stuck. I did not know what to do. The door was shut and I just wanted to walk out of the room. How could I be treated like that? I am a British citizen and my government was threatening me and throwing allegations at me.'

Emwazi was finally told he was free to leave and handed back his luggage. Scraping together just enough money to pay for three train tickets to London, the friends set off home.

It is clear that Emwazi was very badly affected by this experience. He must have had suspicions that the security services were following him. His conversations with Sakr and Berjawi and his association with other members of the network and their reported contact with MI5 and the police would have served as a warning that his turn would come.

The interviews in Tanzania, Holland and Dover now showed Emwazi exactly how the British authorities viewed him. The angst in his voice on the tapes reveals that he believed judgement had been cast on his behaviour without allowing him to properly defend his actions or explain his views. He was being forced into a corner and he didn't like it. Whatever his real intentions for his visiting Tanzania, Emwazi didn't believe he had done anything wrong. When he met Berkjawi, Sakr and Magag to discuss how his trip had gone, one can only imagine their mutual indignation at the 'feds'.

But Emwazi appears to have felt the injustice of their treatment much more than the others. By his calculation he had had a night in the cells, a potential holiday ruined and £500 wasted, and then he had been subjected to a series of humiliating and abusive interrogations. All because he was hanging out with the wrong crowd or someone had told the police he was an extremist?

As far as the security services were concerned Emwazi was just the sort of person they should be targeting. 'He was mixing with extremists and his travel to east Africa raised real suspicions. He was clearly of concern,' a security source told me. But Emwazi was seething. He now wanted justice and no doubt revenge.

About this time an old school friend bumped into Emwazi sitting in a café on Edgware Road, which has long been a favourite haunt of young Arabs who frequent the bars and restaurants to socialize with each other. Emwazi was one of three people wearing long, white Islamic robes. The girl remembers: 'I asked him how he was but he didn't really say anything. He was a bit zoned out, like a zombie. There was a void behind the eyes. It was awkward. I left pretty quickly.'[30]

*   *   *

Emwazi quickly discovered that he and his friends were not the only British Muslims to have come forward to seek advice from CAGE. Asim Qureshi, the then director of research, told him that there were ten or so others who had similar experiences when travelling to east Africa. CAGE decided to investigate these cases as a group, and published the results early in 2010 in a report entitled *The Horn of Africa Inquisition: The Latest Profile in the War on Terror*. In it CAGE's director, Moazzam Begg, the former Guantánamo Bay detainee, explains the problem facing the West. He says in the foreword:

Following the 7 July 2005 attacks the government introduced new policies and legislation which further undermined civil liberties and more blatantly targeted Muslim communities, following the logic that the men responsible were not only mostly of South Asian origin but, that they were all Muslim. Two weeks later, the failed 21 July attacks were also attributed to Muslim men, this time originating from the Horn of Africa.[31]

Begg says that shortly after the attacks on London the head of British Transport Police, Ian Johnston, made a damaging admission about policing policy: 'We should not waste time searching old white ladies. It is going to be disproportionate. It is going to be young men, not exclusively, but it may be disproportionate when it comes to ethnic groups.'[32] Begg added:

Despite the assurance that some government ministers later made that the Muslim community would not be singled out for police scrutiny, Mr Johnston's words have continued to ring true for anyone who happens to look like a Muslim. Since Islam is a religion and not a race this has proved to be one of the most controversial and quite ludicrous measures employed by the government in trying to tackle terrorism. Worse still, the latest community feeling the brunt of the most draconian legislation in the history of Britain are the Somalis – most of whom have fled severe hardship to seek sanctuary in the UK ... Scores of men and women from this community have been detained and questioned at ports of entry and exit in the UK or elsewhere or received veiled and direct threats of imprisonment, deportation and harassment from the intelligence services for refusing to spy on their own community.

The Horn of Africa report also helps to throw more light on the activities of other members of Emwazi's network. Among those featured was Bilal al-Berjawi and his own disrupted safari trip to Kenya. Under the name of Abu Omar, Berjawi tells CAGE how he was held by Kenyan security services in Nairobi for four days, accused of planning to blow up an Israeli-owned supermarket in an attack sanctioned by Osama bin Laden. This goes much further than what had already been revealed about his trip to Kenya.

It is apparent that the Kenyans believed Berjawi and Sakr were part of a plot to attack a supermarket, causing mass casualties, four years before the infamous al-Shabaab massacre at Westgate shopping centre which killed sixty-seven people. Berjawi was captured at a friend's house. Police surrounded the building, arrested him at gunpoint and threw him into the back of a van.

According to Berjawi, during his interrogation the Kenyans told him: 'So you came here to blow yourself up? Because of your seventy-two or seventy-three or whatever the fuck they are virgins? My friend, let's get to the story: you come here, you plan to blow up the Kenyan people. You're a terrorist, you're an al-Qaeda member. We believe you've been to Afghanistan.

Listen, we have pictures of you in Afghanistan, in Chechnya, in Iraq, in Somalia.'[33]

Berjawi says: 'As I looked at him, he kept throwing many names – Abu Ahmad, Abu this, Abu that . . . lots of names.'

The interrogators continued: 'We're telling you: you used this name in Afghanistan, and you used this name in Iraq, and you used this name in Somalia, this name in Israel.'

Berjawi told CAGE that by now he felt sure all the questions were being fed to them by MI5. But the Kenyan interrogators were not bound by the rule of law. One of the burly Kenyans moved towards him and shouted: 'What would you feel if I was to come over to you now and squeeze your balls? You don't exist. You have to understand this. You know the "War on Terror"? You've heard about this? Yeah, you people, you have no rights. You don't exist. In our world, you don't exist. We can do and take you as we will.'

Then another interrogator threw Berjawi a mobile phone. 'So you recognize this mobile? It's got your fingerprints.'[34]

Berjawi told CAGE that they were trying to frame him: 'Then that's when my face went red, because now I thought, "They've stitched me up, they've set me up." Then he goes, "It's made calls to bin Laden. You were planning to attack a supermarket. One called Nakona."' Berjawi explained to CAGE: 'Nakona is very famous there, and according to him, it's an Israeli supermarket. That's what he said. "You've come to hit Israelis and the Israeli embassy. The phone here, this phone, has phoned bin Laden to confirm that the mission is almost accomplished."'

Berjawi claims that during his time in the detention centre he was visited by a British woman from the embassy in Nairobi: 'She was very interested in how my family knew that I was arrested. That was her main priority now. She wasn't interested in my health, or food, just "Who knows?" I felt like I was being interrogated by her.'[35]

Berjawi and Sakr were eventually deported. Berjawi later told CAGE: 'When I arrived in the UK literally ten to thirteen big white built men came on the plane with suits. They escorted us off the actual aeroplane and they explained themselves, "We are MI5". Took my fingerprints, took pictures.'

He says he was left in the airport without money, barefoot and his clothes in bin liners. 'The way I was dealt with was not nice to be honest. It's like I felt I was a man with no rights. They just left me at the airport like that,' he said.[36]

Among the other cases profiled in the Horn of Africa report were the Kentish Town group who had bravely put their names and pictures in the public domain. Mohammed Emwazi also wanted his case to be included in the report. But he insisted that CAGE didn't use his real name as he didn't want his family and friends to know about his contact with MI5 and the police. So he gave his name as Muhammad ibn Muazzam.

Emwazi had read my original articles in *The Independent* on the Kentish Town men. So when CAGE discussed with him about taking his case further they agreed they should ask me to write up his story.

After Asim Qureshi had sent me the Horn of Africa report I asked if I could speak to the individuals named. Qureshi said he would check and come back to me. When he did I was told that none of the three were prepared to speak to me at this stage. Neither were any of the three men willing to have their photographs taken or to provide any of their own pictures. Where CAGE has not used real names in its case studies in the Horn of Africa report it almost always identifies them as *noms de guerre*. But in the case of Muhammad ibn Muazzam the report gives the impression that this is his real name.

After my report ran in *The Independent*, Qureshi said the men, including Emwazi, were pleased with the impact as it gave the impression that the three innocent friends had been harassed while on a safari holiday simply because they were Asian. That wasn't how MI5 regarded these men. As far as the security services were concerned it was obvious that the British men had no intention of going on a safari holiday to watch lions and tigers. MI5 believed Tanzania was a cover for their true destination – Somalia and al-Shabaab.

CHAPTER 4

FACE TO FACE WITH JIHADI JOHN

In October 2009 the Sakrs received an unwelcome knock on the door from officers from Scotland Yard's Counter Terrorism Command. The elite unit set up to keep tabs on terror suspects across the country had lost track of their son.

Gamal Sakr told the media: 'The police came asking: "Where is Mohamed?" And I said: "I don't know." That was the honest answer, I didn't know where my son was.'[1]

Mohamed Sakr and Bilal al-Berjawi had managed to slip out of the country unnoticed and by the time SO15 had realized they had gone the two men were already in Somalia. How they had done it remains a mystery and represents a serious failing on the part of the police and MI5. By the security services' own assessment Sakr and Berjawi were key suspects in a terror network which was financing terrorism abroad and represented a serious terrorist threat to the UK.

Sakr and Berjawi were linked to a bomb plot in Kenya and

had shown every intention of joining al-Shabaab. Berjawi had married a Somali in London, and Sakr had been engaged to a Somali girl. They had already made an attempt to leave for Somalia. Berjawi had even been in Somalia two years earlier training with al-Shabaab and by his own testimony it is clear that the Kenyans thought he may have even taken orders from Osama bin Laden.[2]

The failure to prevent two well-known extremists leaving Britain to join terror networks abroad was to become part of an all-too-familiar pattern. Over the next seven years dozens more, some even on control orders, where their movements were restricted by curfews and electronic tags, have managed to evade the attentions of MI5 and SO15. One of them was of course Mohammed Emwazi.

A few weeks later, Sakr contacted his parents from Somalia and told them that he and Bilal were alive and well.

The security services now believe that Sakr and Berjawi's February 2009 'safari' visit to Kenya was intended to 'prepare the ground' for the real trip later in the year.[3] They also discovered there was a third man with them who can only be named as K2, another member of the west London network.[4] An MI5 report on the three men says they had 'engaged in a variety of terrorism-related activities linked to al-Shabaab activities, including terrorism-related training and fighting against forces belonging to the African Union (AU) Mission to Somalia, a peacekeeping mission operated by the AU in Somalia with approval by the UN'.[5]

In July 2010 al-Shabaab was blamed for two suicide bomb attacks in neighbouring Uganda. As tourists and locals settled down to watch the World Cup final between Spain and the Netherlands two bombs ripped through a restaurant and a rugby club, killing seventy-four people. The attack was seen as revenge against the Ugandan forces' presence in Somalia and al-Shabaab were quick to claim responsibility. It was the first al-Shabaab operation outside Somalia and immediately triggered suspicions that the terror group had received outside help. Very soon local newspapers had named the three British new arrivals as being behind the operation. Although there hasn't been any hard evidence to support these claims, it did have the unintended side effect of raising the profile of the three recruits in the region and at home in Britain.

British counter-terror chiefs decided to act against the trio. Perhaps it was the embarrassment of having let the three men slip through their fingers, or perhaps they posed a genuine threat to the UK. Because the men were dual nationals – Sakr had retained his Egyptian identity and Berjawi could still assert the right to Lebanese citizenship – they were both vulnerable to a little-known law that had been passed by the previous Labour government in 2006. Under these powers, the home secretary can remove a passport from any dual national if he or she believes the individual is a threat to national security. Where an individual has no genuine ties to his country of birth this can prove to be a very effective weapon which renders the individual an exile.

In 2011 the new Conservative home secretary, Theresa May, wrote to the men's families informing them that they had been stripped of their British citizenship. The letters claimed they were 'involved in terrorism-related activity' and were on a list of 'Islamist extremists', which included their own names. But the charges were broad with no mention of any specific plots or allegations relating to terrorism.[5]

The Sakr family were astonished when they received the letter as they had a very different view of their son's reasons for being in Somalia. Nor had they ever thought of their son as being anything other than British. 'For the kids,' said Mrs Sakr, 'it never crossed my mind that they would have anything other than their British passports. I know they are British, born British, they are British, and carried their British passports.'[7]

The Sakrs remain defensive about the claims of terrorism. 'Have they done anything? Have they been caught in anything? Have they been caught in any action? Do they have any evidence against them that they have been involved in this or that? I haven't seen. And they haven't come up with it,' Mr Sakr told the Bureau of Investigative Journalism.[8]

'It [the letter] says they took his freedom away because he knew Bilal!' said Mrs Sakr. 'Does it mean that because I know a bad person it means I'm bad, or know good people that I'm good? He'd known Bilal since he was twelve years old!'

Mohamed Sakr told his parents to fight the deprivation order and the family instructed lawyers to go to court to get the order overturned. Berjawi sent a scrawled handwritten note to his lawyers in London also instructing them to fight the case.[9] But in the end the legal action fizzled out and instead Gamal Sakr pleaded with his son to come home.

'He said: "Daddy, it is impossible for me,"' recalled Mr Sakr. 'He said: "If I go from here, they've already taken my passport from me, maybe they will catch me somewhere, and you will never hear from me again." He knew something could happen to him.'[10]

Members of the west London network who remained at large in the UK were reporting their own problems with the security services. When Mohammed Emwazi was interviewed at Dover it was made clear to him that his phone was being monitored and his movements watched. Perhaps he had half-assumed this anyway. What he hadn't anticipated was that the security services had also begun approaching his family and friends. The contact had been deliberate so as to let him know that he was a watched man. There was little intelligence-gathering value in stopping friends in the street to ask them whether they knew a Mohammed Emwazi. But these approaches did make life a little bit more uncomfortable for him.[11]

Emwazi's friends were almost fair game as some would have been part of a network of like-minded Muslim men who shared a glowering contempt for the authorities. Confrontation with the police was part of being a young Muslim man in west London. But when the police came knocking on his family's door to tell his shocked parents that they thought their son might be involved in extremist activities, Emwazi believed a line had been crossed.[12]

After leaving university Emwazi had begun a relationship with a young Somali girl, a year or two his junior, who he had met through a family connection. She lived only a few miles from the Emwazis' west London home. Emwazi was very serious about the relationship and before he left for Tanzania he had proposed to her. They were now officially engaged and the families were planning a wedding that summer.[13] He later said that MI5 must have known he was hardly likely to be heading to a dangerous war zone like Somalia if he was planning to marry a Muslim girl in the UK and settle down to married life.[14]

But at some point while Emwazi was being questioned in Tanzania, Amsterdam and Dover, two MI5 officers went to her address to speak to his fiancée. The girl's family were deeply upset by the visit and even more concerned as to what it implied about Emwazi and his connections. They were a middle-class, traditional Muslim family who had lived a conventional life, uninterested in the Islamist issues engulfing the Middle East and some Muslim communities in London.[15] They had had no contact with the police before so the unannounced arrival of two MI5 officers on their doorstep had spooked them. Sometime in the summer of 2009 they ordered their daughter to call off the wedding. For Emwazi, this was a cruel blow indeed, as it was the last he would ever see of her. It left him depressed and angry.[16] He complained bitterly to his family about what had happened and begged them to try to save the relationship. But it was no use as the girl's parents considered the matter closed.[17]

Seeing their son so distraught and concerned about the continuing attentions of MI5 and Scotland Yard, Emwazi's parents encouraged him to leave the country for a while to let the situation cool down. One of Emwazi's west London friends who had retired to the Middle East was already living in Kuwait and urged him to join him: 'I knew Mohammed wanted to get away from the UK and I told him that Kuwait was a great place to come and chill. He didn't need much persuading.'[18] And so, in September 2009, Mohammed Emwazi flew out of Heathrow airport for Kuwait City, where his family still had many relatives, friends and, crucially, useful contacts to help their eldest child restart his life away from the intrusive gaze of MI5. Instead of moving into the centre of the city Emwazi chose to live with his grandmother, who his family say he was very close to. His grandmother lived in a basic apartment just outside Kuwait City in the run-down Tayma'a neighbourhood, where the Emwazis had once lived. A friend with him in Kuwait said: 'Even though he could have stayed with his cousins (who had comfortable beds), he stayed with her even though her living conditions is terrible. It was rough . . . bite marks and ants crawling over your face.'

But Mohammed still had to find a job for himself. Clutching a CV in one hand and an introductory letter in the other he traipsed around Kuwait City knocking on the doors of suitable employers. As a newly qualified IT graduate from a London university he was an impressive candidate on paper and it didn't take long before he was offered a job by a computer company called al-Alyal, which had been advertising for a computer programmer who could also do some selling on the side.

Emwazi appears to have fitted in well with the company and his employer declared him to be a model employee.[19] The Kuwaiti boss said that although his new recruit was rather quiet and withdrawn he had a natural gift for the work. 'He was the best employee we ever had. He was very good with people. Calm and decent. He came to our door and gave us his CV.'[20]

Emwazi was given a three-month probation period, earning three hundred Kuwaiti dinars (£657) per month, plus fifty dinars (£109) expenses, and was promised five percent commission on business he brought in.[21] The modest salary was nothing like what he could have expected as a graduate starting out on his first job in the UK.

'Muslim and Arabic people travel from here to London or the US, and they stay two years looking for a job or even a place to stay,' said the boss. 'It always puzzled me. Why would he come here?

'But it seemed as though he faced some problems, maybe family, social or psychological. I didn't really ask. He wanted a good job (in London) and he wanted to get married, but he couldn't and it made a problem for him.'[22]

Emwazi's British passport meant that he was paid an enhanced rate over that of the local workforce.[23] And he impressed his employer by having a combination of fluent Arabic and developed social skills, which he used to persuade potential customers to buy the company's IT products.[24]

His employer recalled: 'He wasn't sociable. He was always earnest. He didn't smile. But he wasn't bad.'

Emwazi's friend from London remembers: 'I sometimes used to see him driving into work in the morning or back home in the evening in his Ford car. We beeped and waved at each other.'[25]

Emwazi didn't socialize with his work colleagues – instead he stayed with his family during the week and then headed to the desert for the weekend. The place he chose was a huge recreational zone where city residents came to enjoy a variety of leisure activities, anything from playing football to tending vegetable patches.[26] 'We used to go to chill in the big tents where everyone just goes to relax. We sat around drinking lots of tea, eating good food and talking about world politics. In these sessions everyone talks about something. But because Mohammed wasn't as old as the rest of us he didn't really say very much,' said his friend.[27]

Three months after his fiancée had broken off their relationship in London, Emwazi used his family contact to find a new partner. It seems his broken heart was mended and he quickly found love with another girl, this time a local Kuwaiti.[28] The friend remembered: 'He really liked this girl and just wanted to marry her. They had a few sit-downs and it was all progressing nicely.'[29]

But towards the end of 2009 Emwazi started to complain of very painful toothache. After exploring dental solutions in Kuwait he decided to return to London to see his local dentist for treatment. 'His teeth were really hurting him badly and he just wanted to get it sorted and then come back and get married.'[30]

His brother Omar recalls Mohammed's dental problems in more detail:

The last time he came back was for his teeth because the Kuwaiti dentists couldn't do anything for him. They said: 'You have to go back to Britain.' So he called up my dad and said: 'I'm coming back for only a week. I'm going to get my teeth checked because they are killing me. I'm going to get a filling and go back.' That was the last time he came back.

He got that done. I always laughed about his tooth because he couldn't sleep at all at night.

With his teeth fixed Emwazi returned to Kuwait in early 2010 and, his family claim, resumed his plans for marriage. But there remain questions about how he spent his time when he wasn't selling computer software, attending tea parties in the desert or trying to get his teeth fixed. In March 2015, shortly after Jihadi John was named as Mohammed Emwazi, a photograph surfaced of him which was taken just before he arrived in Kuwait.[31] It shows a young man with stubble wearing a baseball hat. Two years later, Emwazi was sporting a full beard – so long, in fact, that he claimed a police officer who questioned him on his final return to the UK in July 2010 was able to grab it with both hands.

While Emwazi was in Kuwait an al-Qaeda cell was active there, operating against Western interests, which had been planning an attack against an American base called Camp Arifjan, the main US military camp in the country, housing fifteen thousand troops and used as a staging post for the post-2003 coalition campaign in neighbouring Iraq.[32] The camp also had a small contingent of British military personnel.

The alleged terror cell's leader was a charismatic Kuwaiti called Muhsin al-Fadhli, who would later return to Syria to lead a wing of al-Qaeda known as Khorasan, which recruited Western jihadis to attack targets in Europe. Emwazi himself may well have had contact with Khorasan in Syria before he went on to join the Islamic State. According to a CIA cable published by WikiLeaks[33] another key cell member was Khalid al-Dossary, a Saudi who was later imprisoned in America for plotting a series of terrorist attacks after moving there as a student. But it may be Fadhli, a Bedoon like himself, who was the real reason Emwazi wanted to move to Kuwait.

Fadhli's presence would also explain why Emwazi chose to spend so much of his free time in the desert, away from prying eyes.

Fadhli was reported to be so close to Osama bin Laden that he was one of only a handful who knew about 9/11 in advance. In 2014 he was targeted and killed in an airstrike aimed at the Khorasan group in Syria. While there is no direct evidence that the two met during Emwazi's visit, there is evidence that they already knew each other.[34] According to Kuwaiti security sources Emwazi had been in Kuwait two years earlier in 2007 when he first had contact with Fadhli. The source told the *Telegraph*'s respected Middle East correspondent Robert Tait that the meeting had a profound effect on Emwazi, hardening his views against the West and providing him with an extremist philosophy.[35]

If this is true it would help to confirm that Emwazi was already on an extremist path before he had finished his studies at Westminster University. And if he had indeed resumed contact with Fadhli and the al-Qaeda cell in 2009, it would help answer questions about why the British security services were so interested in him. It would also explain a strange phone call he received from his family in March 2010.

Emwazi said that his father phoned from London to tell him that a woman was at the family home who wanted to speak to him. The woman in question was from MI5 and wished to know when he was returning to the UK as she wanted to speak to him. Emwazi told CAGE in an email in June 2010: 'She stated she was from MI5, then later that she was from the anti-terrorism department. She started to ask me what I am doing and said she would like to speak to me when I reach London, but I refused and told her to leave me alone!!'[36]

It's not clear why MI5 had taken the highly unusual step of contacting Emwazi so openly through his family. But it raises questions about what they had found out about his activities in

Kuwait and what intelligence their secret service colleagues in Kuwait had passed on to them.

In May 2010 all six of the Kuwaiti terror suspects on trial for the plot to blow up the US military, including Fadhli, who was still on the run, were sensationally acquitted by the Kuwaiti courts. A few days later Emwazi returned to the UK. He claims he came back to see his family and arrange his paperwork before making the final move to Kuwait, where he planned to live. But his friend says his teeth were still playing up and so he wanted to give west London one last go before finally settling in Kuwait: 'His father called him and asked if he could come. I said that I didn't think it was a good idea as he was lucky that he didn't get blocked from returning to Kuwait. I said to Mohammed: "Look, after all the trouble you have had in the UK why take the risk?" But he just said he had to help his dad sort a few things out and he would be back.'[37]

As he passed through passport control at Heathrow airport Emwazi was stopped by immigration officers. When he presented his passport to be checked, his name was taken down and he was asked to stand to one side. The officer also made a note which Emwazi wasn't able to see.

Everyone went through apart from him. A few minutes later, two immigration officers met him at the desk and asked to see his passport again. They also took his phones and SIM cards, which were taken away and then returned to him. Emwazi was then questioned, in front of the other passengers, about what he had been doing in Kuwait. When he asked why he was being questioned he was told that this was simply a routine passport check. Emwazi claims he didn't complain because he just wanted to get home to see his family.[38]

Emwazi said he spent the next three weeks with his family in west London making final preparations for his new life in Kuwait.[39] Omar Emwazi remembers the day his brother left:

'The day he was about to go back to Kuwait he never said good-bye to me.' 'He just left. But he called me from the airport saying his plan was to stay in Kuwait for a long time. But I was really upset with him. And I said: "How can you not say goodbye properly? I'm not going to see you for months. The only time I ever see you is when I fly to Kuwait." So he said: "Yeah, sorry, man, I was in a rush. You weren't to be seen. So I am saying it now, goodbye." And I said: "OK, good luck, man, take care."'

On 2 June Mohammed and his father drove to Heathrow airport, but when he lined up at check-in and took his turn at the desk the airline official asked him to stand aside as a message had come up on her screen saying someone wanted to see him.[40] He waited quietly while everyone else checked in. After fifteen minutes three men and a woman, all in black suits, approached him. They told Emwazi they were police officers and would need to interview and search his belongings under powers conferred on them by the Terrorism Act.[41] He was told he was to be subject to a routine check and was asked to surrender his laptop computer, all his phones and SIM cards.

The officials continued to question Emwazi in front of the queues of passengers. His flight was leaving at 8.40 p.m. but the officers told him that he would catch the later 10 p.m. flight because they needed at least two hours to interview him properly. Emwazi told his father to go home as they had assured him he would be leaving on the later flight.

The officers began by removing all his belongings from his suitcase. After that he was told to repack his suitcase and then accompany them to an interview room where he was photo-graphed and his DNA and fingerprints were taken. Emwazi told CAGE: 'I sat down on a chair whilst one officer started to ask questions, the other writing down my answers and the rest searching through my bags.'[42]

They probed him intensely about his life in Kuwait. Who his friends were. Which mosque he prayed at. Whether he had attended any Islamic lectures. They also wanted to know whether he was a *hafiz*. They sought his opinion on world events, a standard line of questioning when MI5 or Scotland Yard wanted to elicit admissions of Islamist extremism. Usually the questioning centred on events such as 9/11 or the individual's views on the state of Israel.[43] Emwazi had of course been here before when he faced a similar line of questioning on his ejection from Tanzania.

Emwazi said he told the officers that all he wanted to do was to return to Kuwait where he had a good job and a fiancée. He later told CAGE in an email: 'Towards the end of this long interview, I told them that I want to be left alone, as I have an ambition of moving from the UK and settling in Kuwait. That is why I found a job and a spouse!! But they laughed.'[44]

He then claimed that one of the officers suddenly became very aggressive towards him. He said a Sikh officer wearing a turban entered the interview room and began searching through his belongings, where he found Emwazi's personal copy of the Qur'an.[45] He told CAGE: 'He reached out for the Holy Qur'an and put it on the floor. I asked him to put it onto the chair rather than the floor. He started to get aggressive, changing his tone of voice. He said: "I have put it onto the chair now, so just shut up," and I replied: "You shut up."'

Emwazi claimed that the officer stood up and walked towards him. Emwazi was also standing now and the officer, his face inches from Emwazi's, pushed him back into his chair. 'At that point,' wrote Emwazi, 'I told the officers that I was not going to answer any more questions until this aggressive and angry person, that had hate for me for no reason, got out of the room.'[46] According to Emwazi the Sikh officer left the room.

Emwazi was then moved to another interview room where

he said CCTV recorded the interview. Here an officer, who said his name was Joe, started questioning him about his aborted visit to Tanzania the year before. Emwazi explained to CAGE in his email that his experience in Tanzania and later his interrogation in Holland and Dover 'completely changed my life'.[47]

What he meant by this 'change' isn't made clear. But in the context of explaining this second interrogation at Heathrow it strongly suggests that, if he hadn't been radicalized before Tanzania, his commitment to Islamist militancy after that 'holiday' was complete. If it had simply been a terrible misunderstanding or case of mistaken identity, as he claimed, then it could hardly have 'completely changed [his] life'. More likely, it was the moment that he realized he was being investigated by the security services and that his activities were being closely monitored. He couldn't simply put the incident behind him because, like other members of his network, he wanted to make a contribution to the violent jihad in Somalia.

The officer pressed on with more questions about the Tanzania trip and asked Emwazi whether he had indeed intended to travel to Somalia. But Emwazi replied: 'I've just graduated and wanted to have a holiday with a group of friends and . . . I didn't want to enter a war zone'.[48]

When the officer challenged him about his knowledge of the conflict in Somalia, he shouted: 'I have a TV and it has a channel called BBC World News.'

Emwazi said that 'Joe' then ended the interview and he was taken back to the first interview room from where he was going to be released. He says while he was waiting in the original interview room a counter-terrorism officer entered who he hadn't seen before. He describes the man as Asian, adding: 'He sat right next to me and asked the officers why I was here.'[49]

At this point Emwazi's mobile phone rang. It was his father who was worried as it was past midnight and he wanted to come to the airport to collect him. Emwazi answered it but he claimed that the Asian officer told him to stop the call and hand the phone to him. 'So when the phone rang I picked it up like usual, but this new Asian officer who had just entered the room told me to give him my phone. I said to him "NO!!" I'm allowed to answer the phone, as the officers have been letting me.'[50]

Emwazi claimed the Asian officer became angry and shouted: 'I don't care, I'm not them.' According to Emwazi the officer stood up and tried to snatch the phone out of Emwazi's hand but was unsuccessful.[51] 'So then he grabbed my T-shirt and threw me onto the wall, grabbing onto my beard and strangling my neck.'[52] He said that the other officers did nothing to help him and remained seated as he was pushed against the wall. Emwazi alleges that it was only when he started having trouble breathing that the officer released his grip. He told CAGE: 'I was absolutely shocked and completely baffled. I took a minute to myself because I didn't know why he had done such a thing, so I asked him why and he said: "You had your phone out and this was a threat to me."'[53]

Emwazi said he was then released from the room, although he kept insisting that they give him their names. He alleged that the CCTV outside the room recorded the officers laughing at him and telling him that 'we don't give out our names, mate'. He also said that the CCTV also recorded the Asian officer looking 'agitated, knowing he had done something wrong'. Emwazi later bitterly described the experience as 'being locked up with caged animals'.[54]

It was approaching 1 a.m. before he finally climbed into his father's car and was driven home. Omar recalls: 'I saw him come through the door. I said: "Bro, you missed me so much you had to come back to give me a proper hug! What happened, man?" He said: "What do you expect? They never accepted me."'

But Emwazi was undeterred. The next day, 3 June, he

returned to Heathrow's Terminal 3 more determined than ever to leave the UK. He had rebooked his flight and once again stood in line to be checked in. But now the security noose was firmly tightened around his neck and Britain's security services had no intention of letting him return to Kuwait.

When Emwazi's turn came to check in he was again told to stand aside. A few minutes later a representative of the airline met him at the check-in desk and apologized for his travel problems. But he told Emwazi: 'Mr Mohammed [*sic*], there's no point in you going on your trip as we have just had a call from the Kuwaitis, saying that they do not want you because you have been deported before and so won't give you a visa.'[55]

Emwazi told the airline official that it was not true that he had been deported from Kuwait and pleaded with him to let him continue on his journey so he could return to his job and fiancée: 'I'm planning to live there for the rest of my life.' But after his experience with the security services the night before he decided there was no point in pressing the issue with the airline. There is no doubt that Emwazi was genuine in his desire to return to Kuwait. And he may have been truthful about wanting a job and a family. But did he also want to use Kuwait as a safe base from where he could pursue his interest in violent jihad away from the scrutiny of the British security services?

Later that day Emwazi made contact with CAGE. He was well known to CAGE after he was thrown out of Tanzania and inter-rogated by MI5 in Amsterdam and Dover in 2009. He subse-quently told their research director, Asim Qureshi, that he felt like he was being held as a prisoner not in a cage 'but in London'.[56]

CAGE had set up a casefile on him and gave him the name 'Mohammed al-Kuwaiti'. Many of the British jihadi fighters who have gone to Syria adopt similar names by giving their second name as the place of their birth such as Abu al-Britani or Abu al-Almani.

That night at 9.46 p.m., just hours after he was prevented from leaving the UK, Emwazi wrote to CAGE asking for assistance with his problem with the security services and the restrictions placed on his entry to Kuwait. He used the name Mohammed al-Zuhary, rather than Emwazi. He told them that he would be taking his case to the Kuwaiti embassy to get some answers to his questions. He asked:

Brothers and sisters from Cage Prisoners [as they were called then], please help . . . I don't want to stay in the UK because I have found a job in Kuwait, found a spouse in Kuwait and thus found a new start to my life in Kuwait. Kuwait is where I am from, I was born their [sic] I just want to go their [sic] and start my new life again!! Brothers and sisters please don't forget my 'little case' but please don't think I'm telling you to neglect the 'bigger' cases.

He then added 'Jazakum-Allah from myself and the entire Muslim *ummah*'.[57]

The following day CAGE put Emwazi in touch with a lawyer, Saghir Hussain, who acts for many of their clients. Hussain was the solicitor who later advised Michael Adebolajo, the murderer of soldier Lee Rigby in May 2013. Hussain advised Emwazi to make an allegation of assault against the police and make a complaint to the Independent Police Complaints Commission.

On 21 June Emwazi wrote to CAGE to update them on the progress of his enquiries with the embassy. He told them that he had discovered from his 'friends' in Kuwait that the reason the airline had refused to take him was because the security service in the UK had put him on a no-fly list.[58] He said they had managed to find a document proving Britain was behind his refused visa which 'clearly states that the order came from the UK'.[59]

If Emwazi had connections with friends in Kuwait who had access to such restricted passenger documents then he was clearly moving in higher circles than had been known before. If he also had contact with any member of an al-Qaeda cell in Kuwait which had been accused of plotting to blow up the US base there, he posed a much greater security risk than anyone first realized. In this context it was understandable why MI5 were taking an interest in him. But if his desire to move to Kuwait was genuine and born out of the harassment he believed he was being exposed to in the UK, the security services were in danger of forcing him into a corner.

According to Omar his father tried to help Mohammed by trying to guide him away from trouble and most of all telling him to stay away from the group of young Muslim extremists who were being watched by the security services. 'He advised him about marriage, about leaving his friends, changing his name on his passport. When you have a child on your hands your whole life changes. You have a big responsibility. This is what my dad was saying to him. If you get married, if you settle down, the way you think, everything changes. You become focused on the family.'

Omar isn't sure whether his brother heeded his father's advice. He believes his brother must take ultimate responsibility for his actions. However, he also believes that the role British and foreign security services played in preventing his brother from leaving Britain for a new life in Kuwait was a key radicalizing factor. 'The thing is they would never leave him alone. When it happens constantly it becomes the norm.' So he says his brother never appeared angry. 'It's not like he is suddenly going to get frustrated again. So this was how it was for him and he just carried on.'

Shortly after his detention at Heathrow on 2 June Emwazi lodged a complaint about the alleged assault he had suffered during his interview. On 22 July Emwazi was asked to attend an address in Putney, headquarters of the Directorate of Professional Standards for the Metropolitan Police Force, which is responsible for handling complaints brought by members of the public. There he met two officers who had been assigned to investigate his allegations.[60]

Emwazi explained exactly what he claimed had happened to him. By now he knew the name of the officer who he alleged had assaulted him.[61] He told the investigating officers that he believed the police constable's name was Anwar and he alleged that the assault against him had been racist. The officers listened carefully to what he had to say. However, they told him that they had already made preliminary enquiries and discovered there was no CCTV in the interview room so the allegation might end up as Emwazi's word against the officers'. The investigating officers said they would report back in a few weeks after they had interviewed all those involved in the incident to see if the complaint could be taken further.[62]

Emwazi wrote back to the officers thanking them for taking the trouble to investigate his complaint. His formal and polite (even over-polite) letter appears to show that he still retained some faith in the police's ability to hold the officer to account and does not betray any hint of antagonism to the West. He tells the officers:

> First of all I would like to take this opportunity to thank you for all your efforts regarding my complaint over specific members of the police force. Thank you for giving a voice to the voiceless, thank you for not tolerating tyranny. Indeed it was of much great help expressing to you my distress over what happened to me in the hands of those particular individuals. I hope that these very few individuals do not represent the entire police force and they learn from that

situation. I also hope that both our efforts put an end of the oppression that so often happens under the hands of those that believe they are above the law, taking advantage of the 'police uniform', acting like 'Robocop' rather than civilized humans. You kindly suggested that I have the right to obtain a copy of the Police record complaint showing that my concerns have been formally recorded. Therefore could you please send me a copy of that record? Once again, thank you for all the effort put forward.[63]

Emwazi's communications with CAGE increasingly show how he had become engaged with the political issues that many Muslims were grappling with at the time. Emwazi is particularly focused on the idea that Muslims have become victims of the Western 'oppressors' across the world.

In one email he included a link to a video clip of abuses against Muslims. He wrote on 31 July: 'I just wanted to share this video with you brothers, notice at the end of the video these evil people start brutally beating old, white bearded, poor men brothers ... Brothers in Cage Prisoners, please keep up your good work and help rescue these people from the hands of the oppressors!!'[64] In another email he attached a link to a video of British men verbally abusing British Muslims. Emwazi sums up the video: 'HAVE IT MATE: Look at the hate.'

Other emails draw attention to atrocities taking place in Chechnya and deride the American use of chemical weapons in Fallujah, Iraq.[65] The next month he wrote again, this time in support of the case of US-trained Pakistani neuroscientist Aafia Siddiqui.

Siddiqui was named by the FBI in 2003 as a courier and financier for Khaled Sheikh Mohammed, the mastermind behind the 9/11 attacks on America. She went on the run and became known as 'Lady al-Qaeda'.

In 2008 she resurfaced in Ghazni, Afghanistan, where she was arrested by local security forces who found she had documents and notes for making bombs. After her arrest she was questioned by American interrogators at a police compound. During the interrogation one of the military guards left a rifle on the floor, which she grabbed and fired at one of the soldiers, seriously wounding him. Another soldier returned fire and shot her in the upper body, critically wounding her. But after emergency surgery at Bagram Air Base in Afghanistan she made a full recovery. The Americans charged her with shooting a soldier and she was put on trial in New York.

It was later claimed that she had been held as a secret prisoner by the Americans for a number of years before her 'arrest' in 2008. Moazzam Begg says he remembers hearing a female prisoner screaming while he was detained at Bagram who he believes could have been Siddiqui. CAGE had also been campaigning for her release and collected a number of notable politicians to the campaign, including MPs John McDonnell, now shadow chancellor, and Green spokeswoman Caroline Lucas.

In September 2010 Siddiqui was sentenced to eighty-six years' imprisonment. The same week her sentence hit the headlines, Emwazi wrote to CAGE saying: 'I heard the upsetting news regarding our sister Aafia Siddiqui. This should only keep us firmer towards fighting for freedom and justice!! So please my dear brothers, keep up your work so that you can say on the Day of Judgment "This is what I done for Aafia Siddiqui ..."'[66]

About his own situation he was much more downbeat and confided in Asim Qureshi that he no longer believed he would be able to get the Kuwaitis to lift the visa restrictions. His friends in Kuwait told him they were too 'scared' to get hold of the document which he believed would prove Britain was behind his blocked visa:

I have been trying to do my best to get hold of that letter from the system that says I've been rejected under 'instructions' from the UK government. No one seems to want to help me because they are obviously scared that they may get into 'trouble'. Knowing this, I'm not going to give up!! I'm going to wait for my dad to come back so that me and him can visit the Kuwaiti embassy in London and ask for what is the reason for my rejection. Going to the embassy myself won't be successful, so that's why I'm just waiting for my dad![67]

However, his father couldn't persuade the embassy to provide any answers other than confirmation that there was a problem with his visa.

By mid-August 2010 Emwazi had become exasperated with the situation and he wrote: 'I really don't know what to do, but *insh'Allah*, I'm not going to lose hope, I've spoken to some family in Kuwait and they said that they are trying their best to move the "refusal" of my name, that is stored in the system. But I can't really depend on that.'[68]

Having explored all the official avenues to have his travel restrictions lifted, CAGE advised Emwazi to make his case 'public'. But he wasn't ready to go to the media and he informed Qureshi that he still wanted to continue working 'behind the scenes' to get the entry restriction removed.[69] However, by late September 2010 he had made no progress and his prospects of returning to Kuwait appeared as hopeless as ever. Qureshi suggested he took more 'drastic steps', telling him: 'There is a lot of emphasis on British complicity in detentions abroad and I would like to see you coming out more openly to speak about all the different things that have happened to you.'[70]

Britain's complicity in the torture of terror suspects made headline news after the revelations of the abuses carried out by the American military in Guantánamo Bay. The avocacy group

CAGE, originally called Cageprisoners, was founded in 2003 to campaign against the war on terror and offer support to victims of America's torture and rendition programmes. CAGE hoped that Emwazi's case would help to show that despite denials Britain was continuing to work with foreign states to subject British citizens to torture, unlawful detentions and harassment, even within the UK.

Emwazi said he was now willing to try everything to get back to Kuwait and so gave his consent to making his case public. Qureshi told him that he knew a journalist who he said would take his case seriously and investigate his claims properly. He asked Emwazi if he could put the journalist in contact. Emwazi agreed.

And so, although I didn't yet know any of what had happened up to this point, Mohammed Emwazi's story became my story, too. Qureshi says he suggested me because we had worked together on CAGE's Horn of Africa report in which Emwazi's experience in Tanzania had been highlighted, although under a different name. But I had also brought the cases of the Kentish Town Community Centre workers to the public's attention. This had raised the profile of the tension between Muslims and the security services in the so-called war on terror. It had also given the victims a voice and put the security services under the spotlight. The ensuing publicity exposed the methods being employed by the police and MI5 to recruit British Muslims as spies. And it did achieve results. In the short term, MI5 had backed off from the Kentish Town group.

The phone calls from shadowy MI5 officers called 'James' or counter-terrorism officers called 'Katherine' stopped overnight. The results helped convince Qureshi that SO15 and MI5 feared publicity. Soon senior staff at Thames House, MI5 headquarters, as well as ministers found themselves facing MPs' questions about the secret operations while field commanders and department heads were asked to justify tactics and their choice of targets.

The service was still smarting from the devastating court case of Binyam Mohamed, who had sued the government over its role in his detention and torture. MI5 had tried to shut down the case by citing the UK's intelligence-sharing relationship with America. In the context of its involvement with Binyam Mohamed, who had been captured in Afghanistan, tortured in Morocco and then detained at Guantánamo, it argued that disclosure of secret evidence would threaten this relationship. But the judges rejected its argument, ordering enough disclosure to show that Britain had been complicit in his torture.[71]

The case triggered a spate of criminal investigations by the Metropolitan Police, which meant for the first time in its history MI5 was the subject of a criminal inquiry. At Thames House the atmosphere was tense as it came under intense pressure from the government, the courts and the media to give a full account of its covert activities in the war on terror.

Over that I summer had worked with other young Muslim men across the country who had been encouraged by the Kentish Town coverage to come forward to tell their stories of encounters with MI5 and SO15. That year I travelled to Birmingham after two Muslim men from the Somali community complained to me they had experienced the same kind of harassment as those in north London. These men, along with Mahdi Hashi, Bilal al-Berjawi, Mohamed Sakr and others, were on a balance point; some seem to have been tipped towards extremism, and others away from it.

In December 2010, when I met him, Mohammed Emwazi had also reached this pivotal moment. After Asim Qureshi had put us in touch, Emwazi and I began an email conversation. He summarized his predicament and some of the history he had with MI5, although crucially he didn't mention his Tanzania escapade. He said he thought I would be interested in his story as I had written about similar cases to his. So he gave me a mobile number to ring to talk further about his case and perhaps discuss how we could take it on.

When I rang the number the voice that answered was calm and measured. He thanked me for ringing him and taking an interest in his story and said that Qureshi had told him about the work I had done. On the phone he was very clear about what he thought the story should be. He said that MI5 had destroyed his life in the UK and now they were trying to stop him from leading a new life in Kuwait. He wanted to meet me so he could tell me in person what was happening to him because there were more details he was certain I would be interested in.

We arranged to meet at a coffee shop near his home in Maida Vale. My memories of Emwazi are of a smart, young man wearing jeans and trainers and a sweatshirt and coat. I think I was early and so found myself ordering a coffee while I waited for him. Emwazi sounded very serious on the phone and his initial outline of his trouble with MI5 had the familiar characteristics of the many other stories I had listened to over the last two years. I wasn't expecting him to blow me away with his story but I knew that it would have to be better than what had already appeared in the paper. And from what he had told me already I wasn't convinced that it would be. As I waited for him I was more concerned with a trip I had planned to Morocco the following week. I also knew that in three weeks' time I was leaving the *Independent* for the *Mail on Sunday*.

Although he hadn't given me a description I had no trouble recognizing him. When he walked into the shop he had a beard and walked with a barely concealed swagger which belied his modest demeanour. I think I offered him a handshake which he duly accepted and then I offered him a drink which he also accepted but then insisted on paying for. He talked carefully and politely, often using my name to emphasize his point.

We already had something in common as I too had been educated at Westminster University (or the Polytechnic of Central London as it was named then). I had studied law but told him computer science would have done me more good.

Throughout our conversation he appeared utterly convinced that he was the innocent victim of a ruthless police state whose actions had destroyed his life. We talked for over an hour about his life in Britain and the events at Heathrow airport. He repeated his complaint that the police and MI5 seemed to be able to stop him without any justification and make him answer questions about his private life before wrongly accusing him of being a terrorist. He said he didn't want to spy on Muslims for the British government and just wanted to get on with his own life.

I asked him to recount in detail the alleged assault by the police officer and the interrogation at Heathrow. And he obligingly took me through it step by step, explaining how the officer had insulted Islam by throwing his copy of the Qur'an on the floor, how the officer had 'attacked' him when he answered his phone at the end of the interview and how they had just abandoned him at Heathrow at 1 a.m. without any apology or promise to help rebook his flight for the following day.

But what aggrieved him the most was the security services' disruptive contact with his family. He said his mother and father were becoming increasingly upset with the anonymous phone calls and visits to his home. 'Look, if they have bother with me, if they want to ask me questions, then they should speak to me about it ... there's no need to involve my family or my girlfriends.'[72]

This was the first mention of girlfriends. And it suddenly made his story unique in a way that departed from the many similar accounts of harassment I had heard from young Muslim men. So I pressed him for more details.

'They caused me to lose two girlfriends, I was engaged to both of them but because they went to talk to the girls' families they broke off with me.'[73]

If this was true, the allegation he was making went further than the claims of harassment I had already written about.

He explained in more detail: 'I had a fiancée in London and one in Kuwait and both times MI5 got to them.'[74]

'How did they do this?' I asked.

'In London they came round to the house to speak to the family about me and told them that I was a terrorist or that they were investigating terrorism and could they answer questions about me. Well, after that the family didn't want her to marry me any more.'[75]

Emwazi said that he believed that MI5 had set out to cause him as much hassle as possible and that they had been very calculating in what they were doing. He said on one occasion they casually dropped into the conversation: 'Oh, by the way, Mohammed, we spoke to your fiancée.'[76]

He said they told him about the visit to his London fiancée just after he returned from Tanzania, which proved to him that they knew his plans never involved Somalia and he always intended to return and settle down. He said he now knew that the intelligence officers had been listening to all his phone calls before he even planned his holiday to Tanzania. He said when he challenged them about listening to his private conversations one of the officers casually shrugged his shoulders and said: 'Well, that's part of our job, mate.'

And so then I asked about the second fiancée and how he thought the security service had wrecked that relationship.

'It was when I was in Kuwait. The family got a phone call from them saying they were investigating me. So my fiancée and her family no longer wanted to see me. It was the same with my job – when they found out about MI5 they didn't want me working for them.'[77]

Omar Emwazi said news of the failed engagement was very disturbing for the family: 'The [Kuwaiti] family members of the girl were friends of us and they said "So-and-so approached us with this and that". They were thinking, if this is happening before the marriage what's going to happen during the marriage? So they cancelled.' But Mohammed Emwazi told a friend it was perfectly natural for them to have second thoughts about the marriage. They were a respectable and wealthy family with a position to protect and they didn't want any trouble with the Kuwait State Security Service.[78] 'Most on his mind was his fiancées,' Omar remembers. 'He was always trying to get married. All his friends had got settled apart from him. That was the thing that hurt him the most.'

Emwazi's account had an air of authenticity about it. After all, he wasn't making allegations which couldn't be corroborated as he promised to put me in touch with the two women concerned. Neither did he exaggerate his story. He was happy to provide detail when it was required and if he didn't know the answer to a question he would say so. And every now and then, throughout our conversations, he conveyed a raw anger about the injustice of it all which helped to make him sound very believable.

When Emwazi spoke about the two fiancées it didn't seem to occur to him to blame them for ditching him on the basis of the untested allegations of the police or MI5 – as many young jilted lovers might have done. Nor did he reproach their families for taking the word of MI5 over their first-hand experience of what he was like. Indeed, if there was anything that might have undermined his story it was his willingness to accept the role of victim. But as a journalist, there was certainly enough in what he had told me to pique my interest. I remember telling him if we were going make the story work and give it credibility his picture would have to be printed in the paper. He said that wouldn't be a problem. I also told him that I would need pictures of both his girlfriends and if possible would want to talk to them about their families' contact with MI5. He said that might be more difficult but he promised to speak to them about it.[79]

Before we parted company he quizzed me about the story. He wanted to know where it would appear in the paper. Would his picture be on the front page like that of the Kentish Town youth workers?[80] I told him that it might but that would all depend on the strength of the story and what other news was knocking about on the day. Then he asked whether I thought it would help solve his problem. I explained that in my experience the publicity did get the security services to back off and I pointed to the experiences of the Kentish Town men as a positive illustration of this point. He seemed reassured by what I had told him and he thanked me for devoting so much time to his case. But most of all he said he was just happy that someone was prepared to listen to him and accept his version of events.

I'm not sure I had accepted everything he told me at face value, and I did challenge him directly about his claim that he had no interest in Islamist extremism. But now that I have read what he was writing to CAGE during this period, it is clear that he was much more engaged in Islamist thinking than he was prepared to reveal to me. Perhaps he considered me part of the oppressive Western state that was responsible for abusing Muslims all over the world. I was after all a white non-Muslim working for the mainstream media. Perhaps he thought he could use me to help further the Islamist struggle by making the security services and Scotland Yard defend themselves against embarrassing allegations. All I can say now is that that wasn't how it seemed to me on the day. If I had been a young graduate who was trying to find a job, go on holiday or find a partner, and had been thwarted at every turn by the government that was supposed to protect me, I probably would have felt just as angry. If it was all just spin, designed to further the interests of al-Qaeda-inspired groups and other extremists, he had certainly mastered his role.

At the end of the meeting Emwazi headed off to his home in Maida Vale and I went back to the office. He said he would be in touch again about arranging a date and time to come to the *Independent* offices to have his picture taken. Later that night, he sent me an email attaching a copy of his police complaint and promised to send me all the documents relating to the findings from the Met's Directorate of Professional Standards: 'As for the photo, I'll go with that as both yourself and Asim kindly suggested or rather advised for that to happen. So just let me know when you want me to come down. Thanks to both for your efforts.'[81]

I wrote back the next morning: 'Good to see you yesterday, Mohammed. Thanks for attaching this letter and I'll be in touch later about pictures. In the meantime if you had a picture of yourself then you could attach that as well. Best, Robert.'[82]

Two weeks later Emwazi contacted me again with an update to his complaint against the police. But he also wrote in detail about how badly his life had been affected by his contact with MI5 and SO15.

From: emwazi_m@hotmail.com
To: r.verkaik@independent.co.uk
Subject: RE: The IPCC document
Date: Tue, 14 Dec 2010 13:59:40 +0000

Hi Robert
    I have just received 2 letters in the post regarding me police complaint. I have attached those as you requested.

Please let me know when you want me to come down for a photo etc . . . also, something i would like to share . . . recently I sold my laptop via gumtree. When I sell anything via internet i always only write my surname in the add, which is Emwazi . . .

I received a call of someone that was interested in my laptop . . . I went to meet that person next to the nearest station to my house, Maida Vale. So that he could have a look at the laptop & if it satisfied him then he would buy it . . . That person to my surprise didn't even bother looking to see of the laptop works or not!!! (when you buy something, from someone you've never seen before you most likely would test the product!!) . . .

Anyway, in a matter of seconds, I gave him the laptop (thinking that hes going to test the laptop) & he gave me the money straight-away . . . We 'shacked hands' & he said 'nice doing business with you Mohammed'. I NEVER TOLD THIS PERSON MY FIRST NAME!! & I NEVER GIVE OUT MY FIRST NAME!! IT WAS IMPOSSIBLE FOR HIM TO KNOW MY FIRST NAME!!

I felt shocked, & paused for a few seconds as he walked away . . . I knew it was them!! Sometimes i feel like im a dead man walking, not fearing they may kill me.

Rather, fearing that one day, I'll take as many pills as I can so that I can sleep for ever!!

I just want to get away from these people!!!

I was in Morocco when I read Emwazi's email. Of course reading it today it takes on a whole new meaning. But at the time I thought his account was rather far fetched and betrayed a state of paranoia. Why would MI5 go to the trouble of buying his old laptop if they had already searched him at Heathrow, where they had twice inspected his phones and computers? Of course, if he was correct and hadn't told the buyer his first name then this was suspicious behaviour. But there could have been any number of alternative explanations.

I don't believe that now. Since I met Emwazi I have met MI5 agents who have told me that this is precisely how the security services work. They can carry out such deep packet searches of computers that this kind of acquisition would be highly prized. Letting slip a target's first name would be the only way you would be aware that they were on to you. Whatever I thought about Emwazi at the time, there is no doubt that he was clued up and highly sensitive to approaches from the security services.

I think I was prejudiced by his use of language, calling MI5 'them!!!', a euphemism that smacked of paranoia. But most of all it was his threat to kill himself that in my mind undermined his story. Earlier that year I had lost my father, who had taken his own life, and I was still very upset about the circumstances in which it happened. When Emwazi threatened to kill himself almost as an off-the-cuff remark I felt nothing but contempt. I didn't think that he had any intention of going through with it and he was using suicide to inject drama into his case.

I had also just returned from a trip from Guantánamo Bay in Cuba, where more than eight hundred detainees were in prison, mostly on evidence they hadn't seen nor would ever see. The camp has a very sobering effect on its visitors and so I couldn't help thinking Emwazi should at least be grateful for his freedom.[83]

Five years later, I believe that I had too easily dismissed Emwazi's vulnerability and desperation. His fears that he was a watched man (if not a 'dead man walking') were accurate. His paranoia derived from the reality of being targeted by people who assert utter control over your life.

I recently spoke to a British man who has been investigated by the security services. Cerie Bullivant was placed on a control order in 2005 after MI5 suspected him of having links to terrorism. He told me that when he read the email Emwazi had sent to me, he broke down in tears. He said it brought back the frightening paranoia which had gripped his own life and caused him to lose his sense of reality. He described how, when you lose control over your own life, your mind turns to black thoughts. He said he had contemplated suicide. When he found himself in prison he tried to use a razor blade to end his life. He says that another terror suspect under a control order had to be cut down from a makeshift noose he had made in his cell. And outside prison there is plenty of evidence to show that those who fall under the suspicion of the security services find their thoughts are controlled by persecution complexes, with many experiencing long-term mental health issues.

A career criminal who has an electronic tag placed on his leg may accept the curtailment of his freedom for what it is – a step up from serving a prison sentence. But a terror suspect who is placed on a control order on the basis of secret evidence which he is never allowed to see can find it easy to conceive of conspiracy and persecution. Under such pressure from a seemingly malevolent state, it is impossible to know how an individual will decide to act.

CHAPTER 5

SUBJECT OF INTEREST

Mohammed Emwazi spent his days aimlessly lolling around the family home, playing computer and video games. He had no money because he couldn't get a job and he feared going out because he didn't want anything to happen to him that might affect his chances of leaving the UK. His brother Omar told me that his parents were beginning to despair of him:

> My parents used to say to him: 'You're dead, you're finished.' Because of the situation he was in. They said: 'You're not supposed to be here, you are not supposed to be in this house. Not supposed to be in this world.' I remember it very clearly. I was in the living room when they said it. They said, every morning we see him when he wakes up. It is as if he is dead. He doesn't care about life any more, because he doesn't have anything any more.[1]

Mohammed Emwazi had a particularly strong and close relationship with his mother. Omar told me:

> My mum could read him like reading a book. It was very easy for her to read him. I would know what was going on in his life but he was always playing around with me and having jokes. But he was very close to Mum. He would always tell her all his problems and how he felt . . . if he was depressed and how he was feeling. They would have lots of strong conversations together. But he wouldn't have that conversation with me and my dad. So my mother knew exactly how he was feeling. So when she said it was like he was dead, I really believe that.

Omar recalled how his older brother had become so detached from the world that he didn't seem to care what happened to him.

> Let's say there was something across the road he had to get. And there was a very busy road. He wouldn't think about getting hit. He would just have to get across that road and get what he had to get. Because he had no life any more. He was rejected from his work, from his marriage and from his community. Even from travelling as well. That hurt him a lot, not being able to go back to his homeland.

On Christmas Day 2010 Mohammed Emwazi wrote to CAGE to tell them that his father was in Kuwait trying to find out why his son had been blocked from entering the country. He said that his father had managed to 'get into the security services in Kuwait and found that my name is not known to them'.[2] Emwazi doesn't explain how his father was able to infiltrate the Kuwaiti security services or on what basis he could categorically state that his son's name was not known to them. It suggests that Emwazi senior still retained influential contacts in Kuwait, perhaps from his time in the police there. Nevertheless, he was encountering problems using these contacts to help his son.

Emwazi continued: 'Anyway, he's saying it's hard to get that on paper ... but many people advised him to try and get some sort of paperwork from the UK stating that I've never been arrested/put in prison for terrorist charges etc ... He's been told that would help a lot.'[3]

His lawyer Saghir Hussain suggested they speak again in the New Year to arrange a 'plan of action'.[4] Emwazi (who insisted on referring to the New Year as the 'Gregorian New Year') asked about a possible meeting with his MP to resolve his predicament. By now Scotland Yard had finished their investigation into his complaint and Emwazi sent me the police correspondence. Emwazi was under the impression that the investigation had found in his favour and that the officer he accused of assaulting him had been reprimanded. But the correspondence with the Directorate of Professional Standards (DPS) showed that the police had in fact exonerated the officer because there was no CCTV in the interview room and so his allegation rested on Emwazi's word against that of the officer, who denied assaulting Emwazi. All Scotland Yard could offer Emwazi was a copy of a letter which showed that his complaint was filed under the police officer's name so that if it were to happen again his superiors could take action.

After I had seen all the correspondence I explained to Emwazi that the officer had not been disciplined and the letter on his file was unlikely to bother him.[5] Emwazi said he wanted to take the case further and so made a complaint to the Independent Police Complaints Commission (IPCC), which oversees police complaints. We discussed whether we should wait for the outcome of the IPCC case before running his story. Emwazi was adamant that I should run it as soon as possible. I told him that without a finding against the officer the story would look weak as we would have to say the police investigated his complaint but cleared the officer of any wrongdoing. I said it would be a far stronger story if I was able to speak to his former fiancées about their experience with MI5.[6] He later told me that he had spoken to both women and neither wanted to co-operate on the story. He said he must respect their wishes and that without their permission it wouldn't be possible to give me their photographs.[7]

At the end of January 2011 I took up a new post at the *Mail on Sunday* as security editor. I knew that the new paper would be less interested in the plight of a Muslim man accused of Islamist extremism who claimed he was being harassed by the police and MI5. Nevertheless, I wrote to Emwazi on 11 January asking him for permission to try his story with the *Mail on Sunday*: 'Sorry not to get to you sooner. I'm in a state of flux at the moment as I am leaving the *Independent* to join the *Mail on Sunday* as the law and security editor. Would it be OK if I took your story to the new paper and tried to get it published there instead?'[8] Emails between Emwazi and CAGE show that he asked for advice and was told that because the *Mail on Sunday* was 'not Muslim-friendly' he should make sure that I 'retained editorial control' over the article.[9]

On 25 January, the day I started my new job, Emwazi emailed me for the final time: 'Hi Robert. No problem I knew you probably was busy because of your move ... I don't know what it is that you want me to forward to you at your new email, but im guessing its the previous attachments??? Thanks again, Mohammed.'[10]

All along Emwazi had insisted that there were other police documents which supported his belief that one of the officers had been disciplined. But the additional ones he now forwarded added nothing new. The letter the DPS had written to the officer was not a finding against him, simply an acknowledgement that Emwazi's complaint had been recorded on his file. Now that I was able to see all the documents I realized that Emwazi had convinced himself that he had scored a victory against the Met. But in truth, all that had happened was that his complaint had been recorded. If there was something to show that the officer concerned had been reprimanded for assaulting Emwazi then it would have been a strong story as it would have corroborated his other claims. But I suspected that he had decided against the media option as a way of solving his problems. He had reiterated his reservations about involving his ex-girlfriends. He hadn't given me enough solid material to pitch an article. The next I heard of him, Mohammed was named as the masked executioner of the Islamic State.

Whenever I think back to those few months in 2010 and 2011 when I knew Mohammed Emwazi, I ask myself whether I could have done anything that might have changed the course his life took. Perhaps I should have made more of an effort to get his story in the paper. Although he never said so, I wondered whether I had been his last hope that the British 'white establishment' could right its own wrongs. But even though he had given up on me, he hadn't given up on CAGE.

On 13 January 2011 Emwazi wrote to Asim Qureshi again, telling him that after spending three months in Kuwait trying to get to the bottom of his travel problems his father had returned to the UK without making any progress.[11] But he also told Qureshi about a friend from London who, like him, had been barred from entering Kuwait: 'After he was living there in a house [in Kuwait] with his kids for months with no problem all of a sudden hes not allowed in, its obviously these people here that made them [the Kuwaiti authorities] refuse entry!!!'[12]

The friend Emwazi is referring to is the one he spent his weekends with in the desert, 'chilling' in tents drinking tea. The friend later told me: 'I told him not to go back to London because I knew they would block him from coming back. I knew it would happen to me too but I had something very important to sort out in the UK and so I had to come back. It was much worse for Mohammed because Kuwait was his country, he was born there. I was born in the UK so although I didn't like what they had done to me too it wasn't as bad.'[13]

News that a second Briton was being targeted by a joint MI5 and Kuwait State Security Service operation was indicative of a growing concern about British links to terror groups in Kuwait. The alleged plot against the American base and the arrival of Muhsin al-Fadhli in the region were significant and worrying developments. Thames House and their MI6 colleagues across the river in Vauxhall Cross decided to take pre-emptive action against any suspects linked to Kuwait.

Two months later Emwazi decided to try to evade British security by travelling to Kuwait with his mother and once again asked CAGE for advice:

My mother will shortly go to Kuwait to visit her family, I was thinking of going with her. Do you think its worth a try, as they will see me travelling with my mother (if that makes a different to them!!). My mother is only worried that when i land in the Kuwait Airport (if i am even allowed to get on the [plane]!!) that they the kuwaiti officials will take my 'fingerprints/photos' and then they will never let me in. Any advice you can pass on to me and my worried mother?[14]

Saghir Hussain, the CAGE lawyer, replied: 'I am afraid no one can give you a definitive answer on this ... but it may be worth trying it out *inshAllah* [God willing].'[15]

On 5 April at 11 a.m. Emwazi visited the CAGE offices in east London for a meeting with Asim Qureshi. Emwazi said he wanted some more help, presumably with his Kuwait problems. After the meeting Emwazi broke off contact with CAGE.

That summer Emwazi did manage to evade the attentions of MI5 and SO15. Travelling as a passenger in a friend's car he went to Folkestone and boarded the Eurotunnel cross-Channel shuttle to Calais. It represented a serious blunder for the government security services, which had kept Emwazi under tight wraps since 2009. He was allowed to escape Britain in the same way that hundreds of thousands of Britons cross the Channel every year. A year later, when the security services started stopping British Muslims at airports who they suspected of travelling to Syria, the cross-Channel route became the jihadi exit of choice. This is also believed to be the way Emwazi left Britain for the final time in 2013.

The 2011 security blunder was made worse by the fact that Emwazi was travelling with a man who should have been of even more interest to the security services than him. The driver was a known jihadist who had been detained in Afghanistan fighting with the Taliban before being deported to Britain only a few years earlier. The Americans had serious concerns about the risk he posed to the United States and as a condition of his release had asked Britain to keep close tabs on him. Meanwhile, Emwazi and his companion sped through France and Spain before linking up with a terror suspect in Portugal. The man they had come to see was a Syrian national who had been imprisoned by Bashar al-Assad. He had fled Syria a year earlier and sought refuge in Portugal, where the national security services had been closely monitoring him.

When Emwazi and his friend arrived, the local security services were naturally interested and phoned the Syrian man to ask questions about his British friends. The Syrian refugee, who was trying to settle in Portugal, was worried about this contact with the security services. To try to reassure them that they did not present a security threat he offered to arrange a meeting with all three of them. Emwazi's friend said he was more than happy to meet them if it would make their Syrian friend's situation easier. But Emwazi, after everything that happened to him, was less than enthusiastic about sitting down with members of another secutiry service. His friend argued that if this meeting would help the Syrian who had to live in Portugal under the scrutiny of the security services then they should do it. Emwazi was eventually persuaded.

So in a café in Lisbon, Emwazi, his British driver and the Syrian all sat down with three officers from the Portuguese security services for a three-hour meeting. Portuguese security officers probably didn't ask MI5 for intelligence on the two British men – if they had, it's unlikely that they would have been quite so relaxed about the arrival of the two Britons. According to the friend's account of the meeting Emwazi remained reticent throughout, letting his friend do the explaining. They reassured the officers that they had no interest in violent extremism and that they were on a European road trip, taking in the sights and catching up with friends. Their candour appears to have satisfied the Portuguese, who let the men continue on their journey.

It is possible that Emwazi was planning to travel to Syria, heading for north Africa and then travelling overland to the Middle East. When he did finally reach Syria in 2012–13 he is alleged to have linked up with a group of Portuguese jihadis who had been radicalized in London.

In July 2014 – thirty-nine days before James Foley became the first hostage to be murdered by Emwazi – one of the Portuguese jihadis posted a message on Twitter that suggested he had advance knowledge of the American journalist's fate.

The tweet from Nero Saraiva, twenty-eight, a former east London council tenant, read: 'Message to America, the Islamic State is making a new movie. Thank u for the actors.' The Islamic State announced Foley's decapitation in a YouTube film called *A Message to America*. European security services reportedly believe that Saraiva and his east London cell may have been involved in filming and disseminating the IS beheadings, including those of the British aid workers Alan Henning and David Haines.[16]

But if Emwazi was intending to make his move to Syria in 2011 it was thwarted – not by MI5 but his own father. While staying in Lisbon he received a phone call from his father, who said that a pressing family matter meant he must return home immediately. Whatever his father had called him about must have been very important for Emwazi to give up his chance to escape Britain. Reluctantly, the two men said goodbye to the Syrian, turned the car around and retraced their route back to the UK.

Back in the UK Emwazi resumed contact with CAGE into 2012. On New Year's Eve 2011 he wrote: 'I hope that this email reaches you in the best of health and Eman. I've been trying to call you a couple of times, however I get no answer? I hope everything is okay *inshAllah*? Akhi, if you have time I would like to see you *inshAllah*? Please let me know if you're free tomorrow via email.'[17] But he did not get a reply from Qureshi who was off work sick.

On 8 January 2012 Emwazi wrote to Qureshi again about his case. The header of this email revealed an empathy for those people who were trying to help him: 'Smile, it's me again?! Sorry for the headaches that I cause akhi ... would you be at your office during the week? I would like to see you *inshAllah* regarding some advice it shouldn't be too long. Anytime is okay with me *inshAllah*.'[18] In these emails to CAGE, it is clear that

Emwazi has managed the change from young teenager with little interest in religion to a committed Islamist.

That month Qureshi and Emwazi met at the CAGE offices in east London where they discussed more options to overcome his travel ban. Exactly what was discussed at this meeting isn't clear. But Emwazi was nothing if not resourceful and so in the summer of 2012 he tried a different tack. Realizing that his computer skills would not help him leave Britain he started looking for another vocation elsewhere in the Middle East. He elected to become a foreign language teacher and began a course in CELTA (Certificate in Teaching English to Speakers of Other Languages), which he passed with good grades.[19] His teachers were impressed with his affinity for the subject, which they credited to his mastery of Arabic and English.

But if Emwazi thought this would be his ticket out of Britain and back to the Middle East he had badly misjudged the lengths to which MI5 were prepared to go to keep him under surveillance. Following his success as a qualified foreign language teacher, Emwazi and two of his friends from the course were offered interviews with a number of English language centres in Saudi Arabia. But while his two friends were given jobs, Emwazi's application was rejected.[20]

The family believe that this was the direct result of the British security services. Omar told me: 'First the person who interviewed him said he did have the job. And on the second interview they rejected him. So they gave him the job at first and then they rejected him.' The second interview was conducted over Skype and Omar sat in with his older brother. 'He was very excited and he had his glasses on and was wearing his nice shirt to look the part. But he was told that he no longer had the job. But I know for sure he got better grades or at least the same grades as the other two.'

Omar recalled that his brother challenged the interviewer

over his failure to get the teaching job. 'So he said: "Why did you reject me? What changed?" They said: "Oh well," they started to get hesitant and she said: "Oh, it is the beard." I think she slipped up. He said: "What about my beard? Does it have a price tag on? Is it unique, is it different in any way [to the others' beards]? Because both my friends who got the job, they both have a beard." She was looking very nervous.' Omar and the rest of the family were in no doubt what had happened. 'It was very simple – it was like two plus two. He got accepted for the job then he got rejected. He knew why.'

Omar says his brother was determined to get back to Kuwait, which he regarded as his 'homeland'. And he explained the appeal of living in Kuwait while also being a British Citizen.

[In Kuwait] you don't get looked at differently. If I was to have a beard you wouldn't look like a stranger. They know why you have a beard – because of your religion. When you are in Kuwait you are dying to go back to UK and when in the UK you are dying to go back to Kuwait. But the reason for him going back to Kuwait was that he wouldn't get treated differently there because everyone's a Muslim there. Everyone's practising, there is always someone in your family household who is religious. You can practise your religion freely there. Another thing is he has his grandmother [on his father's side] there. He loves her dearly but she is very old now. He can't go and see. And to this day he still cares about that and it bothers him. He was always calling her and she would say why don't you come and see me and he would just say he can't. But he didn't get her worried so he just said he can't come now because it is not the right time.

But while Emwazi continued to make the case that he was an innocent victim of state oppression, the security services now firmly believed he was part of a dedicated network of Islamist extremists who were supporting terrorism activities in the UK and Somalia. MI5 surveillance teams were working round the clock to monitor the network, which had grown to more than twenty members since it was first identified as a terror threat in 2005. And it was no longer contained to the UK. The sudden reappearance in 2009 of Bilal al-Berjawi, Mohamed Sakr and other Britons among the ranks of al-Shabaab in Somalia meant the group had a direct link to the UK-based members, giving the network international reach and making Britain an obvious target for attacks against the West.

British militants had recently renewed their association with al-Shabaab at a training camp in Baidoa in the south central Bay region of Somalia where they honed their skills in weaponry, bomb-making and covert communications.[21] According to an al-Shabaab video of the men's exploits they made good progress and within a few weeks were able to take part in a number of difficult operations including firefights and hit-and-run engagements with government troops. The attacks on Kampala during the 2010 World Cup were reported to be linked to operations supported by Sakr and Berjawi.[22]

But it was their fundraising and recruitment roles which proved of most use to the insurgency. So during the next few months the British fighters were pulled off frontline duties and assigned to command and control. Of the two, it was Berjawi who demonstrated the stronger leadership qualities. He rose through the al-Shabaab ranks and, by the end of 2011, had emerged as a senior commander able to influence the political direction of the group. And by his side, just as he had been ever since their west London school days, stood his loyal friend and compatriot Mohamed Sakr. Local media reported that Berjawi was second only to Fazul Mohammed, the head of al-Qaeda's operations in east Africa.[23] The American jihadist Omar

Hammami even claimed in an interview that Fazul, who was based outside Somalia, was kept abreast of developments in Somalia through contacts with Berjawi and Sakr.

Given both men's prominence in this well-resourced and highly motivated terror group it is easy to see how Western intelligence would have identified them as key targets in the war on terror. Britain's historical ties to Somalia meant the region was still in the British sphere of influence. MI6 had established a network of agents among the terror group and the US-backed Somali government. It could call upon SAS units stationed in neighbouring Kenya to intercept British jihadists. It was claimed that one of these units snatched Michael Adebolajo, who murdered soldier Lee Rigby in Woolwich, when he tried to cross into Somalia from Kenya to join al-Shabaab in November 2010.[24] But al-Shabaab had quickly recognized the threat posed by these agents and had developed sophisticated counter-surveillance tactics, dividing their forces and commanders into tight-knit units only communicating through secure and trusted channels.

While some British intelligence had been useful in the early years of the campaign it was subject to the law of diminishing returns. In reality America held the whip hand in the region. The US's counter-terrorism operations in east Africa were controlled out of its military base in the small state of Djibouti, a former French colony. At the American military's disposal was an arsenal of Predator and Reaper drones, pilotless missiles which can be guided directly onto their target by US personnel sited thousands of miles away in the Nevada desert. The drones' secret technology couples satellite and video screening with a deadly warhead capable of destroying buildings and moving vehicles at the press of a button.

The Pentagon increasingly relied on these drone attacks for its surgical assassination operations. In some cases Britain is alleged to have supplied intelligence which linked suspects to mobile phones or names to suspects but it was the American drones which delivered the killing blows. By 2011 the targeting of individuals by US drones had become mired in controversy. Human rights groups, led by Reprieve and Amnesty International, accused the Americans of conducting a policy of extra-judicial killing outside the rule of law. And they accused Britain of complicity through the supply of intelligence.[25]

The British government had already had its fingers burnt over its secret agencies' links to the US rendition and torture programme. Political pressure had forced a succession of ministers to stand up in the House of Commons and deny that the UK had been party to torture or rendition. But damaging details implicating MI5 and MI6 in these programmes had deeply embarrassed the government and forced an investigation by a judge-led inquiry.[26] Mounting pressure for further disclosure forced the UK government to issue a statement making clear that UK forces restricted all its drone operations to Afghanistan, where it operated a small squadron of them.[27] It did not take part in targeted operations outside this theatre of conflict.

America had no such sensitivities and regarded the drone strikes as an important part of its counter terrorism offensive in east Africa. In 2010 it was claimed that CIA commanders had stepped up US operations in that region by drawing up a list of individual suspect targets linked to al-Shabaab. Berjawi and Sakr were right at the top. This presented the UK security services and their political masters in London with a new problem. It was one thing to be accused of helping the Americans to kill foreign terror suspects but it was quite another to arrange the assassination of British citizens. The UK had a duty to protect a British passport holder from extra-judicial assassination (although subsequent British drone strikes in Syria against

UK citizens fighting for Islamic State shows that government policy had moved on by 2015).

In September 2010 the new Conservative home secretary, Theresa May, sent letters to Berjawi's and Sakr's parents revoking their citizenships 'on grounds of conduciveness to the public good'. They were no longer British citizens.[28] Less than a year later, in June 2011, Berjawi was injured in a US drone strike. With the help of Sakr he slipped across the border to Kenya where he received hospital treatment and was able to lie low for a while. By this time, counter-terrorism operations against al-Shabaab and murderous infighting had eliminated a number of senior commanders, including Fazul Mohammed.

When Berjawi sneaked back across the border in 2012 he was regarded by many as the new leader of al-Shabaab. News of Berjawi's rapid promotion to such an exalted position in the new Islamist militia was greeted among the jihadists of west London with genuine reverence. The fact that one of their own had scaled the heights of international jihad re-energized the network. But Asim Qureshi doubts whether Berjawi ever held such a high-ranking commander's role in al-Shabaab: 'Look, he had no real field experience, had spent most of his life in London and did not know the lie of the land. He was well versed in the Qur'an but you couldn't call him an Islamic scholar.'[29]

For MI5 and Scotland Yard these were small points because the risk of an al-Shabaab attack on home soil had never seemed greater. Court documents show that, throughout his adventures abroad, Berjawi continued to remain in touch with the London network, further fuelling suspicions about their capabilities and intentions.[30]

In 2011 the security services presented evidence to a High Court judge reviewing the terms of a control order placed on CE, who was part of Emwazi's extended network.[31] In his statement to the court, CE said he had been made aware of the drone strike which injured Bilal al-Berjawi but refused to give any more information to the security services in case it might further endanger his life.[32] It was the clearest evidence yet of the influence which Berjawi wielded over the network. In the document, the only intelligence on the west London group in the public domain, the judge described the group as a 'network of United Kingdom and East African based Islamist extremists which is involved in the provision of funds and equipment to Somalia for terrorism-related purposes and the facilitation of individuals' travel from the United Kingdom to Somalia to undertake terrorism-related activity'.[33]

For the first time the security services openly stated that they regarded Emwazi as more than just a peripheral member of the network.[34] MI5 told the judge that Emwazi regularly met with the group at a flat owned by CE's wife.[35] The group was observed adopting counter-surveillance tactics, such as leaping onto Underground trains at the last second to avoid being followed or using code names when discussing Somalia or other members of the group.[36] At one point, according to court documents, surveillance teams had established that Emwazi was one of three network members who had used a friend's wedding party in 2011 as cover for a meeting.[37]

Emwazi, said the report, had turned up with another man, Mohammed Mekki, and is thought to have discussed 'extremist activity' with CE.[38] The papers state that the bride's mother was a solicitor named Jaqueline Nuth who rejected the idea that extremist activity had been discussed at the party. However, the security services pointed out that 'Ms Nuth left shortly after the arrival of Mekki and Emwazi at about 10 p.m. and so cannot speak of what occurred after her departure'.

Another man named as being part of this network was Aydarus Elmi, who I had interviewed two years earlier when I met the Kentish Town group. The Elmi link drew in by association the other members of the Kentish Town group and one member in particular. Mahdi Hashi had left the UK at the end of 2009 ostensibly to care for his ailing grandmother. He had claimed harassment at the hands of MI5 and SO15 and wanted to start a new life in Somalia. In 2010 he met his future wife, by 2011 the couple were married and the following year they had a son. But Hashi's story was not over, as he would soon discover.[39]

At the start of 2012 the American drone hunters were closing in on their targets. On the morning of 2 January Berjawi called one of his drivers, Yasin Osman Ahmed, to take him to a local market to purchase weapons. Afterwards they drove to meet an unnamed 'emir of the *mujahideen*' but stopped to make a phone call. Berjawi's wife had days earlier given birth to a child at St Mary's hospital in west London and he was anxious to find out how she and their baby were doing. So he took a risk and phoned her directly.[40]

High above the vehicle a circling drone had already homed in on the phone signal. The American drone pilot confirmed the target and released the Hellfire missiles. Berjawi was killed instantly, prompting claims that Britain's secret listening station at GCHQ in Cheltenham had passed on details of the telephone call to the US trackers.[41]

But another explanation for his demise has since emerged. It is alleged that Berjawi's trusted driver was working for Western intelligence and had led the drone to its target.[42] A month later an almost identical scenario played out, when another agent, a fighter called Abdirahman Osman, helped guide a drone to Mohamed Sakr and another group of foreign fighters.[43]

Within less than a month Berjawi and Sakr had died in American drone strikes. Their families strongly suspected that when the home secretary signed the men's citizen revocation orders she had in effect also signed their death warrants.

News of the deaths of the two west London men, who for so long had struggled against MI5 and SO15 only to be blown up by American missiles, sent shockwaves throughout the London network. The drone attacks had significantly raised the stakes for the British-based militants. Travel disruption, surveillance and control orders were all part of a long-running game of cat and mouse with the authorities but targeted assassinations were seen as an inflammatory act of betrayal by the British government.

Back in Somalia among the ranks of al-Shabaab the deaths of Berjawi and Sakr helped trigger a power struggle which split the group in two.[44] After Berjawi's death, hundreds of foreign fighters reportedly left Somalia. Many of the Somali Shabaab commanders had openly resented the way Western fighters held sway among the leadership.[45] This led some of the foreign fighters to question the circumstances surrounding the deaths of Berjawi and Sakr, which had so 'conveniently' been laid at the doors of the Americans.

But for MI5 the link between the London militants and al-Shabaab had been broken and the immediate threat of a Somalia-inspired attack against the UK had been lifted. Nevertheless, there was a real human cost for the hard-line policies deployed against the British men drawn to the Horn of Africa extremism.

In 2012 Mahdi Hashi was caught between the militant internecine break-up and the cross-hairs of the US-led counter-terrorism offensive in east Africa. His arrival in Somalia could not have been more badly timed. Like Berjawi and Sakr, Hashi had been stripped of his passport by the home secretary, exiling him from the country where his family lived and making him vulnerable to American counter-terrorism operations,[46] although he later confessed that he would take American inter-rogation over interrogation by al-Shabaab any day.[47] Hashi, no longer able to return to the UK, had moved to Mogadishu where he was making a fist of starting a new family. When he failed to return from a visit to a family member in another part of the country his wife feared the worst.

A few days into his journey Hashi had made contact with al-Shabaab – whether he set out with that intention only Hashi can say. Acutely sensitive to the intelligence failures which had allowed drones to eliminate their commanders, the terror group now viewed all newly arrived foreign recruits with suspicion. And it wasn't long before al-Shabaab matched Hashi to my report in *The Independent* of his complaints that MI5 had tried to recruit him. In al-Shabaab's eyes, this only corroborated their suspicions, and he was imprisoned for three months, witnessing the execution of three fellow prisoners.[48] Hashi escaped but was arrested in Djibouti, where he was handed over to American security forces. He claims he was tortured before being flown to New York where, in 2015, he admitted a charge of belonging to a terrorist group.

While he was in Somalia in mid-2012 Hashi's family in London were sent a letter by the Home Office, explaining that they must inform Mahdi that his citizenship had been revoked on the grounds of alleged Islamist extremism. Hashi, according to his family, felt he had been abandoned by Britain to an alien country he did not fully understand. What happened to him after he was picked up by al-Shabaab on his way to visit his relative is not entirely clear. He claims he was taken prisoner by al-Shabaab and after finally making his escape was kidnapped and became victim of a 'horrific' ordeal at the hands of the secret police in Djibouti, who he claims worked closely with US interrogators.[49]

He says he was so frightened by the threats of torture that he signed a confession demanded by his American interrogators. He also claimed he was made to watch as a Swedish detainee was beaten in front of him: '[The man was] stripped to his underwear and hung upside down. They beat the soles of his feet, poured cold water on him and said they would electrocute him. There was screaming all around me and it was pretty horrific.'[50]

Hashi claims that the next day he was taken out of his cell and warned that if he did not co-operate he would be abused and beaten in the same way.[51] He says the Djibouti interrogators then stripped him to his underwear, blindfolded him and told him he would be sexually abused. During the first three weeks of his detention, he claimed he was interrogated only by Djibouti officers in a cell in the intelligence headquarters near the US embassy in a downtown area of the capital, Djibouti City. Other detainees sharing his cell told how they had been tortured. He said many had been forced to endure 'beatings, being sexually abused, being pinned down naked and their testicles beaten'.[52]

He says he was then handed over to the Americans. He described how the first team of two US interrogators ignored his pleas to alert the British authorities to his detention and torture.[53] He claims they knew that he had been badly treated, but let him believe that he faced far worse if he refused to co-operate. A second team of three American interrogators – who he says treated him better – then persuaded him to sign a confession and 'disclaimer' in which he agreed to waive his right to silence.[54] After his alleged four-month ordeal, he says he was shackled and put on a plane to the US, where he has pleaded guilty to charges of terrorism.[55] Hashi's family believe he was a victim of circumstance, caught in a dangerous country at a dangerous time. But the Americans, who have not answered the allegations of rendition and complicity in torture, believe Hashi was a committed terrorist.

Documents released by the US Attorney's Office of the Eastern District of New York show that Hashi and two Swedish men were detained in Africa by 'local authorities' in August 2012 before being handed over to the FBI on 14 November the same year and flown to New York the following day.[56] They accuse the three men of providing material support to al-Shabaab, which is fighting a war against the US-backed government in Somalia.[57]

According to the FBI Hashi carried out weapons and explosives training with al-Shabaab and was 'deployed in combat operations to support military action in Somalia'.[58] The document adds that he allegedly participated in 'an elite al-Shabaab suicide bomber programme'.[59]

After Hashi's detention in Djibouti his family spent months trying to locate him. It was only when another prisoner managed to get a message to his wife that the family became aware that he was in prison. The note contained claims that he had been 'mistreated' and was being interrogated by men working 'for America'.[60] After the prisoner was released, he made his way back to Somalia where he contacted Hashi's wife. Although Hashi's mother-in-law travelled from Mogadishu to the Djibouti prison in a bid to contact him, prison staff refused to say whether he was there. The family also approached the US authorities, but were told that they had no information about him.[61]

Hashi's family say they only discovered the harsh terms of the order revoking his British citizenship when they approached the Foreign Office for help to find him. On 10 October 2012, the Foreign Office wrote back, saying: 'It is our understanding that Mr Mahdi Mohamed Hashi is no longer a British national, and as such has no right to receive Consular assistance.'[62]

On the morning of 12 May 2015 Mahdi Hashi was brought from a high-security cell in New York's Manhattan Correctional Facility, where he had been held in solitary confinement since 2012, and asked to answer the charge of providing support to al-Shabaab. Hashi told the judge he wished to plead guilty. His conviction marked the end of a three-year investigation, which the FBI was quick to trumpet as another success in its battle to win the war on terrorism.

Yet the case of Mahdi Hashi may not be all that it seems. His journey from the streets of Camden, where he worked as a community youth leader, to a New York terrorism court room has taken in encounters with MI5, claims of torture in an east African prison and an American interrogation and rendition programme that was supposed to be outlawed by President Obama.

After his arrest in east Africa in 2012, Hashi had first faced allegations that he was part of an elite al-Shabaab suicide squad planning chemical weapons attacks on the US. But in 2015 US federal prosecutors accepted a plea to the controversial charge of providing material support to terrorism, an offence that imposes guilt by association. Hashi's supporters claim that he had been visiting family in Somalia in 2012 when Theresa May stripped him of his passport under Britain's own controversial powers against terror suspects. When he later tried to leave war-torn Somalia, he was picked up by an 'unnamed' east African security agency before being handed over to the Americans. His lawyers say that he was detained in Djibouti where he was illegally interrogated and threatened with physical and sexual abuse in order to force him to co-operate. Finally, the FBI arranged for Hashi, now no longer a British citizen, to be flown to New York where he was held for three years before being put on trial for terrorism. His supporters say that such harsh treatment and all those years in solitary confinement left him little choice but to end his ordeal by pleading guilty.

In the long-running war on terror, all this has a very familiar ring. But because cases like Hashi's are nearly always wrapped up in issues of national security in which intelligence against a suspect remains secret, the full story is hardly ever told. But the case against Mahdi Hashi is more illuminating.

In a post-conviction statement released by the FBI, it is clear that Hashi has admitted to something that demonstrably cannot be completely true. The FBI says that 'between approximately December 2008 and August 2012, the defendants [Hashi appeared with two others in the case] served as members of al-Shabaab in Somalia, where they agreed with others to support al-Shabaab and its extremist agenda'.[63] But in May 2009, a year after the FBI said he was in Somalia supporting al-Shabaab, I met Hashi in London when he complained of harassment by MI5. In fact, part of his complaint was that the security services in the UK and Djibouti were making it impossible for him to visit Somalia. He denied being involved in terrorism and claimed that he felt he was being targeted simply because he wanted to travel to Somalia, where some of his family lived.

The leader of the community centre where Hashi worked in 2009 believes the home secretary's decision to take away his citizenship was ill judged and left him exiled in a country where he was not equipped to survive. Sharhabeel Lone, chairman of the Kentish Town Community Centre, remembers:

Let down by his own country and at the mercy of a foreign power's skewed judicial system – three years of solitary confinement have extracted a confession from Mahdi that he was a member of a terrorist organization in Somalia for four years. But that can't be true because, for nearly two of those years, he was helping young people out of gang crime and drugs as a junior youth leader with our organization.[64]

The second part of the public case against Hashi released by the FBI was that he 'was a close associate of American-born al-Shabaàb leader Omar Hammami'.[65] This was a key element in the offence of providing material support to al-Shabaab. Hammami was an American Islamist, also known as Abu Mansour al-Amriki, who had joined al-Shabaab in 2010. But he was aligned to a more moderate wing within the terror organization, and before Hashi had arrived in Somalia in 2012, he had left al-Shabaab after expressing misgivings about its violent direction. In 2013, Hammami was killed by the al-Shabaab leadership for what they regarded as his betrayal.

Hashi was one of a number of young Somali Muslim men interviewed by *The Independent* in 2009 and 2010, each of whom claimed they faced intimidation by the security services. It is difficult to argue that none of them were interested in Islamist extremism or had had some contact with terror suspects. Yet at the time not one of these men had a criminal record and all appeared genuine in their wish to lead violence-free lives while living in the UK. There are hundreds, maybe thousands, more young Muslim men today wrestling with what they perceive to be contradictions between their religious and British identities. A tiny number may feel the need to join terrorist groups to resolve these issues, and they must be properly investigated by our security agencies. But the vast majority want openly to engage with the arguments without fear of harassment and intimidation.

CHAPTER 6

ROAD TO SYRIA

Bitter internecine purges among the higher ranks of al-Shabaab and the resulting exodus of scores of foreign fighters from Somalia to Yemen left the dream of a caliphate across east Africa in tatters. Almost overnight the Islamist jihadi quest switched from Somalia to another hotbed of insurrection and instability – Syria.

Pictures of Syria's suffering began energizing British Muslims who arranged aid convoys to travel out to the troubled state. A small number of British jihadists had already answered the cry for military help as Syrian Muslims rose up against President Assad. Syria was now the only jihad in town.

In the wake of the deaths of Bilal al-Berjawi and Mohamed Sakr, Mohammed Emwazi's network of west London jihadists started making their plans to join the struggle. By the middle of 2012 the network of young jihadists numbered more than twenty interlinking associates, placing a huge strain on the security services, who were struggling to contain the group. A heady mix of testosterone, zealous ideology, a desire for adventure and the radicalizing influences of a few extremist clerics made the call to military jihad irresistible.[1] Combine this with an ease of travel to the conflict zone and tacit support by Western governments and it's easy to see why so many foreign fighters signed up to the cause.[2]

The limited intelligence resources available to monitor their movements and correspondence meant it was essential that the security services prioritize the suspects, some of whom were more committed to foreign quests than others. While MI5 could claim some satisfaction in staunching the flow of terror suspects to the Horn of Africa it was no longer certain which part of the Muslim world they would turn to next. And as the door to Somalia closed the Arab Spring opened many others.

Uprisings across the Middle East added a new spur to the group's activities. By the end of February 2012 rulers had been forced from power in Tunisia, Egypt, Libya and Yemen. Civil uprisings had erupted in Bahrain, Algeria, Jordan, Kuwait, Morocco and Sudan. There were also minor protests in Mauritania, Oman, Saudi Arabia, Djibouti, Western Sahara and Palestine. But it was to Syria where British Muslims were drawn. While most rebellions across the Middle East were about reform and democratic governance, Syria was different. The plight of the Syrian Muslims under the harsh repression of Bashar al-Assad's regime made the country an obvious choice for jihad.[3] Moreover, the revolutionary groups in Egypt, Tunisia and Algeria had limited their ambitions to establishing new power-sharing governments whereas Muslims in Syria were gathering under a flag of a new Islamic caliphate.

A myriad of Islamist brigades, perhaps as many as 250, had set up bases in Syria. And they were all competing for new Muslim fighters to bolster their ranks. In 2012 the internet was awash with propaganda setting out how all good Muslims must answer the call to jihad.

And among the brigades were groups with strong ties to the UK. The best-known was Kateeba al-Kawthar, run by a hard-line Islamist from Britain called Rabah Tahari, who also used the Islamic name Abu Musab. He boasted that his brigade comprised fighters from more than twenty countries all seeking to impose an Islamic state.[4] Its Twitter account was written in English and Tahari, and by all accounts he's a charismatic and bewitching figure who used YouTube to post propaganda films in which he softly narrated the footage of Kateeba fighters in battle against Assad's forces. He complained 'it was not easy' to build an Islamic state and urged British Muslims to send money and food for his fighters.[5]

Another brigade made up of British fighters, Rayat al-Tawheed, similarly exhorted young British Muslims to come to Syria to perform their Islamic duty. Their understanding of the importance of propaganda set the scene for the later successes of the Islamic State. They appealed directly to the British Muslim community for support. Their slick videos, accompanied by rousing soundtracks, presented an image of heroic deeds being done in Muslim lands, presaging the propaganda videos so popular with the later Islamic State. Both Kateeba al-Kawthar and Rayat al-Tawheed posted pictures of their dead fighters, praising them as *shuhada* (martyrs) who would be honoured by Allah. They also filmed their fighters committing atrocities including, in the case of Rayat, a British fighter retrieving the decapitated head of an Assad soldier from a bag.[6]

One of the first to answer the call was one of the west London group's newest recruits. Like Emwazi, Ibrahim al-Mazwagi was a recent university graduate. He studied business administration at Hertfordshire University in Hatfield where he was an enthusiastic member of the Hurricanes, the university's American football team, posting photos of himself wearing the team kit on his Facebook page. Emwazi too liked American sport and in the first image of him to emerge after he was unmasked as Jihadi John he wears a Pittsburgh Pirates baseball hat.

Mazwagi was of Libyan descent and had gained heightened status in the group after he had travelled to Benghazi to take part in the uprising against Colonel Gaddafi in 2011.[7] A year later he was back in Britain looking for a new cause to follow. He told his parents that he was joining an aid convoy for Turkey to help the Syrian refugees. His friends describe a gentle young man who cared deeply for the people he was going to help. 'I don't think there was a single person who wasn't a fan of his,' Joe Thompson, a friend and former teammate, told the *Sunday Times*. 'I knew that he was a fairly religious man but obviously not to the extent that he would go out and fight.'

But Mazwagi can be forgiven for believing he had his country's blessing. After all he had been in Libya fighting alongside British-backed militias supported by British and French fighter-bombers. David Cameron had gone on television to praise all those who had helped to bring down Gaddafi and after the victory had flown to Benghazi to personally thank the rebel fighters. A year later when another tyrant dictator, this time Assad, was threatening to suppress a revolution, Britain's foreign policy had hardly changed.

In January 2012 David Cameron described Bashar al-Assad's treatment of 'his people' as 'appalling', saying the Syrian leader had 'lost [their] consent'.[8] The British government later committed itself to using military action against Assad. And in the run-up to the ill-fated Commons vote in August 2013 in which Cameron failed to get backing for British intervention, the prime minister made a number of increasingly bellicose statements.

A few months later, having travelled through Turkey with the aid convoy, Mazwagi turned up on a Channel 4 documentary where a film crew followed him as he lived and fought with a militant brigade in Syria.[9] In the film Mazwagi came across as likeable and spoke eloquently about why he was in Syria. But most of all he came across as young.

Next to leave for Syria were two friends who had recently been released from prison, Mohamed El-Araj and Choukri Ellekhlifi. El-Araj was an engineering student who was arrested in January 2009 at a violent pro-Palestine protest outside the Israeli embassy and sentenced to eighteen months' imprisonment. He came from a middle-class family in Notting Hill, not far from David Cameron's London home. His father was an antiques dealer who sent his son to the fashionable Holland Park School where he overlapped with two other members of the network, Mohammed Nasser and Hamzah Parvez, who both lived a few streets away and had attended the same mosque – the al-Manaar cultural heritage centre in Acklam Road, Ladbroke Grove.[10]

Ellekhlifi, of Moroccan descent from Paddington, had gone to school with Mohammed Emwazi. He was on bail in 2012 after being arrested for a series of robberies in which a group of youths targeted affluent victims in Belgravia by robbing them and then making their escape on bicycles.[11] It was a crime that belied Ellekhlifi's non-violent background and a passionate interest in art. 'He wanted to work in an art gallery or somehow find a way to sell his paintings,' said a Ladbroke Grove resident who knew Ellekhlifi well.[12] The cash from his robberies and his artwork was used to fund his trip to Syria.

Whatever personal and family stake both men had in Britain, by the end of the summer of 2012 they had decided to forsake it all for the Syrian cause. Ellekhlifi and El-Araj are both thought to have followed their friend Mazwagi, serving with Rabah Tahari's Kateeba battalion.[13]

Tam Hussein, the journalist who knew some of these men in west London, says in his own investigation:

> The communities in Ladbroke Grove through a mixture of faith and heritage were profoundly connected to the affairs of the Middle East, especially the Israeli–Palestinian conflict. The US invasion of Iraq in 2003 resulted in Salafi-jihadi thought having a greater resonance in the community especially amongst the young ... These young men were profoundly affected by the images coming out on social media. After all this is the most mediated conflict that the world has ever seen and anyone with a heart would find it hard to bear witness to the despicable acts carried out by the Syrian regime ... Those who are less wedded to aspiration and the good life, might have little to lose and a lot more to gain by going. Especially as the promise for them is either paradise or *ghanima*, war booty.[14]

But Hussein says that this is not enough for so many young men from the same area to leave to fight for a common cause. He argues there had to be a recruiting figure among the group. There was, he said, 'a mysterious convert, not unlike Ras in Ralph Ellison's *Invisible Man*, who packed up his bags and joined the then named ISIS. This Ladbroke Grove Ras, rootless, charismatic and confrontational had gathered around him a group of young men in Ladbroke Grove who would eventually follow him. These young men recruited others through WhatsApp and other messaging services. It was chain migration in reverse.'[15]

Hussein won't say who this man is, only that he was killed in 2014 or 2015 by a jihadist group of fighters opposing the Islamic State in the east of Syria.

The three departures – of Mazwagi, El-Araj and Ellekhlifi – had injected an unstoppable momentum within the group. Next up was Ibrahim Magag, the former Tube conductor who was still subject to tight surveillance controls under the terms of his anti-terrorism order. He had been living in the West Country but had been allowed back to west London when the coalition government had relaxed the surveillance regime for keeping tabs on terror suspects.[16]

On Boxing Day 2012 Magag had been praying at a mosque in north west London when he broke free from the electronic tag on his leg, jumped into a black cab and disappeared out of the country. His departure led to questions in the House of Commons when the home secretary was asked to account for such a deeply embarrassing security blunder.[17]

Of the four group members who had left for Syria, Magag was closest to Emwazi. And to have departed while under such close attention from the security services may have seemed little short of heroic to the remaining members of the network.

Throughout 2012, Emwazi was also plotting ways of getting to the Middle East. The Emwazi family naively thought that the only obstacle to their son returning to Kuwait was his surname. So in a final, desperate bid to get to Kuwait, Emwazi's father suggested he change his name by deed poll. In early 2013, Emwazi filled out the form and six weeks later he had legally changed his name to Mohammed al-Ayan. With a new passport and new name he once again made travel arrangements to leave the UK.

Omar Emwazi recalled what happened when his older brother and father arrived at Heathrow one more time:

He tried to leave again and that's when they interrogated him and my dad. My dad has never been in a British police station in his entire life. Never ever been arrested, never had to go to a police station in his life. That was the first time. It was at Heathrow. He got rejected. They took my brother to a room and they took my dad to a room and interrogated them. It was the security services, not normal police.[18]

Emwazi's family say one week after he made his last attempt to get back to Kuwait in January 2013 he did finally manage to leave Britain.[19] In that last year, his worldview had changed dramatically. Perhaps spurred on by the efforts of Magag, he had given up on Kuwait and instead told his parents that he was in Turkey helping with the refugee crisis.

It isn't clear how he left Britain. There are reports that he went via the channel rail link at Folkestone or the port of Dover, where he had originally started out on his ill-fated 'safari' to Tanzania in 2009 and his grand tour of Europe in 2011. He may have even travelled with Mohamed El-Araj and Choukri Ellekhlifi, who left around the same time. Emwazi's family say that he disappeared in 2013 but one of his friends believes it could have been earlier, possibly even the summer of 2012. Whatever the circumstances of his disappearance, Emwazi had once again, after his trip to Portugal, managed to evade the close attention of the security services.

Omar Emwazi remembers one of the last conversations he had with his brother. It turned out to be very telling, warning Omar not to follow in his footsteps: 'He wasn't the type of guy to complain ... but he would say certain jokes to me, saying: "Don't be like me." He was always saying: "Learn from other people's mistakes." He would basically say: "Look where I am. I can't get married and I can't get a proper job. I can't travel and I can't go nowhere."'

Emwazi was one of scores of British Muslims who in 2013 were leaving the UK for Syria. But the security services were slow to formulate a policy to counter this jihadi migration. It wasn't until later in the year that the government realized that these jihadists were returning to the UK with battlefield experience and now represented a threat to Britain's national security. One Whitehall source explained: 'In 2012 there were lots of people leaving the UK for Syria. Some were going to help with the humanitarian aid effort, others were going to join the Syrian Free Army. Very few appeared to be going to set up a caliphate or join terrorist groups.'

With hindsight it is possible to say that more should have been done to monitor those leaving the UK, especially men like Emwazi who were already on a watch list. But ever since 2013, when the security services decided to take a zero-tolerance approach to Syria-bound travellers, too many determined jihadists have found a way to evade national border security.

CAGE claims that the family was so worried about Emwazi that after three days of waiting for his return, his parents reported him as a missing person. 'It was four months before the police visited the family home. They explained that they had information that he had entered into Syria. The father said that this could not be true, as far as they were concerned; their son was in Turkey assisting refugees with the limited contact they had managed with him during that period.'[20]

Emwazi was now one of an estimated two hundred British fighters who were in Syria aligned to a multitude of jihadi militias. For the members of the west London network, the jihadi group of choice was Kateeba al-Kawthar. We have already seen how its charismatic leader, Rabah Tahari, had strong links to the UK and its propaganda was written and spoken in English. His fighters also had access to the latest battlefield weaponry. In one of the group's videos, fighters are shown parading a stockpile of thirty Soviet-era SA-16 missiles – at the time the most advanced anti-aircraft weapon yet seen in jihadist hands.[21] During the propaganda video, which was aimed at a UK audience, Tahari and his rebel fighters are seen brandishing a black flag and one balaclava-clad fighter is filmed casually lobbing a grenade into a compound of buildings; another is shown running away from an explosion that destroys a communications tower.

During one firefight an English-speaking extremist is heard shouting: 'Run, Forrest, run' – a quotation from the movie *Forrest Gump* – as another fighter sprints for cover under fire.[22] The camera pans around a large room apparently being used as an arms dump by the jihadists. Hundreds of assault rifles are shown in a large pile alongside grenades and boxes of ammunition. During the video, Tahari thanks the group's British supporters for helping the 'brothers in the field in Syria' but admits the fighters took heavy casualties during an assault against one of the Syrian regime's military bases. 'To establish an Islamic state, brothers and sisters, that's not easy. It needs big effort, it needs all the sacrifices you can give, money-wise, health-wise, blood-wise.'[23]

By the summer of 2013 Kateeba al-Kawthar had become part of a much larger fighting force called Kataib al-Muhajirin (KAM) and numbering more than one thousand non-Syrian fighters. We know this because Tahari makes a number of high profile appearances in KAM videos and propaganda. And interestingly he is joined by Ibrahim al-Mazwagi, Choukri Ellekhlifi and Mohamed El-Araj.

Around this time a Channel 4 producer secured unprecedented access to the group. In a series of interviews Mazwagi explains why he has come to Syria and what he is fighting for. He justifies his decision to come to Syria by saying: 'Well, I've always known about jihad, seen the *mujahideen* on TV and everything.' Later he adds: 'We can't accept enemies of Allah . . . killing us, abusing our religion, belittling it, taking our lands. So the *mujahideen*, those who practise jihad, are those who defend the Muslims.'[24]

Filmed over several months, Mazwagi is shown firing weapons, going shopping and joining a key battle for a Syrian army base called Sheikh Suleiman in western Aleppo. At one point he is asked if his mother knows where he is and he replies: 'I remember I called my mother once. I told her I am going on an operation tomorrow. She said, "Make sure you're not at the back. Go to the front."' Laughing, he adds, 'I don't think my mother loves me that much. No, I'm joking. She must love me for her to say that.'[25]

During his time with KAM, Mazwagi is seen preparing to marry a Muslim woman from Sweden and is filmed choosing a sheep for slaughter for his wedding banquet. He is shown on his wedding day celebrating with a group of well-armed jihadists, many in combat fatigues and balaclavas. But Mazwagi and the other British fighters hardly appreciate that in spite of their high Islamic ideals, the emirs of IS regard them as little more than cannon fodder. In 2013, Mazwagi, Ellekhlifi and El-Araj were all killed fighting in northern Syria. They died in the same battle just yards from each other.

Around this time, a second film, released by one of the KAM fighters, provided what some believe is the first tantalizing glimpse of Emwazi in Syria. The footage is of two bands of fanatical fighters joining forces under the command of Omar al-Shishani, a red-haired bearded fighter from Chechnya.[26] At the front stands a man thought to be Mohammed Emwazi. He makes a pledge of allegiance when another band of militants, the Army of Muhammad Brigades group, of which Emwazi is believed to have been a member, joins forces with KAM. The figure sporting the now familiar balaclava which masks his face shouts out the call to arms in front of a crowd of armed fighters. As a smiling Shishani proudly looks on arm in arm with two other foreign fighters, the speaker proclaims: 'This army announces unity within its ranks for the sake of implementing the shari'a and returning this blessed land to God the Most Glorified and the Most High under the leadership of the emir Omar al-Shishani.'[27]

Many believe this film captures the critical period in Emwazi's transition from jihadist to jihadi butcher under Shishani's grisly tutelage. Shishani, whose real name is Tarkhan Batirashvili, is an ethnic Chechen from Georgia, specifically from the Pankisi valley, a centre of Georgia's Chechen community and once a stronghold for militants. He fought in the brief conflict between Russia and Georgia in 2008 and became a jihadist having been discharged from the Georgian military on health grounds after contracting tuberculosis. Although he made a good recovery the Georgian army barred him from re-enlistment. In September 2010, he was arrested for keeping a weapon in his home and imprisoned. After his release in March 2012, he travelled to Istanbul to join Chechen rebels in the Syrian conflict. Once there he established himself as the commander of KAM, which was initially aligned with al-Qaeda's Jabhat al-Nusra.

The Chechen fighters were not only experienced in waging a violent insurgency. They also had little compunction in employing brutal means to secure their ends. In this light it is easy to see how Shishani's background as a battle-hardened veteran might have impressed Emwazi. Many British and other Western jihadists rallied around the Chechen leader. They trained in military camps based on those in Afghanistan where they were shown how to fire weapons and blow up trucks and checkpoints. Emwazi was still establishing himself within the group and those who knew him already regarded him as a cold and callous fighter.

A man calling himself Abu Ayman described to the BBC his encounters with Emwazi.[28] He said he first saw Emwazi at a town called Atmeh in northern Syria, which was a sprawling, desolate refugee camp built on a hillside.[29] The jihadists had taken over nearby homes and enjoyed greater comforts than the civilian population. Abu Ayman said the British fighters were always hanging out together. At the time the Britons called it their 'five star jihad' – and they posted pictures on Twitter and Instagram to glamorize their new lives while acting as propaganda to recruit more fighters. But Ayman, who said he often visited the British fighters in their homes, remembers Emwazi was 'odd' and refused to mix with the other Western fighters: 'He was cold. He didn't talk much. He wouldn't join us in prayer,' he said. 'He'd only pray with his friends … the other British brothers prayed with us, but he was strange … The other British brothers would say "Hi" when they saw us on the road, but he turned his face away. The British fighters were always hanging out together, but he wouldn't join them.'[30]

To reinforce his rejection of Britain, Emwazi adopted the Islamic name of Abu Muharib al-Yemeni.[31] This was not only because he wanted to distance himself from Kuwait, which he also blamed for his travel disruption and banning order, but because his mother had Yemeni family.[32] It meant he could legitimately lay claim to a Yemeni heritage in his new Islamic identity.

In another interview there is evidence that Emwazi had already developed a ruthless streak which betrayed his contempt for life. One militant remembers an encounter between Emwazi and fighters of the Free Syrian Army (FSA), who also held territory in the region.[33] The man recalls how Emwazi and some of his colleagues were held up at gunpoint at an FSA checkpoint, where guards demanded they surrender their weapons and valuables. According to the story, Emwazi calmly pulled out his own pistol and aimed it at the head of one of the FSA soldiers, telling him if they didn't let them go he would shoot. The high-risk strategy worked and the men were allowed to pass through. But the fighter who witnessed the incident said the cold look in Emwazi's eyes and his complete disregard for his own life had completely mesmerized the FSA soldiers. The story of the incident and Emwazi's role passed among the jihadist ranks, enhancing his reputation as a brave fighter.[34] It also won him the respect of Shishani, who had just been appointed commander of the region by the ISIL leader, Abu Bakr al-Baghdadi.

Two British medics who had known Emwazi in London and met up with him again in Syria described him as a quiet man hiding an adrenaline junkie streak and a gung-ho attitude. The British men were working at a hospital in Syria near the Turkish border when they came across Emwazi in 2013 while he visited friends who had been injured in the fighting.[35] They told ITV that Emwazi wore his full combat gear at all times, even in safe areas during the heat of summer, and he earned his high-ranking position through his aggressive behaviour. He was, they said, a man who was 'always ready for war'. One of the medics said he had to ask Emwazi to remove his weapon while he was in the hospital. 'From what I've heard, from the way that he deals with difficult incidents, is that he seems to be someone with not really much to lose.'[36]

Speaking on condition of their anonymity, the men said they had previously known of Emwazi in London but never met until they came across him separately during stints in the war-torn country in 2013, some months before he became known as Jihadi John. He was unmarried and he was 'caring' towards his friends in hospital, bringing fizzy drinks, Haribo sweets and ice cream for them – contrasting sharply with the expensive gun and extra rounds he carried into the health centre. Emwazi had a strong dislike of Britain, they said, and scowled when the country was mentioned. He would only

admit to being 'kind of' British when asked, and usually identified as Yemeni-Kuwaiti, speaking Arabic as his preferred
language. He was evasive and avoided enquiries about where
he had come from, growing suspicious of the medics' questions
before starting to quiz them instead: 'He told me clear cut he
had no intention of returning to London. He said no way and
if you ask him if he was British he would say kind of. He didn't
say yes.'[37]

Shortly after Emwazi had pledged his support to Shishani,
the group found itself on the cusp of a damaging schism. A new
terror group, formed around al-Qaeda in Iraq, had established
itself in northern Syria. The Islamic State of Iraq and the Levant
(ISIL), the name given to the Islamic State before it declared its
caliphate in the region, applied a ruthless and uncompromising
brand of violent Islamist extremism to the revolution. It also
put the creation of a caliphate at the centre of its manifesto of
terror.

ISIL's early successes under the charismatic leadership of
Baghdadi, an Iraqi terrorist who had come to power with
al-Qaeda in Iraq, meant that the group had a heightened profile
which had attracted many foreign fighters. Emwazi was more
than aware of the group as his own network in London had
held heated discussions about the legitimacy of its barbarism.
He had sided with those who argued that the executions and
tortures were justified because of Western military action which
had killed so many Muslims in the region.[38]

Moazzam Begg, the British Guantánamo detainee released
from the US naval base in January 2005, had also travelled to
Syria in 2012 and 2013.[39] In one picture released by KAM,
Begg is sitting around a table with Shishani, Rabah Tahari and
other militants, apparently sipping coffee. The photo is believed
to have been taken at the group's camp in northern Syria in
December 2012. This was Begg's first trip to Syria, where he

was investigating the victims of torture under Assad in which he claims there was UK complicity. He visited a number of camps and witnessed at first hand the birth of ISIL. He recalls how he heard that jihadists believed to be aligned with ISIL were torturing a Muslim prisoner. He said he pleaded with them to stop the torture – but to no avail. Later he wrote: 'I have more reason than most to oppose ISIL. They have tortured and executed several of my friends in Syria, including a rendition victim and a man who welcomed me into his family home where I stayed for months.'[40]

Begg's feelings were not universally shared within KAM. Shishani and Tahari were both courted by ISIL and in May 2013 they announced KAM's allegiance to the new terror group. The announcement ended in the break-up of KAM, with Shishani and Tahari taking a loyal band of foreign fighters to ISIL.[41] One of these fighters was Emwazi. He may have been joined by two brothers from west London, Fatlum and Flamur Shalaku. The brothers had worshipped in the same mosques as Emwazi and had left for Syria around the same time. Like many of the British fighters they told their parents they were doing aid work in Turkey.

But not everyone followed Shishani and Tahari. Another Chechen, Sayfullah al-Shishani (no relation to Abu Omar al-Shishani), appears to have broken away from the group to set up an independent faction fighting alongside Jabhat al-Nusra.

Abu Omar al-Shishani's military experience and ruthless tactics allowed him to control a broad stretch of territory in northern Syria right up to the Iraq border.[42] But he and his band of fighters based themselves in a large villa owned by a businessman in the town of Huraytan, just north west of Aleppo. There are pictures of him enjoying the villa's swimming pool and reports of him spending hours in the jacuzzi.

According to the *New York Times* Shishani was also in charge of a number of high-value prisoners whom ISIL had started to detain.[43]

Around this time there were reports of a prison near Aleppo.[44] We know that one of the prisoners was a Belgian fighter, Jejoen Bontinck, twenty-three, who had been one of the KAM jihadists who had refused to join ISIL. When he tried to leave the group, they imprisoned him and accused him of spying. His father travelled to Syria in 2013 and helped negotiate his release.[45] Back in Belgium Bontinck was arrested and convicted for fighting for a terrorist organization. Court documents from his trial include his testimony about the time he spent in the Aleppo prison between August and September 2013.[46]

Bontinck claims that two Western hostages were imprisoned with him: a British photo-journalist and an American journalist, James Foley.[47] Here he says that for a few weeks he was held with Foley and others in a cramped cell where they were left starving and given dirty water to drink. He has also spoken of a British torturer the prisoners nicknamed 'Pinocchio', because he always lied to them before they were about to be tortured, and other guards known as the 'butcher' (because he tortured them with blunt instruments) and 'the butcher's assistant' (because he was always helping the 'butcher').

Bontinck says Foley was waterboarded, given electric shocks, hit with blunt instruments and made to stand up for three days at a time, leaving him so delirious he didn't know where he was. Pinocchio 'came from Great Britain and had dark skin – he was of Pakistani or Bengali origin.' Pinocchio's penchant for torture and his British background makes it very likely that he was one of the so-called 'Beatles', the British ISIL torturers whose number included Emwazi.

Bontinck says a second torturer at the IS prison was called Abu Horeia, whom Foley and others nicknamed 'Very Good'. 'They called him "Very Good" because they once saw him torture someone and he then said: "Very good."' He says the first ISIL prison complex was next to a shari'a court which was in an urban part of Aleppo screened by high buildings. And there is evidence that Shishani and his men had recently occupied a warehouse in the centre of Aleppo, which helps to place them in the vicinity of the prison.

Other prisoners have also described how they were held by the 'Beatles' in an industrial complex in Aleppo.[48] Describing the cell in which the hostages were held, Bontinck says:

> It was an ordinary room with pale brown walls, a pale brown floor in stone and a ceiling of the same colour. There were mattresses and reed mats and we had some books. I think it was about four metres long and eight metres wide. There was electricity and light. It was half underground and the sash window was overlooking a huge dead wall. We had to eat in our cell. Apart from going to the toilet, we had to stay there all day. But still I think of all the prisoners, we were treated the best.[49]

That all changed when the British jihadists were put in charge. The men were forced to swap their clothes for orange jumpsuits and the tortures aped the abuses carried out by the Americans on their extra-judicial prisoners. These included waterboarding, shackling and sensory deprivations. The inmates had no doubt that they were supposed to regard their prison as a mini-Guantánamo. And they were all given numbers and told to address their jailors as 'sir'.[50] They passed the time by playing games such as Animal, Vegetable, Mineral, in which they took turns to guess who or what the actor was pretending to be.

Bontinck added: 'They had already been prisoners for ten months. That means it must have been around December when they were taken prisoner. They were tortured by al-Nusra [al-Qaeda].'

During his three-week detention with the two Western hostages, Bontinck says they became good friends, exchanging addresses:

> Our conversations were about the present and the future ... that James had better get married and the like. We also talked about what I want to do with my life. I wanted to do something involving computer games. John told me that he had once worked for Sega testing computer games ...
>
> I know that people from the PKK [Kurdish fighters] were imprisoned in the corridors of the court. I think their fate had been decided. I suspect they were executed. When I was in the third cell I saw, through the gaps in the door, clothes lying in a pile down the corridor, whereby I recognized clothing of people who had previously been chained up in the corridor ... Sometimes we heard a shot or a few shots in the cell; we suspected that these were executions.[51]

Bontinck also claims the two journalists were moved on several occasions and 'tortured' while 'barely getting enough to eat', before they were handed over to an IS group in Raqqa. That group, which included Emwazi, may well have been personally headed by Shishani.

Evidence of Shishani's involvement is supported by a little-publicized American Treasury statement which was released on 24 September which claimed: 'Batirashvili [Shishani] oversaw an ISIL prison facility in al-Tabqa, close to al-Raqqah, where ISIL possibly held foreign hostages.'[52]

And wherever Shishani went Emwazi went too. By the summer of 2013 the two men can be placed in Raqqa, the heart of Baghdadi's bloody empire. While Shishani would make his name as a ruthless commander of jihadi fighters, Emwazi was given the job of guarding and torturing prisoners.

CHAPTER 7

BEHEADINGS THAT SHOCKED THE WORLD

Mohammed Emwazi had spent his teenage years drinking and clubbing. He had shown no interest in the teachings of Islam until he left school. And even when he discovered political Islam through his connections with the west London network there is no evidence that he was interested in violence. But after the leaders of the group started plotting murder and terrorism in Somalia, Emwazi was caught in the cross-hairs of a domestic counter-terrorism operation designed to smash the group. Prevented from travelling to his Kuwaiti homeland and denied the chance of work and marriage, Emwazi sought relief and escape in the violence of a jihadi war zone. His journey from misfit schoolboy to committed jihadist had taken him to the epicentre of the most fearsome terror organization in the world.

Under Abu Omar al-Shishani's attentive tutelage, Emwazi was able to commit himself to a brutal and merciless jihad. Western fighters joining the Islamic State were mostly treated as foot soldiers to be thrown at the enemy and very few were given positions of authority or influence. But Emwazi could speak fluent Arabic, had a gift for computers and was committed to the cause. He also harboured a bitter hatred for the West and their allied Arab states, born out of his own encounters with the security services, police and Kuwaiti bureaucracy. And he had no hesitation in using violence in the name of his new masters. Along with other British jihadists, he was tasked with guarding the valuable Western hostages now being held by the Islamic State.[1]

The reported atrocities committed in north east Syria at this time shocked the world. Emwazi was a young British university graduate whose only experience of violence had been gang fights on the streets of west London. The horrors of the Syrian battlefield, including the slaughter of civilians and prisoners, must have eaten away at any residual sense of respect or empathy he had for human life.

On a warm, early spring evening in 2014 a convoy of dozens of jeeps, cars and military vehicles carrying hundreds of ISIL soldiers and their families moved out of Aleppo. In one of the lorries were the Western hostages. Underneath the hostages were boxes of explosive and sitting with them on the long journey was a jihadist wearing a suicide belt.

Javier Espinosa was one of the hostages handcuffed in the back of the lorry. 'If our Moroccan [the jihadist with the suicide belt] pushed the button,' he said, 'the vehicle, and us, would blow up. As if that was not bad enough, the dates we were fed, which were all we had to eat, gave most of us diarrhoea.'[2]

Espinosa was one of the first to fall into the hands of the Islamic State. He is the kind of special correspondent who editors refer to as 'seasoned' and 'battle-hardened' before they send them out to risky conflict zones. He had been covering Syria since the start of the war and, in 2012, was lucky to escape from the bloody siege of Homs during which Assad's artillery had killed several other journalists, including the *Sunday Times'* war correspondent Marie Colvin.

So when he was captured nearly two years later by a rogue al-Qaeda group, as he made his bid to cross the border into Turkey, Espinosa had already witnessed many horrors in Syria. But the brutality demonstrated by the group of terrorists led by the British fighter Jihadi John surpassed anything that had gone before: 'They had me sat on the floor, barefoot, with a shaven head, a thick beard and dressed in the orange uniform that had made Guantánamo, the American prison, famous. Jihadi John wanted maximum drama. He had brought along an antique sword of the kind Muslim armies used in the Middle Ages. It was a blade of almost a metre in length with a silver handle.'[3]

In his account of what it was like to be at Emwazi's mercy he gives a vivid insight into the pleasure Emwazi extracted from his victims. It's an encounter that Espinosa can't stop replaying in his mind.

He caressed my neck with the blade but kept talking: 'Feel it? Cold, isn't it? Can you imagine the pain you'll feel when it cuts? Unimaginable pain. The first hit will sever your veins. The blood mixes with your saliva. The second blow opens your neck. You wouldn't be able to breathe through your nose at this stage, just your throat. You'd make some amusing guttural sounds – I've seen it before, you all squirm like animals, like pigs. The third blow will take off your head. I'd put it on your back.' Then he drew his pistol from his leather holster and placed it against my head and pulled the trigger three times. Click. Click. Click. It's called a mock execution. But not even this terrifying intimidation seemed to satisfy him.[4]

A second Spanish journalist has also testified what it was like to be Emwazi's prisoner. Marc Marginedas had been taken on 4 September 2013 by rebel jihadists close to the city of Hama, in western Syria. He had entered the country three days before, through Turkey, accompanied by members of the Free Syrian Army (FSA). Like his colleague Espinosa, he too was a veteran. In his accounts of his torture he confirms what other hostages have said: that all the 'Beatles' spoke with British accents, but he adds this point – that they named them the 'Beatles' because they liked beating people, not simply because they were British.[5]

Marginedas and Espinosa were among a group of twenty-three hostages who were held in Raqqa, northern Syria, where the 'Beatles' had set up a room next to the prisoners, separated only by a broken glass door and a curtain. Marginedas said the three masked 'Beatles' liked to burst into their cell shouting and threatening the prisoners, and always ended up beating at least one of the hostages.[6]

On one occasion he recalls how Emwazi carried out a particularly savage attack on one of the hostages who had been told by the 'Beatles' to approach the prison door.[7]

Once in position, [Jihadi John] took a red pen and began to draw a sword on the [unnamed] hostage's face, letting him know in this macabre way he would end his days in Syria, beheaded. The pen tip broke before he finished the sketch, but Jihadi John wanted to finish his work with [a] sharpened pencil, already cut almost like a knife, tearing the skin of the cheek with a vengeance, and leaving a visible wound in the face, outlined by the scar.[8]

Despite Emwazi's new-found talents for violence he was not the jihadist in charge of the guards. This role went to another British fighter dubbed 'George', another of the 'Beatles'. George was also British and may well have known Emwazi in London and even travelled with him to Syria. The journalist Tam Hussein speaks of a 'mysterious radicalizing' figure among the west London network who played a central role in the recruitment of the London men to the Islamic State. Hussein does not say who this man is.[9] But could this London jihadist be the leader of the 'Beatles' who the Western hostages called George?

The third 'Beatle' was nicknamed Paul or Ringo according to differing hostages' accounts. There is some evidence that he may have been one of the Shalaku brothers, who had left London at the same time as Emwazi. Tam Hussein says that '[police] officers were particularly interested in the two [brothers] following the revelation of the identity of Jihadi John'.[10]

Marginedas, the Spanish hostage who had been marked with the pen for beheading, would later be released. He has returned to working as a foreign correspondent, and told me he is trying to rebuild his life with his family. In a series of articles he wrote for his newspaper he says he believes that the 'Beatles' were put in charge of the prisoners only because Islamic State commanders couldn't spare hardened fighters from the battlefield.

Indeed Emwazi would have had no contact with the emirs of the Islamic State who controlled the region around Raqqa. They would have had little time for or interest in a British recruit who had no fighting experience. The Islamic State leadership is dominated by a clique of Sunni Iraqis who trust no-one outside their circle. Emwazi's failure to win the respect of the 'sheikhs', as the foreign fighters called them, must have played on his mind.

Marginedas thinks that this may have been a great source of grievance to the 'Beatles', which only served to fuel their cruelty. The jihadi who seemed to feel it the most and who revelled in this cruelty was the one they called John.[11]

According to Marginedas, Emwazi was a 'manic-depressive'. To all the prisoners he was a psychopath who took great pleasure in eking out as much fear and terror from his captives as he possibly could while also showing a complete lack of understanding of how his captives saw him. Marginedas says Emwazi would, on rare occasions, completely forget the tortures he had inflicted on the men and would try to seek their friendship and emotional help when he was having bad days.[12]

Marginedas recounts an incident in February 2014 when Emwazi visited the hostages and claimed that he had been wounded in combat: 'Once, on a February evening, he appeared in the room and began walking in circles around the silent hostages. He said: "I wonder what you would do to me if you were in my position," hinting for the first time that he was aware of the suffering he was inflicting on the hostages while at the same time offering a motive for his cruelty.'[13]

Marginedas says the jihadists' psychopathic behaviour is further demonstrated by another episode in which the 'Beatles' gave the leftovers of their food to half the starving hostages while the remaining hostages were ordered to watch their fellow prisoners eat. This, he says, was designed to sow bad feeling among the prisoners – which it did, with bitter recriminations against those prisoners who had played the 'Beatles'' game by eating the food. 'I know you eat the remains of their food because you are forced to, but do not do so avidly!' scolded one of the starving hostages.[14]

Marginedas was the first of the 'Beatles'' hostages, who came from eleven countries, to be released by the Islamic State. He recalls how Emwazi first told him the good news: '"Marcos, Marcos (is the name on my passport), are you ready to go?" he asked in a quiet, mellow voice. "Yeah," I replied, instinctively looking up at the surprise news that he was giving me and forgetting that when we spoke to the "Beatles" I had to keep my eyes focused on the ground, fearing that we might end up identifying these three masked men. "Do not look at my eyes!" he shouted, lifting his hand.'[15]

Marginedas and Espinosa were among sixteen hostages to be released by the Islamic State in February, March and April 2014. The circumstances of their negotiated freedom, during which France and Spain broke ranks with Britain and America to pay multi-million-pound ransoms to the kidnappers, is mired in controversy. The accusation against the negotiating nations was that they had undermined the long-held position among Western states of not dealing directly with terrorists. When ransoms have been raised for the release of British or American hostages it has been through the use of private funds or insurance companies.

Regardless of the political implications of capitulating to ransom demands, these freed hostages were able to give vital intelligence to the security services about the conditions of detention of the other prisoners. These debriefings of the released prisoners were led by the hostages' own national security services and shared with the CIA and MI6. What emerged was a truly worrying situation in which the health of, and threat to, the British and American hostages was much more perilous than first understood by the spy chiefs.

It also exposed a collective intelligence failure at the heart of MI6 and the CIA, who had been unable to establish a credible network of reliable informants among the high-ranking echelons of the Islamic State. They had badly misjudged the ruthless operational nature of a terror group which had emerged from al-Qaeda in Iraq as a well-organized and well-motivated force capable of defeating the Iraqi military with barely a shot fired in anger. The Islamic State may have grown out of al-Qaeda in

Iraq but it was apparent that it wanted to be much more than an al-Qaeda franchise and its determination to achieve this forcibly made the group unpredictable. The horrific accounts of torture, waterboarding, mock executions and deteriorating medical conditions of some of the British and American hostages led to a rethink in Washington and London about how to save their nationals. The continued beatings and punishments suffered by James Foley and David Haines (who were both identified by IS as having military connections) made them obvious targets for their captors. But it was the fate of Russian engineer Sergei Gorbunov which showed that the Islamic State jihadists were capricious and capable of killing for pleasure.

Gorbunov had been working on an aid project in northern Syria in October 2013 when he was captured by Chechen militants near a military airport in Hama. Eventually he was passed on to the Islamic State and found his way to the Raqqa prison run by the 'Beatles', where he shared a cell with Espinosa and the other hostages. Many of the foreign prisoners had begun their captivity in the hands of criminal gangs who sold their captives to the highest bidder or with jihadi factions who wanted to prove their allegiance to Abu Bakr al-Baghdadi by gifting prisoners to the Islamic State. One day, early in 2014, Gorbunov was taken from his cell and never seen again.[16]

A few weeks later Emwazi visited the prisoners carrying a laptop. He set it up on a table and called Espinosa over, saying he had something he wanted to show him. 'What do you see in the photo? Tell the others!' When Espinosa refused Emwazi provided his own narration: 'The sheikh [a high-ranking IS commander] shot him with an explosive bullet.'[17] Then he asked Espinosa once more to describe the gory spectacle. 'Tell me, what do you see?' he shrieked.

Espinosa replied: 'I see Sergei, he's dead, there's blood, bits of brain on his beard.'

'Yes, and don't you see the enormous hole made by the bullet?' Emwazi said exultantly. 'You might end up with him. We'll make you dig him up and put you in another tomb where you can sleep with him.'[18]

It was a telling exchange which revealed to the Americans, from the debriefing of the released hostages, that unless they acted quickly they might be too late to save those remaining. Added to this concern was the dawning realization that 'Jihadi John' was the same militant kidnapper who had revelled in the video killing and was also involved in the hostage negotiations. The hostages' situation looked more perilous than ever.

A media blackout had ensured that the British and American public were completely unaware of the dangers facing Western hostages held captive in Syria by the Islamic State, or that British jihadists were torturing their fellow citizens. But in early July 2014 American intelligence chiefs believed they had recovered enough information from the former detainees to pinpoint the location of the prison where the remaining hostages were being held. President Obama ordered a meeting of his intelligence chiefs and then gave the green light for a high-risk rescue operation.

On a moonless night on 3 July 2014, at an undisclosed military base in an unnamed country bordering Syria, several dozen US Army Delta Force commandos mounted their Black Hawk helicopters. As the helicopters lifted off, Obama relocated to the situation room with secretary of state John Kerry and national security adviser Susan Rice to follow the mission's progress minute by minute.

Some of the Black Hawks carried Delta Force troops while others were 'direct action penetrators', or DAPs, which do not carry personnel and are modified with rocket pods, 2.75-inch rockets and chain guns. All of the aircraft entered Syrian airspace and headed toward the site near Raqqa.[19]

As the helicopters approached the rendezvous point, two armed Predator drones joined the operation, circling overhead while missile-armed jets remained on standby. As soon as the helicopters touched down the special forces fanned out towards their target – an oil storage facility a few miles outside Raqqa. As soon as they approached the building they engaged a small group of jihadists, eliminating two of them in a short firefight. The Delta Force soldiers carried on towards the oil facility and smashed through the perimeter doors.

Once inside, rescue teams made a desperate search of the building, room by room. The sketches drawn by the hostages matched the location perfectly and the Delta Force commanders were sure they had found the right place, but they didn't encounter any of the hostages. They stayed an hour on the ground making sure they hadn't missed anything, but in the end had no choice but to leave the prison empty handed except for a mobile phone and a couple of blankets.

The American rescue mission was too late. The Western hostages had been moved to another prison just a few days earlier.

The mission's failure not only confirmed the Americans' reliance on stale, outside intelligence but they had been forced to prematurely show their hand. For several weeks, nothing was heard from the kidnappers and the situation became very difficult to read.

For the family of James Foley the waiting was agonizing. They had been in contact with the kidnappers since November 2013. The first email was only four lines long. It had arrived on 26 November via an encrypted, untraceable email account and was addressed to Michael Foley (James's brother) and Phil Balboni, Foley's editor at the GlobalPost news website. The kidnappers struck up a friendly, in retrospect sinister, tone:

'hello. we have james. we want to negotiate for him. he is safe: he is our friend and we do not want to hurt him. we want money fast.'[20]

The picture suddenly became horrifyingly clear after 7 August 2014, when President Obama authorized American airstrikes in Iraq to rescue the stranded Yazidi minorities and protect US headquarters in Irbil and Baghdad. Following sixty-eight strikes from jets, bombers and drones, Obama announced that Iraqi and Kurdish forces, with US air support, had retaken a strategic dam north of Mosul from the militants and that they had been pushed back from Irbil. Within hours of that announcement, the Islamic State posted an online message warning it would attack Americans 'in any place' in response to the airstrikes. 'We will drown all of you in blood,' it said.[21]

On 12 August the Foley family received this ominous email from the kidnappers: 'This is the last email you are going to receive from us.' Then, on 19 August the Islamic State delivered on its blood-curdling message. A video entitled *A Message to America* was published on the internet. It claimed to be produced by the Islamic State's media arm and what it showed made shocking viewing.[22]

A Message to America, the now infamous beheading video of James Foley and the direct threat to his fellow American captive Steven Sotloff, got the reaction it was looking for. President Obama gathered his trusted security advisers so he could issue a speedy riposte to what the American public felt to be as every bit as horrifying as al-Qaeda's attack on the Twin Towers. Like 9/11, the killing of James Foley was an act of terrorism beamed unedited into the living rooms of the world.

Foley, aged forty, had been missing in Syria since November 2012. But before that he had been imprisoned in northern Libya in 2011. Foley, together with fellow American Clare Morgana Gillis, a freelance reporter, and Spanish photographer

Manu Brabo, were detained near Brega by forces loyal to Gaddafi. Another photo-journalist, Anton Hammerl, had been killed in the attack in which Foley, Gillis and Brabo were captured.[23] When the shooting started, Foley and Gillis both heard Hammerl yell out 'Help!' But Hammerl was killed and the other three journalists were beaten by the pro-Gaddafi forces and then taken as their prisoners.

Foley said afterwards: 'Once I saw Anton lying there dead, it was like everything had changed. The whole world has changed. I don't even know that I felt some of the blows.'

Gillis remembered: 'We all glanced down at him as we were being taken by, and I saw him just lying in a pool of blood. And then we were put into the truck and our heads were pushed down. We weren't able to see anything that happened after that to him.'[24]

Foley was finally released from jail after forty-four days. But his experience had done nothing to dim his enthusiasm for the on-the-ground reporting in Syria and he returned to the increasingly unstable region where he was captured and then executed by Emwazi.

Foley's death confirmed what Washington and London already knew – that they had lost control of the hostage crisis. Overnight the operation had switched from a finely balanced hostage negotiation between the Foley family and the Islamic State to an international manhunt led by the FBI. On the news of Foley's execution, some of the released captives now felt compelled to speak to the media about the man who they knew was responsible for their colleague's death. They had been warned by their Islamic State kidnappers that once they were released they should not speak to the media or they risked the lives of their detained comrades.[25] But the killing of Foley had loosened the hold the 'Beatles' still held over the released Europeans. All eyes were on the masked terrorist in the video who spoke with a London accent. Now he was to be given a name.

Didier François, a former hostage who was released by IS in April 2014, told the radio station Europe 1 he had some idea who the killer could be. According to a translation the 53-year-old French journalist said: 'Recognized is a very big word. I see roughly who it is.'[26]

François said he had been held with Foley from August 2013 until April 2014 and that he was also held for almost nine months with fellow journalist Steven Sotloff. He said that Foley 'was an extraordinary person with a strong character. He was a pleasant companion in detention because he was solid and collective. He never gave in to the pressure and violence of the kidnappers.'[27]

He had not spoken of Foley and Sotloff until now because he was warned upon his release that if he told the public he had been held with them, reprisals would follow against them. He said: 'Their exact words were: "They'll be punished."'[28] But now Foley was dead, François decided to speak out. In an interview with Reuters he said: 'The guy who killed him is the guy who took him from the start.'[29]

Nicolas Hénin, an independent reporter released by IS around the same time as François, also came out of the shadows and told *L'Express* magazine that Foley had been treated worse than the other captives, after militants searched his computer and discovered his brother was in the US Air Force. 'Because of that and as he was American he got extra bad treatment. He became the whipping boy of the jailers, but he remained implacable,' Hénin told the magazine.

But Hénin went further than any of the former hostages about the nature of the relationship between the hostages and the Islamic State captors. Shortly after his release he told the BBC about discussions between the prisoners and their captors.[30] Such interactions were often important to secure vital food and medicine. But they also revealed jarring details about their captors' backgrounds and interests: 'I noticed that these jihadists have little to do with the local culture – Arab or Muslim culture – they are children of our societies. They speak our language, they have the same cultural references we do. They watch the same movies as us, play the same video games our children play. They are products of our culture, our world.' And they watched everything, Hénin said, 'from the *Teletubbies* to *Game of Thrones*.'[31]

Hénin refused to talk specifically about Mohammed Emwazi, then known only as Jihadi John, on the grounds that a British journalist was still being held hostage by the group. He remembered the execution of Gorbunov, who was killed during his time there, and a small ceremony held by the rest of the prisoners: 'Everyone paid tribute to him. The British journalist spoke first and then we held a minute's silence.'

Talking to some of his captors during his ten months as a hostage, Hénin said he saw flickers of doubt 'and a lot of bad faith, because they had to justify it to themselves, and some of their acts [were] impossible to justify'.[32] He said he believed that many jihadists began with a genuine desire to help victims in Syria. But, he went on:

these are fragile people. As soon as they arrive, [their recruiters] hook them and push them to commit a crime, and then there is no way they can turn back ... I remember with a couple of [the captors], we had discussions that showed their convictions were a bit fragile and that they maybe even had regrets about what they were doing. Beyond that, connection was very difficult. A bit of chat might help, but no pity for sure because they are totally closed to pity. [Asking for pity] is the worst thing you can do. It's stupid. Never try it.

It is not clear which hostage was the first to describe James Foley's executioner and give him the nickname 'Jihadi John', but the fact that the black-clad executioner was British was quickly confirmed in London. The British prime minister, David Cameron, who broke off his holiday in Cornwall to return to Downing Street, said it seemed 'increasingly likely' that the killer was a UK citizen: 'Let's be clear what this act is – it is an act of murder, and murder without any justification,' Cameron told reporters at Number Ten.[33] Acutely aware that the Islamic State held three British hostages, he stressed there would be no 'knee jerk' escalation of British military involvement, warning that the West faced a 'generational struggle' against Islamist extremism. 'I have been very clear that this country is not going to get involved in another Iraq war. We are not putting combat troops, combat boots on the ground, that is not something we should do.'[34]

Using what meagre intelligence resources they could muster in the region, MI6, MI5 and GCHQ had been monitoring the IS kidnappers. British intelligence had also shared in the debriefings of the released hostages. The truth is that Cameron had known the nationality and possibly even the identity of Jihadi John weeks before. But nothing could have prepared the security agencies in London and Washington for how far IS was prepared to go to market their reign of terror. The beheadings were the propaganda centrepiece of the Islamic State's asymmetric war against the West. And such is the power of social media that the Islamic State was able to give 'Jihadi John' star billing in a series of hostage snuff movies. Much has been made of their slick production skills but the video executions were a deliberate tactic that matched America's own 'shock and awe' strategy so devastatingly deployed in Iraq, where the IS commanders had learned their trade. In Mohammed Emwazi, IS deliberately created a monster who became the most wanted terrorist in the world. Not since the hunt for Osama bin Laden had America and its allies devoted so much intelligence and resources to capturing or killing one man.

The execution of James Foley had changed the rules of terrorism propaganda. For journalists, it's impossible to ignore the echoes of the killing of Daniel Pearl, the *Wall Street Journal* reporter executed in Pakistan in 2002. Pearl and Foley were almost the same age when they died. Both were working for American news outlets. Both were captured by Islamist extremists and had video recordings of their executions released. Perhaps the grimmest similarity of all, however, is the horrific way both men were killed. Foley, like Pearl, was beheaded.

While it brought the practice to widespread attention, there were certainly instances of Islamist groups using beheadings before Pearl's death, notably during the first Chechen war, in which Abu Shishani had served. In 1996, for example, Russian soldier Yevgeny Rodionov was filmed as he was beheaded by his rebel captors after refusing to convert to Islam. His death led to calls for the Russian Orthodox Church to canonize him.[35]

Some historians have argued that the act of beheading can be linked to Middle Eastern culture. 'The religious and cultural symbolism that the sword carries with it in the eyes of the Muslims, particularly in the Middle East, is an important factor in determining the terrorists' choice to behead hostages,' Pete Lentini and Muhammad Bakashmar of Monash University's Global Terrorism Research Center explained in a 2007 academic paper.[36]

Others have found even deeper roots. Writing in the conservative *Middle East Quarterly* in 2005, Timothy R. Furnish noted that the 'Pearl murder and video catalysed the resurgence of this historical Islamic practice'. Furnish argued that justifications for beheadings can be found by looking to the Qur'an or Islamic history, though he also noted that Islam was far from the only force in history to make wide use of the practice (the French Revolution being an obvious historical example, though modern groups such as Mexican drug cartels have also made use of the practice).[37]

The Islamic State has justified its beheadings with theology and history, but Max Abrahms, a senior academic who studies jihadist groups, argues that by using high-profile beheadings, it could be attempting to link itself to Khalid Sheikh Mohammed, a Guantánamo Bay detainee and September 11th mastermind who is now thought to have killed Daniel Pearl.[38]

Pearl's death was particularly shocking as he was a Western, non-combatant journalist. After his death, the use of this tactic seemed to spread, most notably into Iraq, where a large number of foreign citizens were captured and later beheaded in the immediate years after the American-led invasion. Some of the deaths, such as that of American businessman Nicholas Evan Berg, were videotaped.

Berg's execution is the prototype of the IS beheadings. Berg is also dressed in an orange jumpsuit and tied up beneath five masked men in a white room. The tape begins with clips of Berg speaking, talking of his family and his home, humanizing him for the audience before he is murdered. One of the men reads in Arabic for much of the tape, the tension increasing as he ploughs on and on with his manifesto. He stops, then cries out "God is great!" and they fall on Berg, picking up the refrain, one man dropping to pin Berg as another carves at his neck, all the while shouting "God is great! God is great!"[39]

Berg's screams begin long before they start cutting, and then there is silence as they lift his severed head and place it on his back.

Four months later, on 16 September 2004, British worker Kenneth Bigley was kidnapped in the al-Mansour district of Baghdad, along with two Americans, Jack Hensley and Eugene

Armstrong. The three had been civil engineers working for Gulf Supplies and Commercial Services, a company carrying out reconstruction projects in Iraq. After their capture, they were beheaded by insurgent leader Abu Musab al-Zarqawi. According to reporters who watched the film, Bigley was wearing an orange jumpsuit and read out a statement, before one of the kidnappers stepped forward and cut off his head with a knife. The bloodied head was then placed on top of Bigley's abdomen.

None of the gruesome history of al-Qaeda in Iraq appears to have been lost on the 'Beatles'. According to Javier Espinosa they pointedly compared Alan Henning, a British aid worker captured in Syria, to Bigley: 'They insisted that Alan Henning had a "great" physical similarity with Kenneth Bigley ... As a result, they started to call him Mr Bigley – "You know who Mr Bigley was? He was very famous in Iraq! If you are lucky, you will end up being very famous!"'[40] Yet nine years earlier, in 2005, a senior al-Qaeda deputy had sent Zarqawi a letter ordering al-Qaeda in Iraq to stop releasing videos of hostage executions. Muslims 'will never find [the images] palatable,' he pronounced.

By 2013 beheadings were back on the terrorist agenda. In May of that year, when two young men in south London attacked and killed off-duty soldier Lee Rigby in broad daylight, they tried to hack off his head with a knife. And in the summer of 2014, when Islamic State militia captured the Iraqi city of Mosul, there were reports of mass beheadings.

It seems that whatever gruesome tortures and butchery al-Qaeda had used to spread fear and terror among its enemies, the Islamic State was determined to take it to another level. In this context the filmed execution of James Foley in August of the same year can be seen as a logical extension of the Islamic State's desire to raise the stakes in international butchery.

Two weeks after the murder of James Foley, on 2 September 2014, IS released its second hostage video featuring Jihadi John. This time, kneeling before the cameras in an orange jumpsuit was the American journalist Steven Sotloff. Sotloff, thirty-one, from Miami, who freelanced for *Time* and *Foreign Policy* magazines, vanished in Syria in August 2013 and was not seen again until he appeared in the Foley video. In a disturbing echo of past atrocities, US media reported that Sotloff was the grandson of Holocaust survivors. In the new video the executioner points his knife menacingly at the camera as he speaks. Clad in the same black garb he wore during Foley's execution, Jihadi John has a pistol strapped under his arm in a shoulder holster. The signature black flag of the Islamic State can be seen waving in the background. Then he utters these words:

> I'm back, Obama, and I'm back because of your arrogant foreign policy towards the Islamic State, because of your insistence on continuing your bombings and ... on Mosul dam, despite our serious warnings. You Obama, have but [*sic*] to gain from your actions but another American citizen. So just as your missiles continue to strike our people, our knife will continue to strike the necks of your people. We take this opportunity to warn those governments that enter this evil alliance of America against the Islamic State to back off and leave our people alone.[41]

Sotloff was filmed calmly reading a statement moments before his murder. 'I'm sure you know exactly who I am by now and why I am appearing. Obama, your foreign policy of intervention in Iraq was supposed to be for preservation of American lives and interests, so why is it that I am paying the price of your interference with my life?'[42] While he speaks, Emwazi menacingly holds a knife at his side and stands next to Sotloff. The video then shows Emwazi placing his knife against Sotloff's throat and graphically appears to be cutting into his neck. The final shot shows Sotloff's severed head placed on his back.[43]

The execution videos during the late summer of 2014 established their own cruel momentum. Direct appeals from both the Foley and Sotloff families were either ignored or had no impact on the death sentences imposed on the two Americans. Days before the Sotloff video, his mother Shirley went on television to beg for her son's life. Reading from a tightly worded script she said: 'I am sending this message to you, Abu Bakr al-Baghdadi al-Quraishi al-Hussaini, the caliph of the Islamic State. I am Shirley Sotloff. My son Steven is in your hands; you, the caliph, can grant amnesty. I ask you please to release my child. I ask you to use your authority to spare his life.'[44]

Referring to Baghdadi as the caliph was controversial, as it conferred legitimacy on what the American and British governments have denounced as a terrorist organization. Shirley Sotloff continued: 'As a mother, I ask your justice to be merciful and not punish my son for matters he has no control over. I ask you to use your authority to spare his life and to follow the example set by the Prophet Muhammad, who protected People of the Book. I want what every mother wants, to live to see her children's children, I plead with you to grant me this.'[45]

Shirley Sotloff had requested a media blackout after her son's capture because IS told her they would kill him if his detention became public. But it was IS who broke the blackout when they released the Foley execution video.

'Steven is a journalist who travelled to the Middle East to cover the suffering of Muslims at the hands of tyrants,' Sotloff's mother added. 'Steven is a loyal and generous son, brother and grandson. He's an honourable man and has always tried to help the weak. We have not seen Steven in over a year.'[46] Her words fell on deaf and merciless ears.

The beheading of Steven Sotloff set in train the next set of beheadings. In a now a familiar portent of the fate awaiting the next hostage, Jihadi John was joined by another Westerner dressed in an orange jumpsuit – this time a British aid worker called David Haines.

Although the video was widely available on the internet the British government urged the media not to name its subject. Foreign Office guidance made clear that the government believed that any public identification placed him in even greater danger. Nevertheless, the attempt to keep his name out of the public eye was hopeless as the American and online media did not feel bound by the same restriction. The next day the blackout was broken, with British newspapers, following the American media's lead, carrying Haines's name.

Haines was working for a French aid agency called Acted when he was kidnapped in Syria in March 2013.[47] He had joined Acted to help co-ordinate the delivery of clean water, food and tents, in order to ease the growing humanitarian crisis in refugee camps near Atmeh, a town in Syria's northern Idlib province, near the border with Turkey. Haines and other aid workers were staying in Atmeh. On 12 March he and an Italian colleague, Federico Motka, were kidnapped after a car chase in which the tyres of their vehicle were shot out. Motka was later released after the Italian government reportedly paid out a multi-million-euro ransom.

Born in Holderness, in the East Riding of Yorkshire, Haines was raised in Scotland and attended Perth Academy. After leaving school, he worked for Royal Mail, married his childhood sweetheart Louise and had a daughter called Bethany. He left the postal service to join the RAF as an aircraft engineer, where he served for twelve years. Later he divorced his wife and moved to Croatia, where he lived with his second wife Dragana and their daughter. Haines served in the United Nations mission in the Balkans, where, according to a family statement, he 'helped whoever needed help, regardless of race, creed or religion'.

It was this military background that may have sealed his fate. He had left the RAF many years before to work for ScotRail and without a reference on the networking site LinkedIn to his time with the air force his captors would have found it difficult to uncover that part of his history. Yet throughout his capture there was no effort to remove his presence on social media.[48] His online business profile also showed that he worked for a US company supplying consumer goods to the military around the world.

It has become common practice for the Foreign Office to seek to remove the social media presence of hostages so why was this not done for Haines? A number of the other hostages have described how Haines suffered some of the worst torture meted out by Emwazi and the other 'Beatles'. He was said to have been beaten so badly that he began repeatedly vomiting and suffering from debilitating bouts of diarrhoea. His kidnappers, fearing he would die before their demands were met, were forced to arrange medical treatment.

The video of Sotloff's beheading, which afterwards cuts to Emwazi threatening the life of the first British hostage, called for a strong reaction from Downing Street. David Cameron immediately said he would chair an emergency meeting of his security officials under the umbrella of COBRA, the acronym for the Cabinet Office Briefing Rooms, the location used for top-secret planning when the UK's security is threatened.

David Haines's family made direct appeals to the Islamic State, saying that they were concerned that they had not heard from the kidnappers. But on 14 September their worst fears were realized. A new IS video began with a news clip of David Cameron talking about Britain's foreign policy. The prime minister is explaining that Britain will be working 'with allies' to combat the rise of IS, which he describes as an 'appalling organization'. The clip then cuts out as if a television is being turned off. A message in Arabic is followed by one in English which reads: 'A message to the allies of America'.

Wearing an orange jumpsuit and in handcuffs, Haines is on his knees in front of the executioner. He appears gaunt and pale. When he begins to speak, his voice is clear, but wrought with emotion: 'My name is David Cawthorne Haines. I would like to declare that I hold you, David Cameron, entirely responsible for my execution.' As Haines is talking, the camera angle changes and shows him from the side. 'You entered voluntarily into a coalition with the United States against the Islamic State just as your predecessor Tony Blair did following a trend amongst our British prime ministers who can't find the courage to say no to the Americans. Unfortunately it is we, the British public, who will pay the price for our parliament's selfish decisions.'

Behind the hostage stands the now familiar silhouette of Jihadi John. He threatens:

This British man has to the pay the price for your promise, Cameron, to arm the Peshmerga against the Islamic State. Ironically, he has spent a decade of his life serving under the same Royal Air Force that is responsible for delivering those arms. Your evil alliance with America which continues to strike the Muslims of Iraq and most recently bombed the Haditha Dam will only accelerate your destruction and playing the role of the obedient lapdog, Cameron, will only drag you and your people into another bloody and unwinnable war.[49]

As he speaks, he continues to gesticulate to camera and wave a knife.

The footage fades out and back in on Haines's lifeless body, as in previous videos. Emwazi then parades a second British captive, charity volunteer Alan Henning. 'If you, Cameron, persist in fighting the Islamic State, then you, like your master Obama, will have the blood of your people [points at Alan Henning] on your hands.'

The video fades to a close-up image of Jihadi John's covered face. In this video, more than the previous two, the voice is recognizably that of Emwazi, when compared with his taped interview with CAGE back in 2009. Although he has deliberately deepened it there are one or two distinctive speech patterns which give away his west London 'gangsta' drawl, which he uses to show his indignation at being questioned by the security services in his interview with CAGE.[50]

In London the latest execution and the threat to a second British hostage left the prime minister with little option but to call another meeting of COBRA. Two meetings in as many weeks gives the impression of action and yet it was plain to see that on the hostage crisis the government was impotent. The respective heads of MI6 and MI5 were in no in better position to advise the PM of a solution to the hostage crisis than they had been a week or even a month before. But of course it is clear that the only thing that might have saved Henning from Emwazi's knife was an immediate withdrawal of British forces from the region, which would have been a disaster for UK foreign policy for years afterwards.

Nevertheless, there were significant differences with Henning's case that offered his family and supporters a realistic chink of hope. He was an aid worker travelling under the protection of Muslims, and there were even reports that he was well on his way to converting to Islam before making his final trip to Syria.

Alan Henning was a Manchester taxi driver who had volunteered to join a Syrian humanitarian mission at Christmas in

2013. He had worked closely with the mission after helping to raise funds to buy the medical equipment that it was taking in a convoy to the refugee camps. But the vehicles were halted by masked gunmen after crossing the Turkish border and Henning, forty-seven, was separated from his friends.

It was his fourth humanitarian trip to the country – the previous one nine months earlier had been trouble free. His abduction while travelling with the relief convoy greatly distressed the group and one of the British Muslims in the group was dispatched to Aleppo to successfully plead his case before a shari'a court. But the ruling in his favour was too late as Henning had already been passed on to a hard-line group of extremists who regarded him as a prize captive who they could ransom or use as a bargaining chip for the release of other prisoners held by the West. It was only later that he fell into the hands of the Islamic State. Throughout most of his captivity there had been a media blackout but Britain's Muslim community knew about the injustice of his situation and some had made direct pleas for his freedom. There was hope that letters written by respected Muslim clerics, even those that the British government had considered to be terrorists, would eventually secure his release.

Moazzam Begg, who had returned to Britain and had been charged with (and later cleared of) terrorism offences, used his time in Belmarsh prison to write letters to Abu Bakr al-Baghdadi in a direct plea for mercy.[51] Begg made his appeal to Baghdadi as a fellow, former prisoner of the Americans also forced to wear an orange jump suit. (Baghdadi had been held in Iraq, Begg in Guantánamo.) But after the release of the Haines video the timeframe for action was narrowing by the day. Henning's wife Barbara decided she had no choice but to make a direct television plea to Baghdadi and the Islamic State. She said her efforts to communicate with her husband's captors had been met only with silence. Her sole contact had been an audio message from Henning pleading for his life.

In her televised appeal she said:

> I have a further message for Islamic State – we've not abandoned Alan and we continue in our attempts to communicate with you. We have had no contact from Islamic State holding him other than an audio file of him pleading for his life. Muslims across the globe continue to question Islamic State over Alan's fate. Their position regarding his statement is unequivocal. He is innocent. Some say "Wrong time, wrong place". Alan was volunteering with his Muslim friends to help the people of Syria. He was in the right place during the right time. We are at a loss why those leading Islamic State cannot open their hearts and minds to the truth about Alan's humanitarian motives for going to Syria and why they continue to ignore the verdicts of their own justice system ... Surely those who wish to be known as a state will act in a statesmanlike way by showing mercy and providing clemency. Alan, we miss you and we're dreadfully concerned for your safety. But we are given so much hope by the outcry across the world as to your imprisonment. We ask Islamic State – please release him, we want him back home. Thank you.[52]

But on 3 October Barbara Henning was confronted with the worst possible news. A video showing Alan Henning's beheading was released on social media.

This time the Islamic State footage begins with an English-language news report broadcast on the night Parliament voted to approve airstrikes against the Islamic State. It then cuts to static and fades to black, before the message 'Another message to America and its allies' appears on the screen in English and Arabic.[53]

After Henning is killed, the black-clad Emwazi reappears with another hostage, Peter Kassig, who is shown kneeling in the same position as the British captive with a caption showing his name. Emwazi then adds:'Obama, you have started your aerial bombardment in Sham [Syria] which keeps on striking our people, so it's only right we continue to strike the necks of your people.'[54]

Downing Street responded quickly and issued a statement saying:'The prime minister was clear that we must keep doing all we can to ensure that these terrorists are found and brought to justice for their heinous crimes and we will keep working with our US partners and those in the region to do this. ISIL's brutality will not persuade us to change our approach.'[55]

Like Henning, Kassig was an aid worker who also converted to Islam. And like Henning, this offered him no protection from the barbarism of the Islamic State. On 16 November the West received video confirmation of Kassig's death.[56] Unlike in the previous videos, all the jihadists' faces are visible, apart from that of Emwazi. The footage also gives away the location of the atrocity – near Dabiq in Aleppo province, with an identifiable village in the background.[57] But in a change of approach it did not show the person identified as Peter Kassig being beheaded. Also unlike previous videos, it did not show other Western captives or directly threaten to behead anyone else.[58]

It was three months before the Islamic State published another hostage video, this time featuring two Japanese hostages, Haruna Yukawa and Kenji Goto. Yukawa, described on Facebook as the chief executive of his own 'Private Military Company', was captured in Syria in August 2014.[59] His father later said that his son had endured a difficult few years when his wife died of lung cancer and he lost his business and house to bankruptcy.[60] One video on his website showed the 42-year-old holding a Kalashnikov assault rifle with the caption 'Syria war in Aleppo 2014'.[61]

Kenji Goto, a journalist, left for Syria in October 2014 with the intention of rescuing Yukawa. He was expressly warned not to go by his own government but ignored the advice and was captured by militants just one day into his rescue mission.

On 20 January 2015 both men appeared in an IS video wearing Guantánamo Bay-style orange jumpsuits beside the all too familiar black-clad figure of Jihadi John. 'You now have seventy-two hours to pressure your government in making a wise decision by paying the $200 million to save the lives of your citizens,' he said, addressing the Japanese public.[62]

The Japanese government held firm. Shinzo Abe, the Japanese prime minister, held the same line as Obama and Cameron, saying Japan would never negotiate with terrorists. On 24 January, IS released a picture of Goto holding a photo of a decapitated Yukawa. In an audiotape accompanying the picture, Goto reads a message in English blaming the Japanese government for the death of his 'cellmate' and claiming that IS will only spare Goto's life in exchange for Sajida Mubarak Atrous al-Rishawi, an attempted suicide bomber who participated in the 2005 Amman bombings and was imprisoned in Jordan.[63]

It marked a new development in hostage negotiations and presented spy chiefs in London and Washington with their first opportunity to seize back the initiative since the failed rescue mission of the year before. The Jordanians indicated to IS they were prepared to negotiate over Rishawi if IS also released Muath al-Kasasbeh, a Jordanian pilot shot down and captured in Syria. The exchange was to take place close to the IS-held town of Tal Abyad near the Turkish border.

CIA and FBI teams were put on high alert while drones, satellites and radio communication posts tried to track the IS convoy which was to bring both hostages to the exchange location. But at the last moment the exchange was cancelled. It is not clear what spooked the terror group. But a combination of

Jordan's prevarication over IS's failure to prove that the pilot was still alive and heightened Western intelligence activity may have led IS to believe they could no longer trust the negotiators.[64] Or it may have been that the pilot was already dead and IS were negotiating in bad faith.

On 31 January 2015 IS released a video purporting to show Goto's beheading. The video returned to the style associated with the first beheadings.[65] The jihadist, now well known as Jihadi John, says:

> To the Japanese government – you, like your foolish allies in the Satanic coalition, have yet to understand that we, by Allah's grace, are an Islamic caliphate with authority and power, an entire army thirsty for your blood. Abe, because of your reckless decision to take part in an unwinnable war, this knife will not only slaughter Kenji, but will also carry on and cause carnage wherever your people are found. So let the nightmare for Japan begin.[66]

Three days later IS confounded those who thought it had plumbed the depths of human barbarism by releasing a video of Kasasbeh being burned to death. Aside from the unremitting cruelty of this act, for nearly all Muslims it is also close to sacrilege. The Qur'an forbids death by burning and Islamic scholars all around the world were quick to condemn the terror group for carrying out such an atrocity.

For the first time in its orgy of filmed executions the Islamic State was forced on the defensive and issued a fatwa justifying the burning of a Muslim trapped in a cage. Part of this justification rested on the need for revenge against one of the pilots whose bombs had been dropped on the Muslim people of Syria, some of whom, trapped in the collapsing buildings, had been burned alive.

Western media remarked that the video could also be distinguished by the absence of Jihadi John, although it was later reported that he was spotted helping to prepare the macabre apparatus, and that he attended the scene of the burning.[67] Emwazi's starring role as the Islamic State's executioner-in-chief may have been coming to an end. There were indications that the strategy of filmed beheadings coupled with threats against the West had played out its effectiveness. The emirs, who must have been aware that they were running out of hostages, were preparing to withdraw Emwazi from the propaganda frontline.

CHAPTER 8

THE UNMASKING OF JIHADI JOHN

Intelligence chiefs discovered the identity of Jihadi John in the summer of 2014. The crucial piece of the jigsaw fell into place when he used a laptop in Syria to download web design software. Instead of buying the software with a credit card, Emwazi used a student code from his degree course at Westminster University to take advantage of a free trial. The number contained unique information which gave his date of birth, what he had studied, and where, and information on his student loan.[1]

For several months the tight-knit circle of spy chiefs and trusted politicians in London and Washington who knew the identity of Jihadi John were able to keep his name secret. But this wouldn't last. On the morning of Thursday 26 February 2015 James Harding, head of news at the BBC, was in Belfast meeting with Ulster Unionists. It was a damage limitation exercise in which he hoped to dampen the anger around the decision not to include the Unionists in a series of television debates in the lead up to May's general election. This involved very sensitive discussions and the BBC news chief had given express instructions that he was not to be disturbed.[2]

Back in Broadcasting House, his journalists had made a major breakthrough in the Jihadi John story. They were confident that they had confirmed his identity and wanted to publish his name. At the start of the week all they had known was that his first name was Mohammed, that he had lived in London and that he had been connected to security investigations into al-Shabaab. They also knew that the *Washington Post* had been working on the same information and had already established his name. But some excellent catch-up investigative journalism and analysis of court documents had provided the BBC team with a name they could put to a senior cabinet source. Although the name was wrong the spelling was close enough for the source to offer them formal encouragement. They went away and this time returned with another name closely resembling the first – this second name was Mohammed Emwazi. They had found Emwazi in a court document connected with a terror suspect who had been placed on a control order. And this time the cabinet official confirmed the identity.

It was a dramatic breakthrough.

The BBC dispatched a team of journalists to the Emwazi family home in Queen's Park, west London, in preparation for publication. Knowing that the *Washington Post* also had the name, it was vital that they lost no more time and published the name and any other supporting details they could muster on the BBC website or they risked losing the story to a foreign newspaper. But the wheels of bureaucracy do not always run quickly or efficiently at a behemoth like the BBC: 'I was informed by an executive that James Harding had to give the final go-ahead but he was unavailable,' a source involved with the story told me. 'So we would have to wait until the top of the hour, which was forty minutes away. I was also told that we had to get confirmation from the police but we really didn't need it as we had Emwazi's name confirmed by someone at the top of government. If we didn't go now I was sure we would lose the story.'[3]

The identity of Jihadi John would soon be out of the bag. The Cabinet Office warned MI5 and SO15 that the BBC were about to name him. The security services reacted instantly and at 11 a.m. plainclothes detectives arrived at the Emwazi home in order to move the family out of harm's way and into a safe house. The BBC journalist on the ground reported this latest development back to Broadcasting House. Now the team had their confirmation from the police.

'Finally someone saw sense and we were given the green light,' the source told me. Just one minute after the BBC pushed the button, the *Washington Post* put their own story online – it had more detail and clearly showed that they had been working on it for much longer.[4]

Around the same time I received a phone call from a contact warning me that the BBC was about to name Jihadi John. I checked my Twitter feed and saw that his identity had been revealed to be Mohammed Emwazi, a 26-year-old Muslim from west London. The name didn't mean a thing to me. Mohammed Emwazi looked like another one among a myriad of false leads and aliases connected to the Jihadi John investigation, which I had been working on over the last six months. I was sceptical that this new name had any chance of being confirmed by official sources. But the BBC had confidently flashed their scoop across its media network and the *Washington Post*, which also claimed the story as their own, had published its own version.

It later emerged that the *Washington Post* had had the name confirmed by security sources in the US and had been quietly conducting extensive investigations in the UK.[5] In its story, the *Post* said that Asim Qureshi of CAGE had confirmed Emwazi's identity.[6] But Qureshi says that after the *Post*'s reporter had pointed him towards Emwazi he had only said that there were strong similarities.[7] In all likelihood, the *Post* had already had the name confirmed by official sources in Washington.

Since in both cases the media outlets relied on government confirmation before running their stories, it seems likely that it served the security services' interests to have Emwazi's name out in the open. MI5 had completed its background checks on Emwazi and his London network while coalition security forces had come to a dead end in their hunt for him in Syria. It may well have suited London and Washington to see what pressure they could bring to bear by publicly exposing him.

Whoever was responsible for allowing the media to name Jihadi John, the fact was that his identity unleashed a media storm. Buried in the *Washington Post* story was the article I had written about three Muslims who had gone on a safari holiday to Tanzania in 2009. One of the three, said the *Post*, was Mohammed Emwazi. For the next hour or so my phone went crazy as every news desk in Fleet Street assumed I must have met Jihadi John. But at this point, as far as I knew, the name in the *Independent* story was different and the article had been written on the basis of interviews conducted by CAGE. I was sorry to disappoint everyone who was ringing me but as far as I was concerned I hadn't met the man.

My main feeling was one of relief, because at last the speculation and 'wild goose' jihadi chasing was over. We had the real name of Jihadi John and the media would no longer keep running daft stories making tenuous links to any old jihadi bragging on social media about bringing death and destruction to the world. Nevertheless, the story was massive. The world's media cleared their front pages to cover the exposure of the most notorious terrorist of modern times.

CAGE hastily organized a press conference for the same day at the P21 Gallery near the British Library in central London. Journalists from all around the world were in attendance and it was covered live by a number of broadcasters. In his opening statement, Asim Qureshi said that the purpose of the press conference was to highlight the relationship between Emwazi and the security services. It was a subject which CAGE had been campaigning on for some time but, in this context, Qureshi and the rest of the group may have lost focus on the dramatic developments of that day.

Qureshi was clearly emotional and when he described his own impression of Emwazi he said: 'He was such a beautiful young man ... He was the most humble young person that I knew. This is the kind of person that we are talking about.'[8] He also said that he found it very difficult to believe that the man who came to see him in his office in 2010 to 2012 brandishing gifts of pastries was the man in the IS videos. It was a serious misunderstanding of the world media's revulsion for Jihadi John and anyone connected to him. Qureshi's characterization of Emwazi gave the impression that CAGE was somehow defending this man when all everybody wanted to hear was unqualified condemnation.

Then Qureshi made another revelation. In detailing Emwazi's contact with CAGE, he said he had put Emwazi in touch with people who could help him in his efforts to return to Kuwait. He said one of those people was a journalist from *The Independent*. As I listened to him speaking, I realized that he must have meant me.

To say I was shocked is an understatement. I tried desperately to separate my recollections of Emwazi from the many other men I had interviewed who had had run-ins with MI5. It wasn't until three days later that I finally found the emails that proved I had met him. Only then did it dawn on me that this was the man whose story I had catalogued in my mind as 'how MI5 harassment cost a British man two marriages'.

I too remembered a gentle young man whose openness and anxiety over his predicament may have made him seem 'beautiful'. But, I thought to myself, it wasn't the first word I would have used to describe him. Sure, he was courteous and friendly, but my first thought was of a man who was obsessed with his problems with the security services. Now I was desperate to know when I had met him and how much contact we had shared. I searched my email account and recovered an exchange of emails with a man called Mohammed al-Zuhary, who had used a Hotmail address which included only part of his real name.

I was astonished. I was amazed. I was worried. Suddenly I was reading a series of emails written by me to Jihadi John. The name he was using was an Islamic alias and using this I could search the rest of my sixty-thousand-message archive which thankfully I had left stored on the server. He had hidden his real name in his email address by using the name Mohammed al-Zuhary. So a search for Mohammed Emwazi did not generate any results. But now I was reading an email written by Emwazi to me in which he was bitterly complaining about how he claimed the harassment by MI5 had left him wanting to take his own life.

Despite all these emails, the full picture of my relationship with Emwazi evades me to this day. I have a recollection of our meeting on at least one occasion and a strong impression of his character. But I can't remember things he must have told me about university or his family life. Later that week, I came under pressure from a newspaper to use Emwazi's email account to make direct contact with him. But I was uncomfortable about doing so while another British hostage was still alive.

This hostage was a journalist like me and the only other British journalist Emwazi had known was me. I felt it was important to seek advice from the security services first before making any attempt to contact Emwazi. They would know what sort of risk this might create. In the end I decided against using his email address in this way.

In the days after Emwazi's unmasking, his life, family and friends became the subject of intense media attention. Anyone who had met him, worked with him or even been at the same primary school was given licence to offer their own insight on his life.

But it was his family who faced the greatest intrusions. His siblings were all located and interrogated. One media report claimed Omar Emwazi was linked to extremists through social media. In the end their father, who was in Kuwait at the time, gave a press conference from Kuwait City. He initially denied that Mohammed could be Jihadi John. He was later reported to have said if he was his son then he should be hunted down like a dog.[9] The whole family were all deeply shocked when they were finally told that the brutal IS executioner was their son. His mother later sued the media after a number of newspapers and broadcasters wrongly reported that she had recognized her son in one of the beheadings videos but had not reported him to the police. Ghaneya Emwazi, represented by top London law firm Bindmans, said that if she had been aware of the terrorist's identity she would have been 'guilty of a serious criminal offence under the Terrorism Act'.[10] The claim form criticized newspapers for not having 'made any or any adequate attempt' to contact her for comment. It said: 'Had this been done, [she] would have stated (as is in fact the case) that she had never seen or heard the videos of Jihadi John and did not know or suspect that her son was Jihadi John until she was informed of media reports to that effect in late February 2015.'[11] The claim also highlighted Twitter users who had tweeted about the story and commented on it. In addition, it made reference to readers' comments on newspaper websites. It said: 'By reason of the publication of each of the articles [Ghaneya Emwazi] has been very seriously damaged in her character and reputation and has suffered considerable distress, anxiety, grave embarrassment and injury to her feelings.'

School friends, university colleagues, teachers and employers were all interviewed in the coming weeks. Most of the stories focused on what a likeable person Mohammed Emwazi had been. But wherever there was a suggestion of potential evil it was these stories which were given greatest prominence.

Among the headlines was one particularly interesting story which portrayed Emwazi as a drunken lout when he had gone to Tanzania on his safari holiday after leaving university in 2009.[12] The BBC said that it had spoken to a Tanzanian immigration custody officer who reported that Emwazi had not been allowed into Tanzania because he had 'brought chaos to the airport' and 'behaved like alcohol was involved'.[13] The officer also claimed that Emwazi's detention had nothing to do with any terrorism investigation or contact with the British security services. He said: 'The three friends had been causing a disturbance. We couldn't let him in.'[14] The officer added that Emwazi had been taken to the airport's cells and left to sober up.

The story, which was on the front page of *The Times*, was followed up all over the world and appeared to cast doubt on Emwazi's whole 'MI5 harassment' narrative – that he was being persecuted by MI5, who had targeted him since 2009.

The BBC continued the coverage the next day with an interview with Tanzania's home affairs minister, Mathias Chikawe, who repeated the details surrounding Emwazi's drunken behaviour. 'We had no information whatsoever from any organization or anybody for that matter,' he said. 'They [Emwazi and his friends] were in a state of inebriation – highly drunk. And they were cursing and saying all the bad words you can think of. So the immigration officers detained them and asked them questions, saying: "Why do you behave like this? Who are you? Why are you coming here?"'[15]

To support its story the BBC even published the custody record, which also named Ally [sic] Adorus and Marcel Schrodl [sic], Emwazi's travelling companions. It was written in Kiswahili and requested that Emwazi and two friends 'be detained after they refused to return back to Amsterdam using KLM 569 after being refused entry to the country'.[16]

Asim Qureshi of CAGE is not convinced about the Tanzania account: 'It seems very strange to me that three practising Muslims should all start drinking and turning into yobs on a plane trip – it looks rather convenient for the security services that just when people are asking questions about harassment and possible abuse this story suddenly comes out.'[17] But Emwazi's brother Omar is open to the idea that his brother may have been over-doing his post-graduate celebrations. 'He was doing all sorts of things then – you've seen that picture of him with the baseball hat, well, that was the sort of person he was when he started university. I'm not saying he did it, but I'm not saying he couldn't.' He explained: 'You see that he wasn't on his religion at the time. There wasn't a single hair on his chin. So he wasn't really practising . . . after that he became more devoted.'

But even if Emwazi had been drunk and rude on the plane that did not justify the abuse he claims he suffered at the hands of the Tanzanian security services. One of his friends who saw him just after he had been thrown out of Tanzania said he was still carrying injuries from the alleged assaults he suffered: 'He was deaf in one ear. He was beaten quite bad and he couldn't hear in one ear.'

Now Emwazi's name was out in the open his cover within the Islamic State had been emphatically blown. He had also lost some of his menacing mystique. Knowing which school he went to or that he was awkward with girls humanized his terror. But the exposure also left him vulnerable to spies – or, indeed, anyone who wanted to cash in on the £6.2 million reward offered by the US Senate for information that led to his capture or death. As a result his Islamic State controllers pulled him back from the propaganda frontline.

Since his last internet appearance in the execution video of the Japanese hostage Kenji Goto on 31 January 2015 there were various reports that Emwazi had been injured in a drone strike, had fled the Islamic State for Libya or was being closely guarded in a safe house in Mosul. In September 2015, before Emwazi's death, I contacted Richard Barrett, a former head of counter-terrorism at MI6 before spending nine years as the co-ordinator of the UN's al-Qaeda and Taliban monitoring team. He thought Emwazi was most likely to be in Syria. He told me: 'He has been very quiet since the exposure of his identity. By having the face beneath the balaclava identified, he lost his power and became an ordinary loser. But the loss of his value to IS need not have led to IS killing him. I expect he is still in Syria.'[18]

At the beginning of November 2015 Emwazi was still the most wanted terrorist in the world and the US administration had prioritized security operations to locate him. It was even reported that American aircraft carrying FBI agents had flown over west London in order to use state-of-the-art listening devices to secure surveillance intelligence from his family and friends on his whereabouts.[19]

In the UK officers from SO15 interviewed his family and

rounded up the network of Muslim men he was associated with in west London. Meanwhile, a bank of operators stationed at GCHQ, the government's secret listening headquarters, waited patiently for him to phone or email contacts and friends. When Emwazi's identity was first made public it was reported that he managed to get a message to his family apologizing for any distress the news may have caused them.[20]

In April 2015 the respected German politician and journalist Jürgen Todenhöfer claimed he had seen Emwazi when he visited Mosul in northern Iraq in December 2014.[21] Todenhöfer had spent months negotiating with the IS leadership for his own safe passage to Syria and Iraq to conduct interviews with foreign fighters. When he finally secured the assurances he was seeking he travelled to the heart of the Islamic State. He claims that the man given the task of driving him around Mosul was in fact Emwazi. He says that it was only after he rewatched the tapes when Emwazi was exposed in February 2015 as Jihadi John that he realized his masked driver was the same man.

Todenhöfer, who was accompanied on the dangerous mission by his son Freddie, said:

I realized Jihadi John was one of our drivers. He was always the masked driver and the boss of our commander. Later I saw him unmasked in a restaurant and they said I had done it on purpose, that I was trying to find out his identity. I said to the ISIS commander, 'What the hell, all the other terrorists take off their masks, why is he so special?' But they didn't answer. The fighters had hours and hours of conferences about the situation, they would not speak to or sleep or eat with us any more, because I had seen his real face, heard his real voice.

He described Emwazi as having long curly hair and an aquiline nose and as being 'the most unfriendly guy we met there'. He added: 'Jihadi John was always masked, you could only see one eye and he had a strong accent, the same accent as the Jihadi John we know from the videos.'[22]

Then, in August 2015, the *Mail on Sunday* claimed it had found the most recent information about his location and appearance.[23] The paper said it had obtained a video shot in June near the IS-held town of Deir Ezzor in south east Syria. In an eight-second excerpt the camera pans away from a flatbed truck upon which a grenade launcher is mounted, to reveal a hooded Emwazi in profile. No sound accompanies the footage, but journalists from the paper were played an audio excerpt from the full video. In it, the jihadi fighter is heard clearly saying, in a British accent: 'I will carry on cutting heads.' The film was secretly obtained by rebel fighters of the Free Syrian Army, who sent it to one of their colleagues, known as Abu Rashid, in the Bulgarian capital, Sofia. In the video Emwazi looks at the camera and announces: 'I am Mohammed Emwazi. I will soon go back to Britain with the *khalifa* [the leader of the Islamic State].' And then he promises to cut off more heads before the camera switches to two jihadis who the paper claims were like Emwazi's bodyguards.

That same month it appeared that the net was closing. Missiles fired from an American drone killed jihadist Junaid Hussain, reported to be only second to Emwazi on the CIA kill list. Hussain, twenty-one, had been jailed in the UK for hacking Tony Blair's Gmail account when he was a teenager. He fled to Syria in 2013 where he quickly established himself as an effective jihadi cyber hacker.

Then, a few weeks later, British drones operating in Syria killed two more British jihadists who David Cameron said had been planning attacks on the UK. The target of the first RAF drone attack was Reyaad Khan, a 21-year-old from Cardiff who had featured in a prominent ISIL recruiting video in 2014. Two other Islamic State fighters were killed in an attack on the Syrian city of Raqqa on 21 August. One of them, Ruhul Amin, twenty-six, was also British. The strike had been approved at a meeting of 'the most senior members' of the National Security Council, and personally authorized by defence secretary Michael Fallon because David Cameron was away on holiday. This was a marked departure from established British foreign policy, which, until these drone strikes against British citizens, had been restricted to attacks on IS fighters in Iraq and Taliban fighters in Afghanistan where the UK had a military mandate.

The drone attacks on British citizens in Syria drew sharp criticism from human rights groups. Cameron justified the assassination on the sovereign territory of another country on the basis that Khan represented a specific threat to UK security and that he, Cameron, had exercised the country's 'inherent right to self-protection'. The prime minister told the House of Commons on 7 September 2015:

> It was necessary and proportionate for the individual self-defence of the UK ... We took this action because there was no alternative. In this area, there is no government we can work with. We have no military on the ground to detain those preparing plots. And there was nothing to suggest that Reyaad Khan would ever leave Syria or desist from his desire to murder us at home. So we had no way of preventing his planned attacks on our country without taking direct action ... The strike was conducted according to specific military rules of engagement which always comply with international law and the principles of proportionality and military necessity. The military assessed the target location and chose the optimum time to minimize the risk of civilian casualties. This was a sensitive operation to prevent a very real threat to our country.[24]

But the big prize was always Emwazi and Cameron had demanded weekly updates from his spy and security chiefs on the hunt for Jihadi John. After the execution of James Foley in August 2014 it was an open secret in Westminster that Cameron had made eliminating Mohammed Emwazi his personal mission. One government source said: 'As far as the PM is concerned Jihadi John is priority number one in Syria.' Secretly Cameron authorized a special Whitehall team, with the cover of legal advice from the office of the attorney general, to locate and kill Emwazi.[25] Military aides and spy chiefs drew up several plans, including sending in SAS sniper teams and mounting a capture-or-kill operation using Islamic State agents working for Western intelligence.

In fact in September 2014 Cameron had already laid the political groundwork for the operation: 'In order to catch Jihadi John, you have to know where he is, right? We know he is in Syria. I very clearly reserve the position that if you need to act immediately, either to secure a vital British interest or to prevent a humanitarian catastrophe, you would act first and go to the House of Commons afterwards.'

Behind the scenes British and American intelligence agencies had been working flat out to get a fix on the elusive Emwazi. Analysts at the government's GCHQ spy agency in Cheltenham had to link unique voice recordings collected by spy planes to Emwazi's own aural profile. Advancements in technology meant this could be as effective as fingerprint identification. At the same time jihadi chatter on the internet (and some of the more brazen communications on mobile phones) had been picked up by Britain's listening station in the Middle East and was being closely studied for clues as to Emwazi's whereabouts. In Vauxhall Cross MI6 collated hundreds of profiles of British jihadis they believed were operating in Syria and Iraq. They created complex computer diagrams linking the suspects' digital footprints to try to uncover the true identities of the individuals behind accounts on Twitter, Facebook, Ask. fm, Surespot, Telegram and many other social media platforms. Where the identities have been cracked the security services can monitor their likely contact with friends and family in the UK. All the intelligence was sifted for clues to the whereabouts of Mohammed Emwazi.

Despite all these efforts, for over a year the Islamic State's security apparatus had proved more than a match for Western intelligence. Only a handful of trusted commanders and couriers are granted access to the leaders of the Islamic State. While Emwazi was not one of these, his propaganda value meant he was given the highest security protection. Everyone entering territory controlled by the Islamic State is subjected to sophisticated vetting procedures not unlike the developed security vetting system in the UK. IS recruits who enter the state are placed in 'holding' buildings while their personal information is thoroughly checked. This can include checks made in the individual recruit's home country. A security source told me: 'I was shocked how much they knew about people in London and what they knew about what was happening in London.'

Later in September 2015 the security services made a major intelligence breakthrough. And like most breakthroughs concerning complex terrorist organizations it came from a human intelligence source. An agent operating in Raqqa, the Islamic State's self-proclaimed capital, had discovered that Emwazi had married a woman with whom he had had a young son. Emwazi's search for a wife and family, a search that began in west London and Kuwait and which had been thwarted by MI5 and the Kuwaiti intelligence services, had ended in Syria. He had after all, as his father had told him to do in 2011 in London, found a wife and started a family. But Emwazi's lifelong desire to marry was to prove his ultimate undoing.

The Raqqa agent had supplied his handlers in Washington with the wife's most recent address. He had also discovered that it was near the IS media centre, with which Emwazi was closely involved, and just a few hundred yards from Raqqa's Islamic court building. Western intelligence may have been unable to get a fix on Emwazi but now all they had to do was wait for him to visit his wife and son.

On 12 November 2015, at 11.41 p.m. local time, Emwazi was identified leaving his wife's apartment. He got into a pick-up truck with another jihadist, possibly one of the so called 'Beatles'. The agent on the ground confirmed that Emwazi was on the move and was heading for the court building.

Security chiefs meeting in the Pentagon knew they would not get a better chance to eliminate the world's most wanted terrorist. Emwazi and his gang of torturers had once before escaped retribution when President Obama had sent special forces to rescue the hostages in July 2014. They were not going to let him slip through their hands again. An American Predator drone, armed with Hellfire missiles, and British and American reconnaissance drones were called into the airspace over Raqqa.

The Predator, controlled by pilots at the Creech air force base in Nevada, may have been several miles away at the time, invisible in the night sky. But just before midnight local time it locked on to the jihadists. As Emwazi started to leave the vehicle the missile, travelling at Mach 1.3 (995mph), tore into the ground, obliterating everything in a seventy-yard radius.

The result was described by one US official as a 'flawless strike', a 'clean hit' that would have 'evaporated' Emwazi, with no collateral damage. 'We are ninety-nine percent sure we got him,' the official said. In Britain, news of the operation led Friday's early breakfast bulletins. David Cameron and Barack Obama both made public statements repeating their respective security services' belief that Emwazi was indeed dead. Cameron, speaking outside 10 Downing Street, was enthusiastic about claiming the operation as a partly British success and for the first time he officially named Mohammed Emwazi.

But he also spoke of Britain acting in self-defence, acknowledging the thorny legal questions surrounding the use of drones to assassinate British subjects abroad. 'Emwazi', said Cameron, 'is a barbaric murderer. He was shown in those sickening videos of the beheading of British aid workers. He posed an ongoing and serious threat to innocent civilians not only in Syria, but around the world and in the United Kingdom too. He was ISIL's lead executioner, and let us never forget that he killed many, many Muslims too. And he was intent on murdering many more people.'

Other leaders also rejoiced in the death of Emwazi. Tony Blair even used it to build the case for British military attacks against the Islamic State in Syria. Speaking to reporters in Jerusalem the former British prime minister, whose war in Iraq had done so much to bring IS about, said that it was important that Emwazi's death showed that Britain and America were taking the fight to the jihadists and this 'hideous extremism'.

In Raqqa the Islamic State acted quickly to limit the propaganda damage done by a strike against a key figure in the heart of its capital. Emwazi's body was hurriedly removed from the vehicle and carried to the city hospital while the site of the attack was sealed. The Islamic State's army of cyber-jihadists promised revenge against the West but the official IS channels were ominously quiet. They were hardly likely to give America and Britain the propaganda victory they were looking for by confirming his death.

The day American and British security forces were closing in for the kill, I was at Scotland Yard meeting a senior SO15 officer to discuss the terror threat posed by the Islamic State and how it was being tackled in the UK. When I asked about Emwazi there was no hint that an assassination operation was well underway in Syria and that the Met's most important investigation for many years was about to reach a dramatic climax.

When I heard the news the next morning announcing Emwazi's death I was surprised how little it meant to me. It was nearly five years since I had listened to his stories about MI5 harassment and he had confided in me that he felt 'like a dead man walking'. He was angry but there was a desperate vulnerability about him too. He came to me looking for help and I had tried to give it. But now I didn't feel any connection with him at all.

The next day some media reports implied Emwazi's death was the trigger for the murder of 129 innocent civilians in Paris the previous evening. But I doubted that his life ever really meant that much to the emirs who had controlled and directed his terrorism. I tried hard to picture Emwazi, married and with a son, spending time with his family. How he got the marriage he fought so hard to achieve. How he had progressed from Islamist agitator to psychopathic mass murderer. Did he really believe he could escape retribution by hiding in the Islamic State? Or did he still feel like a dead man walking?

CHAPTER 9

THE TERRORIST THREAT

In terms of the evolving world crisis caused by the troubles in the Middle East the picture is surreal. Hundreds of thousands of Muslim refugees are streaming across Europe, fleeing the Islamic State. On their way, they pass fellow Muslims heading in the opposite direction towards the very horrors from which they are escaping. How can this be? And given the relentless warnings of danger and the grisly images pouring out of IS strongholds like Raqqa, why would they want to go?

I have been told about a British man who travelled to Raqqa in 2015 to take a look at the Islamic State. He spent two days in a security vetting facility in Tal Abyad on the Turkey–Syria border. He was quizzed by two British members of the Islamic State's own security service, set up along similar lines to MI5, before being cleared for travel to Raqqa, where all foreigners must go before being dispatched to the frontlines, hospitals, schools, factories and training camps. He didn't like what he saw so he came home.

It's an extraordinary story which tells us two things about the fight against the Islamic State. The first is that the relatively free movement of fighters to and from the Islamic State should be of great concern to our own security. How can someone leave the UK, cross the border into Syria, join IS and then come back to London without our own security services knowing anything about it? No doubt others who have made the journey are less well disposed to the West.

The second concern raised by this man's experiences is the deep knowledge and interest IS's own 'security service' has in the UK. The two IS security agents who interviewed the man wore black masks throughout their conversations with him. They confiscated his iPhone, his passport and his money, and then they took a sample of his blood. This is what he told my security source: 'They knew who I was and they knew people I know. They follow the media and use spies to report on the terrorist trials in the UK ... and they are clever. They can see who is working with MI5, who might be a double agent. They have contacts with lots of people here and they definitely want to kill people in the UK. They keep saying, "We want to do something in the UK – something big".'

This is the very real threat facing the UK. It isn't the Islamic State 'crazies' who use social media to make wild claims about chopping off David Cameron's head or blowing up the Houses of Parliament. What we have to guard against is the sophisticated plots directed from inside Syria by cold, calculating terrorists who know how to strike to cause the greatest number of deaths. The Paris attacks in November 2015 graphically demonstrate what happens when the security services fail to disrupt terrorist plots.

MI5 conservatively estimates that more than 750 British Muslims have travelled to Syria and Iraq to join Islamist militant groups, including the Islamic State. In addition, the security services have concerns about three thousand individuals linked to terrorism in the UK and are actively monitoring another three hundred.

Jihadi John wannabes are springing up across the Middle East and the greater Maghreb – all bent on the destruction of the West. The massacre of thirty Britons on the beaches of the Tunisian holiday resort of Sousse in June 2015 shows how exposed British citizens are when they leave these shores.

But the reach of the Islamic State stretches into the heart of our cities too. Fighters from the frontline of the caliphate in Syria and Iraq keep in regular contact with jihadists and family at home. Some of this contact is blatant and conducted on mobile phones. Other militants use what they believe are safe encryption apps or coded messages sent through third parties. There is a brazenness about this contact that suggests the security services are losing the battle of surveillance and intelligence gathering.

One British man whose family come from Tunisia told a source he regularly speaks to his brother in Iraq, where he is fighting with the Islamic State. 'He rings me on his mobile maybe a couple of times a month. He likes to know about the politics of Islam in the UK. He wants to know which imams are supporting the Islamic State and which ones are against them.'

Western security agencies are in a constant technological arms race with terror groups like IS to monitor their communications. IS depends on encrypted messaging, utilizing apps such as Surespot, Kik, Telegram and WhatsApp. But it also understands the capabilities of the West, especially since the disclosures of the American security contractor Edward Snowden.[1] Not only must top secret listening stations located in countries surrounding IS be able to monitor and process millions of communications but analysts working for GCHQ and the US National Security Agency, who pick up this intelligence, must also understand the significance of each message. IS change their codes every day and frequently engage in false messaging.

So although some intelligence gathered in this way has resulted in successful counter-terrorism airstrikes, the overall integrity of the IS security apparatus remains operational and a direct threat to the UK. The vote in Parliament on 2 December 2015 authorizing British warplanes to bomb the Islamic State in Syria has made us even more vulnerable to terrorist attacks.

The tightening of border security preventing home-grown jihadis from joining the caliphate may have even added to the numbers prepared to carry out attacks inside Britain. Charles Farr is the government's most senior adviser on counter-terrorism. He is a former MI6 officer and in November 2015 was named as the chair of the Joint Intelligence Committee, which sets the intelligence priorities for MI5, MI6 and GCHQ. He told me that he believes that the threat posed by the Islamic State is different to anything that has gone before because it is opportunist and carried over the internet.

> ISIL's propaganda is more varied and diverse than the propaganda of al-Qaeda. Where AQ's narrative focussed on themes of oppression and violence ISIL can purport to offer a non-violent message, appealing to people to travel, live in and help to build the so called caliphate. Propaganda of this kind can appeal to a much wider range of people than the social media of Al Qaeda. Young, impressionable Muslims will be told that they have no choice but to join ISIL and defend a nascent state. Of course some ISIL propaganda is explicitly violent. We need to counter ISIL propaganda of all kinds.[2]

And the Islamic State is not the only terrorist agency threatening Britain. Al-Shabaab in Somalia, where Mohammed Emwazi and his network first chose to travel, remains a significant threat. The numbers of British fighters joining the Somali conflict may have dropped as a direct result of events in Syria, but they continue to present a threat to British interests.

In one revealing social media interchange a British fighter based in Somalia, calling himself Saahibul Hijratain, says that al-Shabaab will continue fighting until all the 'invading infidels' leave and the 'apostate government' cedes power to an Islamic one. On 11 January 2014 he explained on the question and answer site Ask.fm that his fighting in Somalia is part of the global jihad, aimed at instating shari'a law not only in Somalia but throughout the world. In his words, after the liberation of Somalia, 'we will fix our gaze on Rome'.

But perhaps of even greater worry is the al-Shabaab nexus with fellow fighters in Syria and the prospect of a jointly co-ordinated operation against the West.[3] Hijratain uses Twitter to chat with foreign fighters in Syria, whom he apparently knows, either directly or through mutual acquaintances. On 20 November 2014 he posted a photo of his jacket and gun which were now in the hands of jihadi fighters in Syria. The caption to the photo reads: 'My former jacket somehow made his way to #Syria & now he's with the Mujahideen. May Allah bless the one who wears it.'[4]

Then there is the extant terror threat presented by the shifting sands of al-Qaeda in the world Osama bin Laden left behind. According to US intelligence the so-called Khorasan cell of al-Qaeda was sent to Syria by al-Qaeda's leader, Ayman al-Zawahiri, not to fight the government of President Bashar al-Assad but to 'develop external attacks, construct and test improvised explosive devices and recruit Westerners to conduct operations'.[5]

Every Monday morning MI5 team leaders and a senior counter-terrorism officer from Scotland Yard meet at Thames

House, on the north bank of the river. Each leader brings to the meeting a growing bundle of pressing terrorist investigations, ranging from inchoate terror plots to suspicious chatter picked up on mobile phones or the internet. At the heart of the discussions are the constantly updated risk assessments. But finite resources mean that counter-terrorism commanders must compete with each other for surveillance teams and the vital analysts who can make sense of the intelligence. Since the start of the war in Syria and the emergence of terror groups such as the Islamic State, these meetings, overseen by MI5's head of international terrorism, have become more heated and last longer. It is easy to see why. Each section leader knows that failing to make a case for security resources could ultimately end in the loss of British lives. And the atrocity in Paris in November 2015 is a reminder that the terrorists will kill as many people as they have bullets and time.

A senior officer with Scotland Yard's SO15 told me that in the eighteen months leading up to the November 2015 terrorist plots, the numbers of British Muslims leaving for Syria and of arrests had both doubled. In November, MI5 and SO15 were involved in six hundred counter-terrorism investigations, the vast majority related to Syria.

'We see this problem increasing,' the officer told me. 'The more people we put in jail, the more people we disrupt, the more people we then have to manage. The more people who get radicalized the more action we have to take … and this means there is a knock-on to other agencies like prisons and social services and CPS [Crown Prosecution Service].'

Speaking in plain language the officer surmised: 'The legacy of this in ten years' time will make the world look like a different place. Borders may change internationally, community views will change. We will look at this in hindsight and see a fundamental shift in lots of aspects of our lives as a result of what ISIS have done. ISIS have established a caliphate and are the only Muslim [terrorist] organization to succeed in this goal and that is a galvanizing factor.'[6]

To counter the IS and al-Qaeda threat the security services, with the backing of ministers, have adopted a zero-tolerance approach to anyone they can link to Syria. The courts have established that it is a terrorist offence to go to Syria, to plan to go to Syria or to help someone planning to go to Syria. Syria has become synonymous with terrorism.

Arrests for terrorism-related offences in 2014/15 rose to 315, up a third from the previous year, which was itself a record year.[7] The courts have also fallen into line. Children considered vulnerable to extremist parents are being taken into care and electronic tags are being bolted onto anyone who shows any sign of leaving Britain for the allure of the caliphate.[8]

But it wasn't like this in the beginning. In the first weeks and months of the Syrian revolution, British foreign policy was still basking in the success of our armed intervention in Libya. Colonel Gaddafi's regime had been toppled and the people of Libya had won their freedom. There were no Allied casualties and the relaxed confidence of the 'new Libya' meant David Cameron felt comfortable enough to stand on the streets of Benghazi and soak up the collective appreciation of the people.

Britain hadn't just sat on the fence over Libya. It had actively waded into the revolution, tipping the scales in favour of the rebels. And it wasn't just our warships, aircraft and special forces which were involved. MI5 and MI6 played their part, too.

I have been told of three British residents born in Libya who were on control orders in the UK because they were suspected of terrorism but who found support from some very unlikely sources. According to my sources, MI5 helped them travel to Libya to join the rebel forces and when two of them got into trouble with rebel militias outside Tripoli, agents from MI6 were on hand to extricate them from their predicament. One terror suspect under a control order for many years, who is known as 'Detainee M', even went on to head up the government security unit in charge of guarding Hillary Clinton when as US secretary of state she made an unannounced visit to Benghazi in 2011.[9] One woman's terror suspect is another's trusted bodyguard.

Almost as soon as Gaddafi had been dragged out of his hiding place in a roadside drainage ditch and executed on the spot, Western eyes turned to another dictator who was oppressing Muslims less than a thousand miles away. At first glance the situation in Syria looked very similar to the one in Libya. A brutal dictator had lost control of his people, who had risen up against him. President Assad's abuses against his own citizens and the brave resistance of fighters such as the Free Syrian Army were widely publicized in Britain. It wasn't difficult to see which side Britain was supporting.

For British Muslims the atrocities carried out by Assad, including the use of chemical weapons and torture, encouraged them to answer the call from the growing band of militias gathering in the north of the country. The West firmly pledged its support to the Free Syrian Army, founded by Assad defectors who offered a secular answer to the Assad problem. An alternative government of the Syrian National Council, backed by the FSA and the West, was ready to step in when Assad had fallen. Western commentators were almost unanimous in their belief that the whole thing would last no more than a few weeks. But the FSA turned out to be an ineffective fighting force, weakened by poor discipline and infighting, while Assad's response to the revolution was murderous, deliberately targeting civilians and foreign journalists.

Islamic charities in the UK organized themselves quickly and soon hundreds of British Muslims were involved in supporting a growing aid effort. Fundraising appeals across Britain sent convoys via Europe to deliver desperately needed food and shelter to the refugees fleeing Assad's repression of their revolution. However, others joined the convoys with the intention of offering military support. Border guards from Britain to Turkey enthusiastically waved them through with few questions asked.

Some British fighters had even come straight from the battlefield in Libya. Among them was Ibrahim Mazwagi, a British Libyan, who had links to Mohammed Emwazi. Like many of the young men who went out to Syria in the first flush of the revolution in 2012, he fought and died in the firm belief he had the blessing of both his God and his government. This laissez-faire approach to the Arab Spring came to a shuddering halt in September 2012 when the security services started to realize the true nature of the groups the British volunteers were joining.[10]

Since the start of the uprising Syria had become the popular jihadist cause across the world with thousands of fighters pouring into the country. Even before the Islamic State emerged on the scene there was already a chaotic mix of jihadist groups, widely ranging in Islamic ideology and political ambition. Among them were a number of terrorist organizations, the most prominent of which was al-Qaeda's affiliate in Syria called Jabhat al-Nusra. This dazzling array of groupings, brigades and militias left British jihadists spoilt for choice. Because many had hitched rides with aid convoys it wasn't immediately clear who was signing up for the fighting and who was solely interested in supporting the aid effort. The division between the two was often blurred as erstwhile aid workers took up military jihad.

By the close of 2012 alarm bells started ringing in Whitehall and the security services quickly mounted a change of tack.

Instead of turning a blind eye to the scores of 'freedom fighters' that were heading out of Britain, instructions were given to stop them leaving. Stops at airports and seaports increased as MI5 and SO15 started to use the full range of counter-terrorism powers at their disposal. But the greatest concern was the numbers who had travelled to a complex war zone and were already on their way back to Britain fully equipped with all the skills required of the terrorist. This is what MI5 describes as the 'terrorism blowback' – fighters returning to the UK intent on carrying out bombings and shootings. One Whitehall security source put it like this:

> All we can know is that they have been in a war zone and come into contact with any number of bad people. They may have been badly affected by what they have witnessed and experienced. So now they are back in Britain after they have done their jihad but how many are just happy to put the whole experience behind them and get on with driving their taxi or whatever they were doing before they left? And how many are planning terrorism?[11]

In April 2013 Abu Bakr al-Baghdadi announced the creation of the Islamic State of Iraq and the Levant, and by August he had established a base in Syria with five thousand fighters.[12] The group was commanded by a cadre of Iraqis who had worked ruthlessly to suppress the Shia and Sunni populations under the dictatorship of Saddam Hussein. This was a terrorist organization the like of which had never been seen before.

Throughout the summer of 2013 Baghdadi spread his message of warped Islam and barbarity through social media. His house-trained clerics explicitly targeted Muslim populations in the West. The films of fighting and jihadi camaraderie were designed to appeal to young Muslim men bursting with testosterone. But most importantly they were accompanied by cod-Islamic justifications for killing and execution.

To secure a credible standing in the Muslim world the leaders of the Islamic State know how important it is to make sure everything they do and say is supported by the teachings of the Qur'an and the prophecies of Muhammad. Because the Qur'an, like many religious scriptures, is open to interpretation this has provided Baghdadi and his followers with a great deal of latitude. So while the vast majority of the world's Muslim clerics declare Islam to be a peaceful religion, the Islamic State has found it very easy to offer its own interpretation to justify a growing list of grotesque punishments and practices, including the beheading of civilians, the sexual enslavement of women and even the burning to death of prisoners. To achieve this it has publicly borrowed from the work of the clerics of al-Qaeda. In 2014, the Islamic State released a video tracing its origins to bin Laden and acknowledged Abu Musab al-Zarqawi, the brutal head of al-Qaeda in Iraq, from 2003.

In this way it was able to build on al-Qaeda's established doctrine of Islam-sanctioned terrorism. Virtually every major decision and law promulgated by the Islamic State adheres to what it calls 'the Prophetic methodology', which means following the prophecy and example of Muhammad, in exacting detail. So while the Muslim world rejects the Islamic State as un-Islamic it is difficult to argue that it is not based on an interpretation of Islam, however skewed.

It was, and probably still is, Muslims with the weakest grasp of Islam who tended to answer the call. Emwazi himself came late to his piety, while others were desperately trying to mug up on the basic tenets even as they travelled across Europe to join the Islamic State. Two Britons, Yusuf Sarwar and Mohammed Ahmed, travelled back from Syria in 2013 and were convicted of terrorism offences on their return. Both lacked any real understanding of religion and before they left Britain they had ordered from Amazon *Islam for Dummies* and *The Qur'an for Dummies*.[13] Some didn't bother to take the trouble of learning the basics and, treated as cannon fodder by IS, were dead within weeks of turning up in Syria. Yet the appeal of playing a jihadi warrior in a foreign field has proved too strong to resist for many young Muslims.

In the summer of 2012 Muslim leaders were aware that young men were disappearing from their communities. There were reports of people taking off in the night without a word to their families and friends of where they were going. It soon became clear that they were heading to Syria. Few imams or members of the mosques' management committees knew about IS or Jabhat al-Nusra. Yet Islamist debate on the streets focused on the ideological differences between them. And for some young Muslim men the real question was: 'As a devout Muslim, which one should I join?'

Among Emwazi's network in west London there was a split down the middle as to whether it was possible to justify the atrocities and twisted Islam of the Islamic State. Asim Qureshi sums up their position like this: 'The group had a falling out over ISIS [in 2012]. At that stage it was about "Should ISIS be condemned or not?" rather than "Should they support them?" Half said they shouldn't be condemned because the West was so much worse. Emwazi was in that group.'[14]

Of greatest concern was that some young Muslims were trying to excuse the atrocities they had seen on the internet as being part of a media conspiracy against Islam. In the summer of 2012 six or seven young Muslim men had left their north London homes and were presumed headed for Syria. As a consequence one leader decided to travel to the region to find out at first hand about this new jihadi grouping then called ISIL. After arranging a briefing with a military Muslim group who had dealings with ISIL his fears were quickly realized. He discovered that ISIL was every bit as bad as he had heard and even more dangerous for the young men who had left his care in north London. To his horror he was told in graphic detail how the ISIL leadership comprised sadistic killers whose plan was to exploit young foreign fighters as child or youth soldiers. He was warned that the most brutal and dangerous of these militants was Omar al-Shishani, the charismatic Chechen whom Emwazi followed and whose brigade, KAM, signed up to Islamic State in mid-2013.

The British community leader who had travelled to the region told me:

He was not the soldier he claimed to be but an evil killer. When he needed to break through a wall during an operation or take out a gun position he would simply call a young follower forward and tell him he was a martyr for Allah. He was told to strap explosives to his chest and then charge at a wall. In this way he used young fighters as 'suicide bombers' to take out a wall at a time and advance on the enemy. Most of his fighters were Islamic illiterates, easily manipulated, and in a few cases [they] had mental health issues.[15]

Richard Barrett, a former head of counter-terrorism at MI6, says young men and more recently growing numbers of women travel to the caliphate because the Islamic State is very appealing to Britain's Muslim youth:

Although there will be common themes – lack of respect, marginalization, alienation and so on – these are common to many more people than those tempted to join IS. Each recruit will have his or her own individual reasons for joining and trigger for doing so. It appears that many have been attracted by the idea of joining something new that offers them a chance to 'be someone', have an adventure, get a sense of belonging, identity and purpose and to escape an environment that they find suffocating or lacking in opportunity. It can often have something to do with a personal desire for reinvention.[16]

Britain's army of foreign fighters in Syria also includes jihadists radicalized in the UK prison system. Choukri Elekhlifi, the 24-year-old Londoner who was killed with two other Britons, funded his travels to Syria by mugging people in London's affluent Belgravia with a Taser-style gun. To take another example, 24-year-old Ali Almanasfi was born into a Syrian family in west London and had a troubled childhood involving gangs, theft, drug and alcohol abuse. His father – a bus driver originally from Syria – had sent Almanasfi back to Syria in an attempt to change his behaviour. In 2009, however, Almanasfi was arrested and sentenced to prison after he attacked an older man while drunk. He was initially sent to Feltham young offenders institution, a prison that has had the leader of the 21/7 London bomb plot cell, Muktar Said Ibrahim, and 'shoe bomber' Richard Reid pass through its gates. It is believed that it was in prison that Almanasfi grew religious, and in January 2013 he left for Syria. Jihadists with violent or criminal pasts only sharpen the terror threat we face from Syria.

Raffaello Pantucci, director of international security studies at the Royal United Services Institute (RUSI), says: 'People with criminal pasts are often drawn to extremist ideologies as a way of atoning for past sins, though often they do not leave their pasts completely behind. But the high instance of people going to Syria with criminal pasts of every sort adds a further worrying dimension to the phenomenon of foreign fighters going to Syria.'[17]

It is very difficult to measure the real threat to the UK until terrorists strike. The security services and the police will always err on the side of caution and put it at the high end. But in the UK there is in place a system for measuring the current threat level. Since 2003 it has been set by the Joint Terrorism Analysis Centre (JTAC), run by a team of counter-terrorism advisers based in MI5's headquarters at Thames House in London. Here counter-terrorist expertise is brought together from MI6, GCHQ, the police, government departments and other agencies.[18]

The JTAC analyses and assesses all intelligence relating to international terrorism, at home and overseas. It sets threat levels and issues warnings of threats as well as producing more in-depth reports on trends, terrorist networks and capabilities. At the time of writing the terrorist threat to the UK is severe, the second highest level, which means a terrorist attack on the UK is 'highly likely'.[19] This threat level reflects the belief of our spy chiefs that the capacity of the Islamic State to direct attacks against UK and the rest of Europe increases every day it remains operational.

Sir John Sawers, the former head of MI6, believes that Islamic State terrorists have changed the business of terrorism. 'They're not trying to fly airliners into buildings. They're doing simpler things,' he said in September 2015. They're picking up Kalashnikovs, pistols or knives and walking into the offices of *Charlie Hebdo* . . . Or into a market, or onto a crowded passenger train, like the man tackled [in August 2015] on the Amsterdam-to-Paris line who brandished a rifle, a pistol and a box cutter. That's much harder to stop and obstruct as an intelligence service.'[20] The Paris attacks two months later showed just how prescient Sawers's warning was.

What worries him greatly is the rate at which European citizens are signing up to IS. 'They can come back radicalized and keen to carry out terrorist attacks in their home countries.'[21] News comes in almost every week of more arrests by British or Turkish authorities of suspects travelling to or returning from Syria. The resources of MI5 and SO15 are being stretched like they have never been stretched before. So barely a month goes by without a media report of a known jihadist on a terrorist no-fly list evading the security services and making it to Syria.

Equally concerning is that we are witnessing a stream not just of hot-headed young men but also of whole families − mothers, brothers, children and grandparents − exiting the UK for a very troubled and dangerous state. One reason for this is the rise in Islamophobia and Islamophobic violence. In the aftermath of the Paris terrorist atrocity assaults on British Muslims in London tripled. In the last year hate crime (including anti-Semitism) has risen by a fifth. A sense of prejudice combined with a fear of physical assault has made Britain an uncomfortable place to live for minority groups. Far-right extremists are exploiting the fears of terrorism and stirring up tension in the heart of our multi-cultural communities. This is why some Muslims have chosen to leave Britain to join a caliphate where they perversely believe they will feel safer. Others will do all they can to defend their communities against racist terror groups. The situation is made more dangerous by the potential for sectarian violence on British streets fuelled by the Sunni−Shia conflicts in the Middle East. We must stop the hatred that underpins the violence in Syria and Iraq from spilling into British mosques and the wider Muslim community.[22]

Today the greatest terror threat we face still comes from Islamist terror cells based in training camps thousands of miles away. But the Islamic State has also found a new way of doing terror in the twenty-first century that doesn't require months of planning, investing in expensive weaponry or even dispatching trained fighters to the West. Just as deadly is the self-radicalized terrorist whose attacks are merely inspired by the propaganda of Baghdadi and his media operation. And these are the terrorists from whom the security services can't protect us. One Whitehall security source put it like this: 'Before we may have focussed on people returning to the UK. Today we are equally concerned about people who have not travelled abroad but are just as capable of carrying out terrorist acts inspired through social media.' So unless we confront the conditions that stimulate Islamic State-inspired terrorism within the UK, by closing off the spaces where flawed ideology and disaffection can take hold in Muslim *and* non-Muslim communities, we will be storing up dangers for generations to come.

CHAPTER 10

HOW TO BEAT
THE TERRORISTS

The November 2015 terrorist attacks in Paris exposed a massive failure in Western intelligence. The French security services have some of the toughest and most intrusive counter-terrorism powers in the world but they were useless for gathering vital intelligence among the marginalized Arab neighbourhoods in the suburbs of Paris and Brussels where the terrorists were sheltered.

President Hollande's response to the attacks was to declare a state of war. Perhaps it was to distract from the failings of his own security services. But declaring war on the Islamic State is playing into the terrorists' hands. A war is exactly what IS wants because it validates the organization as an enemy state. Wars, including the war on terrorism, also force people to choose sides, when really there should be only one side, the side that opposes all terrorism.

The idea that some thirty thousand Islamic State fighters pose what David Cameron has called an 'existential threat' to

Western democracies will have Jean-Paul Sartre turning in his grave. Neither does defence secretary Michael Fallon's fondness for calling the RAF's campaign in Syria the 'new Battle of Britain' help us to understand the threat we face when IS doesn't even have an aeroplane, never mind an air force. When Britain stood alone in 1940 facing a Nazi invasion there really was an existential threat to our way of life. This deliberate exaggeration of the strength of the 'enemy' only helps IS in its own terrorist recruitment campaign. What is required is a proportionate response to a terrorist group that has already secured a disproportionate hold on the rational senses of our politicians.

But we have been here before.

When Tony Blair famously said after 7/7 that the rules of the game had changed, Britain's security services were effectively given a green light to use newly enacted terror laws to shake down Muslim communities. In their haste to make up for their own intelligence failures, MI5 and SO15 used a blunt instrument to crack a misunderstood phenomenon – militant Islamism. Doors were broken down, hundreds of unlikely suspects were pulled in and Muslim neighbourhoods were disrupted.

A zero-tolerance approach to extremism didn't work then and it isn't working now. The government's flagship policy on countering radicalization, the Prevent initiative, is failing to stop Britons heading for one of the most dangerous war zones on earth. It seems that whole sections of Muslim communities have become disengaged with authority and entire families are choosing the horrors of the Islamic State over a safe and peaceful life in Britain.

One reason for this is that communications have broken down between parts of the Muslim community and government agencies. These communities have stopped listening to

Whitehall-vetted Islamic groups, turning instead to their own leaders, who share their sense of marginalization.

Since the outbreak of the Syrian conflict in 2011 there has been no let-up in the arrests of British Muslims for terrorism offences, nor in the numbers of people who have evaded the security services and left to fight in the Middle East and Africa. So how do we stem this exodus and confront the threat of home-grown terrorism? Should we give our security services greater powers of surveillance as set out in the investigatory powers bill of 2015? Should we go further and set up internment camps similar to those used in Northern Ireland to combat the IRA? Or should we engage with the underlying causes of radicalization?

There is no simple counter-terrorism policy to defeat extremist ideologies, because there are as many reasons why a person turns to 'extremism' as there are jihadists fighting in Syria. We must accept that the extremist problems we face are complex and entangled in socio-economic conditions, which means the business of identifying terrorists before they commit acts of terrorism can never be a precise science. Perhaps I can best illustrate this point by saying that I have shaken hands with both Mohammed Emwazi and the spy in charge of catching him. The spy was confident and engaging while Emwazi was diffident and unassuming. Both men came across as friendly and my first impressions of them were positive. In fairness, most people put their best foot forward when they are talking to a journalist. But I wouldn't claim to know either man. I can't really tell you very much about their intentions, nor even how much reliance I should place on the words they used to answer my questions.

If I had both men under surveillance I could probably tell you a little more about them. Where they live, how they converse with their friends and family and what they like to do at the weekends. But surveillance won't reveal people's innermost secrets. With Emwazi, this is what really matters. Understanding him for what he became is very important. Is there always something about a person that tells you he is capable of killing another fellow human being in cold blood? Can you spot a murderer before he kills? Much depends on when you meet him. If you come across someone who is hours or even days away from committing a criminal act then he may give himself away. He may say things that raise suspicions about his behaviour or he may do things that betray his intentions.

What if he is months, or even years, from the moment he commits his crime? The whole business of prediction falls prey to unknowable intervening events. I have thought about this a great deal because I met many young Muslim men who the security services were investigating in connection to terrorism, or who had expressed extremist ideas. But I can't say that I heard anything or observed anything which raised my own suspicions, unless you count asking questions about the morality of going to war in Iraq, or the possibility of 9/11 being an inside job.

One of these men was Mohammed Emwazi, who showed himself capable of committing the worst kind of atrocity. He used a knife to slit the throats of at least six innocent men, some of whom he had known well and he must have understood presented no threat to him or his religious cult. Perhaps he was harbouring these dark thoughts when I knew him. Perhaps he was planning to murder me. After all, I am a journalist just like James Foley. I could have been so wrapped up in the story that I failed to push him hard enough about his real views on terrorism and his real intentions. But terrorists generally don't go to the media to complain about police harassment, especially while they are in the throes of planning terrorist atrocities.

Emwazi came to me as a British citizen who was able to convince me that he had genuine problems with the security services and that his single goal was to find a way of bringing his 'harassment' to an end. I wanted to help. If I hadn't changed jobs while we were corresponding, it is very likely that his story would have been told in print. If I had stayed at *The Independent*, which had already covered the role of MI5 interventions in the Muslim community in great depth, I'm sure his picture and story would have appeared in the paper. After the media coverage, perhaps our security services and the Kuwaiti authorities would have softened their engagement with Emwazi and left him alone to resume his new life in Kuwait. Failing that, perhaps he would have accepted the publicity as some sort of vindication, which would have allowed him to put the bad times behind him. From time to time I ask myself this question: if Emwazi's story had been published, would he have gone on to murder innocent people in Syria? Had I done more to get Emwazi's story out there, would we have ever heard of Jihadi John? Or was Emwazi in 2009 already a violent extremist who could not be diverted from his path towards terrorism?

The security services don't deal in these kinds of 'what if' scenarios. After all it would be impossible to conduct an effective counter-terrorism strategy if they were required to take account of such imponderables. How could they thwart terror plots if they were forced to follow a non-interventionist approach?

I'm sure when the security services first investigated Emwazi they didn't believe he was capable of beheading innocent men. He did not have a violent history or even a criminal record. Emwazi's name only appeared on MI5's radar because they had decided to map the lives of a loose network of young Muslim men in west London who could be linked to a terror organization based in Somalia. Emwazi was obviously different – he could carry out acts of terrorism that go beyond our own understanding of humanity. My own view is that his radicalization was brought about by a complex series of events and experiences in his life. He was drawn to Islamist extremism through his contact with a west London network of extremists, which in turn brought him to the attention of the security services. But this did not make him a killer. The key radicalization factor was his encounters with hardened jihadists and killers from the violent Islamist militias who were roaming northern Syrian in 2012 and onwards. Of course now that he is dead we will never know what happened to him in Syria that turned him from a jihadi militant to a cold-blooded terrorist. But he must always take full responsibility for his actions. Moazzam Begg makes the point well when he says he was radicalized in Guantanamo but it didn't turn him into a terrorist. Radicalization can never be a justification for terrorism.

Many of the other Muslim men who I met after they had encountered the security services were interested in exploring political ideas and the exigencies of faith that underpin their religion. One of these men was Mahdi Hashi, the youngest of the Kentish Town group, whom I met in 2008 and who told me that his life in Britain was being strangled by the close attentions of the police and MI5. He had model looks and really was a 'beautiful' young man who has become a poster boy victim of disaffected Muslim youth. Three schoolgirls from Bethnal Green, east London, who left their families to run away to Syria in 2015 had downloaded pictures of him on their social media accounts. Hashi, too, had complained about MI5 and police harassment. The security services considered him such a serious threat to national security that they asked the home secretary to remove his passport, leaving him exiled in Somalia, a country he barely knew. One year later he was picked up by the FBI in

Djibouti, convicted in America on charges of supporting al-Shabaab and imprisoned.

Then there is Mohamed Aden. He was another of the Kentish Town men. He was the most reticent of all those I interviewed and yet his picture ended up on the front page of *The Independent.* After I met him in 2008 he moved out of Kentish Town to live in Slough with his mother. His father had died when he was a child and he had found it difficult to adjust to living in his adopted country. One of his friends claimed that even after the publicity around his case the security services continued to take an interest in him. He also found it difficult to escape the public attention his case attracted after his story and picture were published in *The Independent.* Perhaps this acted as an unintended radicalizing factor. He disappeared in 2014 and is now believed to be in Syria fighting for one of the Islamic militant groups, perhaps even the Islamic State.

The security services will argue that since these three men later became caught up in terrorism, MI5 was right to take an interest in them. But we must also ask whether they could have been turned away from the lure of terrorist ideologies before they had developed a serious interest in joining violent Islamist organizations.

What happened to these three men between the time they were growing up and the time they found themselves embracing terrorism is now fashionably described as 'radicalization'. There is an academic industry devoted to explaining it. The best research looks at all forms of extremism, because it is important to realize that many of the push and pull factors which lead to extremist violence are shared across cultures, from white supremacists to isolated cults. But the government has hijacked the concept of radicalization. Instead of looking at the social and psychological causes of radicalization, the principal focus is now on Islamic ideology. The Home Office's programme comprises four elements that make up the UK's post-9/11 counter-terrorism strategy (known as Contest). They are:

- Prepare for attacks.
- Protect the public.
- Pursue the attackers.
- Prevent their radicalization.

Of these, Prevent is the most controversial as critics say it targets people based on their religious faith. In the wake of the 7/7 attacks in London, the Labour government stepped up the programme, spending tens of millions of pounds on hundreds of schemes across the country. But many of these initiatives came to be regarded by Muslims as a cover for police spying operations where organizations, dependent on government funding, competed with each other to gather the most incriminating intelligence from their local communities.

In Birmingham, for example, a CCTV network in a Muslim part of the city was found to have been funded out of the Prevent budget. Instead of stamping out extremism, the Prevent programme was actually alienating Muslim communities who began to view the strategy with deep suspicion. In one case related to me a leading Prevent-funded organization actually tried to entrap young Muslim men by offering free air tickets to Afghanistan. By pointing to the understandable high take-up of its offer the organization was able to say it had uncovered dangerous extremists and so justify the huge sums it was receiving from the government.

In the face of the threat posed by the Islamic State and other terrorist groups based in Syria and Iraq, the coalition government decided to push Prevent to the fore. Since then there has been an alarming rise in the number of terror arrests in 2014 and 2015 and a constant stream of British Muslims heading to Syria.

The government's reaction to this is to push harder. In 2015, ministers relaunched Prevent accompanied by a set of policies once discarded by Tony Blair as too radical. These included a clampdown on all 'non-violent extremism', the creation of a Home Office unit to target radical speakers and an investigation of shari'a law in the UK.

Since 2012, more than four thousand people, mostly young Muslims, have been referred to the Channel counter-extremism programme. A referral will usually require the subject to take part in a series of intensive de-radicalization sessions. In cases of children it can lead to a change of school or even removal from a family.

Between September 2014 and August 2015, four hundred Channel referrals were made for London teenagers and children under eighteen. At the heart of the referral system is a new statutory duty on public bodies, such as schools, hospitals and councils, to prevent people being drawn into extremism. But what we still don't really know is the basis on which these referrals are being made. Are some politically motivated to justify continued government funding, or made to settle community or religious disputes?

Rizwaan Sabir is a lecturer specializing in counter-terrorism and insurgency at Edge Hill University in Lancashire. In May 2008 he was arrested with another man under the Terrorism Act and accused of unlawfully being in possession of the al-Qaeda Training Manual (AQTM), which had been downloaded from the US department of justice website to help in his postgraduate research on terrorism. But it is not a crime to possess the AQTM, which is used by academics all over the world. The manual is freely available from the university library and can even be purchased for £20 from WHSmith. Sabir says:

> The document was discovered on the computer of my friend and mentor Hicham Yezza by a member of staff. It was reported to the university management, who, without conducting any internal inquiries or risk assessments, reported us to the police. On 14 May 2008, the police arrested my co-accused and I for being involved in the 'commission, preparation or instigation of acts of terrorism'.[1] The only evidence used to launch and justify the arrest was this one document. After seven days' detention, I was released without charge.

In 2011 Sabir won a legal settlement of £20,000. But in 2012 it emerged that the police had 'made up evidence' to justify his arrest and detention. The case was later investigated by the Independent Police Complaints Commission. Sabir explains:

> The underlying 'cause' for my arrest, I believe, was based on a racist and Islamophobic assumption that because I was a Muslim and in possession of this document, I was using it as material for nefarious purposes as opposed to academic research. Because of this assumption, the university and police felt it was entirely justified and legitimate to arrest and investigate me on the very serious charge of terrorism. With the current Prevent strategy now being introduced via the CTS [Counter-terrorism and Security] Act 2015, what happened to me could well happen again.[2]

Sabir wants the government to urgently change the direction of its counter-terrorism strategy. He wants more to be done to recognize that other factors like Western foreign policy or its war on terror can play a role in the radicalization of all kinds of people, not just Muslims:

> Rather than accepting that government action, including foreign wars and unfair social, political and economic policies, may be responsible for creating conditions that facilitate a person's attraction to terrorist ideology, Prevent wrongly claims that ideology is what ultimately drives terrorism when there is no scientific evidence to prove this point. Prevent is therefore based on a flawed evidence base that fails to engage with the real drivers of terrorism. It will fail in making us any safer.[3]

Charles Farr has been the government's most senior adviser on counter-terrorism policy. He was the architect of the post 7/7 Prevent programme and until December 2015 the director general of the Office for Security and Counter-Terrorism. He takes issues with Prevent's many critics and strongly maintains that the government's deradicalization policies are succeeding and this success is demonstrated by the figures. In a democratic state no counter-terrorism policy can be 100 per cent successful. But there are nearly 3 million Muslims in Britain, of whom about 800 of interest to the agencies have travelled to Syria. Even taking into account some under-counting that is a very small percentage.

Farr points out that forty thousand people have come into contact with Prevent-related programmes in the past year. 'That is a lot of people,' he says 'to be removed from the terrorist radar. We believe the programme as whole is successful in stopping people from becoming terrorists or supporting terrorism.' Farr also claims that the flow of Muslims leaving Britain for Syria has slowed, and that 'the profile [of British Muslims going to Syria] has ... changed. They are now younger and there are more women.'

Farr does not accept that the government's Prevent strategy is criminalizing Muslims.

There are misconceptions surrounding the Government's terrorist prevention programme. The purpose of Prevent is not to criminalise or spy on Muslims and Muslim communities. The purpose of Prevent programmes is to protect Muslim and other communities and avoiding them being drawn into criminal activity and the criminal justice system. These are safeguarding programmes. ISIL and other militant Islamist terrorist groups are focussing on Muslim communities and it therefore follows that we need to do so too. The Channel programme has had proven success in diverting people away from terrorism and dissuading them in particular from travelling to Iraq and Syria. The programme is voluntary; if someone doesn't want to take part then we can't and won't force them.

Farr adds.

Over 70% of those who have attended Channel have been successfully directed away from extremism. The others, where vulnerabilities still remain may, if appropriate, be referred on to further programmes or back to the police. Referrals to Channel (not every referral is accepted onto the programme) have increased in the last two years, due in part to events in Syria but also the new statutory duty which has led to more referrals from some statutory partners. Channel is extremely effective for a very low cost. It is an essential part of Government counter-terrorism policy.

Today, ministers continue to justify the levels of intrusion and disruption to people's lives by claiming that Britain is under attack. After the attacks on France in November 2015 it is an easy message to sell. But the stakes have been raised so high that little notice has been taken of the damage done to Muslim communities by heavy-handed policing and intelligence gathering. Muslim communities have become distrustful of these policies while many regard the security services' 'harassment' of individual Muslims as part of an invidious informant recruitment programme. Deradicalization programmes led by Muslims that lack credibility, or worse, by white, middle-class men and women (like me), can't ever expect to win the trust of young Muslim communities. The debate among many young Muslim men isn't how we can be better citizens who subscribe to a British version of Islam imposed by government-funded organizations. Far from it. On the streets the real, worrying conversations are about which is the more legitimate representation of Islam in Syria, the al-Qaeda affiliate Jabhat al-Nusra or the Islamic State.

In the school playground the warrior codes of the Islamic State feed on teenage testosterone. Muslim youths brag about how they are going to join IS. IS has also charged classroom racism with a terrorist vernacular so that Asians who are insulted as 'Pakis' have the effective riposte 'Shut your mouth or I'll behead you'.

All this needs to be addressed. And it needs to be addressed in the open, in mosques, at Islamic centres and, yes, in schools. But the imams and the mosque management committees have been cowed into silence, avoiding the tough questions in case they are reported to the authorities.

It is not just the leaders of the mosques who are afraid to engage in the debate. In researching this book I have been able to hold discussions with Britain's most secret security agencies. But when I approached the University of Westminster, where Emwazi and I were both educated, I was met with suspicion and obstruction. The university told me that they couldn't talk to me about radicalization or any other part of this book because they had a duty to protect Emwazi's human right to privacy. Westminster's reluctance to engage is typical of the cowardice many of our educational establishments have shown (perhaps understandably in response to government messaging) in confronting radicalization and the difficult terms by which it is defined.

Jihad must no longer be a concept swept under the carpet because it is now considered to be synonymous with terrorism. It needs to be explained carefully that it can be used as a justification for 'military action or self-defence', but that is countered by tenets of Islam that impose duties of peace and non-violent action. In the current climate these debates are being forced underground so that a warped version of Islam is reaffirmed by internet propaganda and self-appointed religious leaders.

The role of the internet has also changed the nature of radicalization, weakening the role played by extremist preachers so that images and films have become dangerous self-radicalizing tools. The government wants service providers to do much more to police the internet. But unless this is done proportionately, banned extremist imagery will be given greater value for the terrorist as contraband propaganda. Bernard Hogan-Howe, the Metropolitan Police commissioner, played his part in this chilling effect by warning members of the public in 2014 that even the act of watching a Jihadi John video was an offence under the Terrorism Act punishable by imprisonment.

It has become much easier for terrorists to recruit from communities where young Muslims are forced to explore their

Islamic identity inside closed groups, away from the police and other agencies. It is partly why many Muslims are beginning to feel detached from mainstream British society, a kind of Muslim fringe, whose views swing between the established media and the pro-violent jihadist propaganda that populates social media. On the one hand they are revolted by the gruesome executions and punishments and yet on the other they applaud the idea of Muslims flocking to a caliphate where they are free to live real Islamic lives unfettered by Western culture. They are desperate for the Islamic State to be a true caliphate and are blinded to its grotesque excesses.

Asim Qureshi says we don't need to worry about the people who dismiss the atrocities as not real or media manipulated. They are at least prepared to ground their beliefs in a moral argument. The ones we have to worry about are those who absolutely believe what they are seeing and still say 'So what'. The numbers who have this worldview may be very small at present but the sceptics are rapidly becoming the so-whats. The so-whats are the ones who are susceptible to radicalizers and recruiters. Today the British state is stoking these sympathies, pushing people to the margins of our society. So what set out as a de-radicalization programme might just as easily be described as a radicalization programme.

Charles Farr rejects this conclusion but acknowledges there are dangers in driving the discussion of extremism underground. He says he recently spoke to a Muslim mother who confided that she was worried that the law did not permit her to discuss the dangers of the Islamic State with her son. 'This is wrong,' says Farr. 'The last thing we seek to do is drive the debate underground. Silence drives people into the arms of ISIL. There is nothing in the law or about Prevent which should stop people discussing the dangers of terrorism.'

The police and Crown Prosecution Service handling of the exodus of Muslims leaving Britain for Syria and Iraq has only exacerbated the problem. A number of desperate families who sought help from the police after their sons and daughters went missing found that press conferences were being used as counter-terrorism events to warn Muslims of the consequences of going to join the Islamic State. Promises that all reports will be treated sensitively and that the police have the missing person's interest at the heart of their investigation have not always been borne out.

In 2013 Yusuf Sarwar's mother Majida found a letter from her son, in which he said he had gone to 'do jihad' with a group allied to al-Qaeda. Mrs Sarwar told the police, who arrested her son, together with his childhood friend Nahin Ahmed, when they returned to the UK. She told the BBC: 'As soon as I found out about the letter I went to the police and co-operated but the police have betrayed me and misused me. I am isolated. If I had known they would put my son behind bars I would not have told them about the letter.'[4] Both men pleaded guilty to terrorism charges at Woolwich Crown Court in London in July 2014. Sarwar and Ahmed were sentenced by Judge Michael Topolski, who described the two men as 'deeply committed to violent extremism'. Mrs Sarwar said her son had gone to Syria with good intentions and asked: 'Is there justice in this? Other mothers are not going to come forward to the police. Nobody's going to hand their son in, knowing that they're going to be behind bars.'[5] The then security minister, James Brokenshire was unbending, responding to Mrs Sarwar's complaint, by saying: 'This case clearly demonstrates the government's clear message that people who commit, plan and support acts of terror abroad will face justice when they come back to the UK.'

In another disproportionate case the young son of a Merseyside police officer was a given a twelve-month prison sentence suspended for two years after he admitted sending his brother in Syria a pair of trainers.[6] Police and government counter-terrorism groups encourage families to stay in contact with close relatives who travel to Syria in the hope that they can encourage them to come back home. But when Majdi Shajira, from Liverpool, tried to keep in touch with his brother he was arrested in a police sting. The trainers were to be sent by a friend who was travelling to Syria on an aid convoy, Help for Syria, over Christmas in 2013. But the rendezvous never occurred, and Shajira ended up being arrested by counter-terrorism police. The judge told the defendant: 'In my judgement your primary motivation was not at its heart sinister – but was born out of a naive wish to help your brother and to maintain a link with him which evidently your mother had lost.'[7]

Shajira pleaded guilty to 'entering into or becoming concerned in a terrorist funding arrangement, as a result of which property would be made available'. Handing him a twelve-month sentence, suspended for two years, with supervision and two hundred hours of unpaid work, the judge said it was a very serious offence.

Politicians who intervene in the debate with inflammatory remarks only serve to discourage families from co-operating with the police. In August 2014 after the beheading of James Foley the then London mayor, Boris Johnson, said that anyone who went to Syria or tried to go to Syria should be presumed guilty of committing a terrorist offence unless they rebutted the presumption,[8] thus ending in one outburst the right to a presumption of innocence that can be traced back to Magna Carta.

But harsh prison sentences only stigmatize families and stir up community grievance. Whenever a British Muslim is given a hefty prison sentence after returning from Syria social media is flooded with posts from enraged Muslims complaining at the injustice of the punishment. These complaints are transformed into hostile grievance when other extremist crimes are prosecuted outside the terrorism laws, even though there may be political and violent dimensions to the offence.

In November 2014 former soldier Ryan McGee was sentenced to two years' imprisonment for making a homemade bomb which contained 181 metal screws and bits of glass.[9] The court was also told McGee kept a journal entitled *Ryan's Story Book* which contained references to right-wing groups such as the National Front, KKK and BNP.

He downloaded a number of extreme videos and his laptop had links to websites including Nazi execution videos, 'French skinheads', 'Russian racism', 'Handguns for sale UK and Germany', and YouTube videos of Nazi youth and EDL marches against Muslims. But the Crown Prosecution Service did not prosecute him under the terrorism laws. In the same month a young Muslim mother of two was sentenced to twenty-four months in jail for trying to send her husband money while he was in Syria with the Islamic State. Amal El-Wahabi, twenty-eight, persuaded her friend to stuff €20,000 in cash down her knickers to evade security checks at Heathrow airport, but she was caught.[10] She was charged under the terrorism laws even though Judge Nicholas Hilliard said he was satisfied that 'the initiative for this offence must have come from' her husband. He even said that she had only committed the crime 'because you were infatuated with him and thought he might provide for you and your two children'.

Such disparities in the treatment of people connected to extremism only legitimize any feeling among the Muslim community that they are being discriminated against on the grounds of their religion. In the bluntest terms, the UK government is now targeting Muslims for harsh treatment in just the way that many jihadist groups wish to claim.

But the most serious condemnation of the government's counter-terrorism strategy is reserved for the treatment of Muslim children. Nearly half of the four thousand Channel referrals across the country relate to under-eighteens and, by the start of 2015, referrals had increased by fifty-eight percent. In one case a fourteen-year-old boy was investigated under Prevent for asking if the government planned to ban halal meat. When he voiced this in the classroom, the teacher alerted authorities rather than address his opinions. A three-year-old boy was reported for saying 'I am going to kill you' as he was holding a water pistol, while a three-year-old girl was quizzed because she did not want to play with boys.

Any community under threat will always feel most protective towards its children. Using the law to target Muslim families in this way will ultimately marginalize young Muslims and force them into the arms of the radicalizers. The current government approach to tackling extremism has also attracted criticism from a broad range of experts in the field of counter-terrorism. One of them is the government-appointed independent reviewer of anti-terrorism laws, David Anderson. In his annual report published in September 2015, Anderson warned that new laws to clamp down on individuals and organizations accused of extremism could backfire. He said that the Counter-Extremism Bill risks provoking a backlash in affected communities, hardening perceptions of an illiberal or Islamophobic approach, and alienating those whose integration into British society is already fragile. The strategy, he warned, risked 'playing into the hands of those who, by peddling a grievance agenda, seek to drive people further towards extremism and terrorism'.

He is not alone among the counter-terrorism establishment to voice concern over the government's approach. Sir Peter Fahy, former chief constable of Greater Manchester Police and until 2015 vice-chair of the police's terrorism committee and national lead on Prevent, has said that there is a danger of smothering free speech. Lord Blair of Boughton, the former Metropolitan Police commissioner who was in charge of the capital's police force during 7/7, told *Newsnight* on 1 July 2015 that he profoundly disagreed with David Cameron's call for being 'more intolerant of intolerance'. He believes it is now critically important to talk to fundamentalist preachers. And Eliza Manningham-Buller, the head of MI5 during 7/7, reminded governments in her book *Securing Freedom* that it is never a good idea to rush to legislation in the wake of a terror atrocity. To tackle terrorism effectively we must first understand how radicalization works.

Jonathan Maynard Leader is the Rank-Manning junior research fellow in social sciences at New College, Oxford, and a world-acknowledged expert on the conditions that create radicalization. He says that radicalization becomes possible when people become secluded in 'small networks of like-minded friends' – usually numbering around eight – who 'cleave off' from mainstream society.

> All humans tend ideologically to conform to what seems to be the 'local common sense' in the circles they move in. If a vast majority of our friends espouse a view, we will often go along with it, especially when it fits well with our existing sentiments. When an individual's social network becomes isolated from broader society, it can consequently twist into an extremist echo chamber, draping an aura of plausibility and common sense over even those ideas that are morally reprehensible and utterly disconnected from reality.[11]

This pattern has been repeated in any number of terrorist radicalization cases. For example, Maynard Leader says the 9/11 pilots hung out exclusively with each other in dorms and a shared apartment in the Hamburg suburb of Harburg, 'affirming and reaffirming each other's progressively more radical views'. He says the same story applies to the 2004 Madrid bombers and to Anders Behring Breivik, the far-right perpetrator of the 2011 Norwegian attacks on a children's summer camp, although he gives the important caveat that Breivik's secluded social network was an online community.

It is almost impossible to stop these radicalizing social networks from emerging. But Maynard Leader's work has convinced him, and many others, that the very worst strategy is to actively discourage students from expressing their views in school and university classes, or indeed in wider society, out of fear that they will be monitored and condemned as 'vulnerable to extremism'. 'But this is precisely what Prevent does: it directly encourages young people to move their politics into exactly the secluded social networks that facilitate radicalization.'[12] He warns that such an approach is 'hugely dangerous', adding: 'It is made worse by the persistent use – by politicians, much of the media, and Prevent – of a comforting but false portrayal of the ideological battle underpinning terrorism as occurring between a set of blatantly awful extremist ideas on one hand, and an incontestable set of fundamental British values on the other.'[13] Once that happens it is only a matter of time before they appear on the radar of the security services.

I have documented elsewhere in this book how MI5 and counter-terrorism police units make contact with suspects. The security services have a twin-track approach, so that any individual who falls under suspicion of Islamist extremism will also be considered for its recruitment programme. Obviously those who are further down the terrorist road are more likely to face criminal prosecution but even these cases can be part of informant deals. A key MI5 *modus operandi* tends to confront the individual with the untested allegations before making any offer of recruitment. It is in the best interests of the security services to be as robust as possible in these first meetings so as to give them a psychological advantage. In the vast majority of cases it means that anyone approached by the security services will at some stage feel threatened by the state. It is a tactic best summed up, not by a terror suspect or man on a terror control order, but by a fellow journalist who found himself targeted in this way.

Multi-award-winning journalist Jamal Osman went public about the pressure he was put under to become an informant over a five-year period: 'The incentives they offer range from a "handsome salary" or a "nice car" to a "big house". I have even been told that they "could help me marry four wives". I have declined all their offers. Their psychological tactics include telling me how easy it is for them to take away my British passport and destroy my career – and even my life.'[14] Nevertheless, there is little doubt that this tactic gets results because we know that MI5 and SO15 rely on intelligence emanating from informants in the Muslim community. And they disrupted seven plots in the year leading up to November 2015. But there are short-term and long-term disadvantages to pursuing this line of attack.

The short-term disadvantage is that it provokes hostility rather than fear, shattering any hope of establishing a working relationship. There are few Muslims who are not already prepared for such contact and many may have even rehearsed their response. There is some evidence that Emwazi himself was fully prepared for his own encounters with the security services, as many of his friends had already received the same kind of approaches. The 'front door' tactics, such as turning up unannounced or trying to frighten people by speaking to their friends and families, not only reinforce prejudices but also undermine the mystique and professionalism of MI5. One community leader put it like this: 'There was a time when if someone was approached by MI5 it was a very big deal. They were supposed to be the elite in the secret service and so whatever you may or may not have done it must be very serious. But not any more. When they behave like "PC Plod" then they are regarded as such. They are no longer feared or even taken very seriously.' The young Muslim street gang members who gravitate between crime and extremist behaviour refer to MI5 as '5-0', in urban slang derived from the US TV programme *Hawaii Five-0*, its sense of mystery long gone.

In the long term the dangers of this approach are of even greater concern. Mutual trust must be at the heart of any enduring informant relationship. But a Muslim who spies on other Muslims may already feel he or she is in breach of Islamic teaching, with one cleric calling it the 'ultimate form of treason ... which takes you out of Islam'.[15]

If the relationship between security service and agent is solely based on fear, then when the agent no longer fears the organization he is working for he is free to dictate his own terms. The reliability of the intelligence may suffer or the agent may even switch sides. There has been at least one high-profile case of a British Muslim working for the security services in this country who has been 'turned' by a terror cell in Syria. And the Islamic State has made plain how much it would treasure a terror victory against a member of the security services.

For Emwazi and a number of the other Muslim men I met, the aggressive approach against suspects who had no history of violence or criminal record amounted to harassment. Groups such as CAGE have argued that this tactic helped to turn Emwazi into the killer he became and that MI5 must be held accountable for its actions.

It is an accusation that has been interpreted as a direct attack on the integrity and professionalism of MI5 and SO15, so much so that when CAGE first made the claim after Jihadi John was revealed to be Mohammed Emwazi, the prime minister not only mounted a knee-jerk defence of the security services but he also turned on the accusers. His spokeswoman said it was 'completely reprehensible to suggest that anyone who carries out such brutal murders [is not responsible for them] – they are the ones responsible and we should not be seeking to put blame on other people, particularly those who are working to keep British citizens safe. The people responsible for these murders are the people that we have seen in the videos.'[16]

Boris Johnson went further and called CAGE 'apologists for terrorism'. And a few months later in July 2015 David Cameron used a speech on counter-terrorism delivered in Birmingham, the home city of CAGE director Moazzam Begg, to single the group out again. This time he called CAGE 'extremists' and urged people not to work with them.[17] Interestingly, behind the scenes Cameron ordered an inquiry into MI5's dealings with Michael Adebolajo, one of the two men who killed soldier Lee Rigby. Did that make him an apologist for terrorism or a politician keen to learn lessons from MI5's surveillance and contact operations?

When the head of MI5, Andrew Parker, was questioned live on BBC Radio 4's *Today* programme about claims that his officers' contact with Emwazi may have alienated or even criminalized him, he would have none of it: 'I completely dismiss that ... it is the sort of thing that our detractors and some people who we need to take an interest in want to say.' The Security Service and SO15 argue that Emwazi's subsequent actions confirm that they had the right man in their sights: 'People who are mixed up with extremism which poses a risk to this country are precisely the kind of people we should be talking to.'

But none of this macho rhetoric addresses the central issue – that people who have no violent history or criminal record and are approached by, or have contact with, the security services still go on to commit acts of terrorism.

I don't support the criticism that the security services always take a heavy-headed approach when confronting the threat posed by Islamist extremists. But the fact remains that of the sixteen or so individuals I interviewed almost all made the same complaint – that they were being unfairly harassed. And of course it is very unlikely that a successful and happy spy will be allowed (or even want) to speak to the media about how well their relationship with MI5 is working.

One former MI5 agent I did interview, who had spent two years spying on terror suspects, added a bit more background to the security services' handling of spies. He once told me: 'They always want to have leverage over you so that if you fall out of line they can rein you in – with me it was a passport, and the promise to let me live as a citizen in Great Britain.' The agent and MI5 eventually parted ways in 2008 but he still hasn't received a passport. What is clear is that MI5 wields considerable power over these young men – it can offer them wealth and wives as well as threatening them with deportation to torture states.

An internal document leaked in 2008, around the same time I was interviewing the Kentish Town group, revealed that MI5 should have been able to operate a much more sophisticated recruitment and disruption policy than their critics give them credit for.[18] The nuanced analysis, based on hundreds of case studies by the Security Service, found there is no single pathway to violent extremism. It concludes that it is not possible to draw up a typical profile of the 'British terrorist' as most are 'demographically unremarkable' and simply reflect the communities in which they live. The 'UK restricted' MI5 report takes apart many of the common stereotypes about those involved in

British terrorism. They are mostly British nationals, not illegal immigrants, and, far from being Islamist fundamentalists, most are religious novices. Nor, the analysis says, are they simply 'mad and bad'.

The research, carried out by MI5's behavioural science unit, is based on in-depth case studies on 'several hundred individuals known to be involved in, or closely associated with, violent extremist activity', ranging from fundraising to planning suicide bombings in Britain. The operational briefing note, circulated within the security services, warns that, unless they understand the varied backgrounds of those drawn to terrorism in Britain, they will fail to counter their activities in the short term and fail to prevent violent radicalization continuing in the long term. But it also concludes that its research results had important lessons for the government's programme to tackle the spread of violent extremism, underlining the need for 'attractive alternatives' to terrorist involvement but also warning that traditional law enforcement tactics could backfire if handled badly or used against people who are not legitimate targets.

What is important now is that the government and its security services don't become disengaged from certain sections of the Muslim community. CAGE and other hard-line Muslim groups aren't going away. Neither are imams who refuse to preach what the government calls a 'British' kind of Islam. Political and personal attacks have only strengthened their position in the Muslim communities.

In the days after the Emwazi press conference, Asim Qureshi received a number of death threats and in one instance the police were called in when a local plumber threatened to rape a member of his family. But CAGE also received record financial donations as well as thousands of expressions of support. By standing up to the media and the government CAGE was seen to be standing up for British Muslims. However, in an ideal world CAGE would not be the best advocacy group for the Muslim community. It has made claims against the security services which are not supported by the evidence, it sees conspiracies in places where there are none and its pursuit of its own agenda means that it does not always tell the complete truth about the cases that it works on. Questions must also be asked about the high number of young Muslim men who have passed through CAGE's doors before going on to commit acts of terrorism. If the security services can be accused of playing a part in the radicalization process of terrorists then so can advocacy groups and journalists who take on their cases.

But of course we do not live in an ideal world so CAGE remains a vital release valve for young Muslims with grievances. It can offer guidance and provide a useful sounding board when an individual is considering extremist action. The government refuses to recognize this and has targeted CAGE's funding, determined to force it underground. By the same token CAGE refuses to acknowledge that the government's actions are directed by its duty to protect British citizens rather than a desire to wage war against British Muslim communities. On the face of it the two sides seem diametrically opposed. But CAGE and the government may be actually working towards the same goal – to stop young Muslim men from adopting the values of violent extremism. They also probably don't realize that they share the view that counter-terrorism policies on their own can't defeat extremist radicalization. CAGE argues that more needs to be done to tackle the underlying causes of radicalization in society, including poverty and exclusion.

Charles Farr told me: 'Counter-terrorism programmes are only one way of addressing the drivers of radicalisation. They cannot deal with some factors that might recreate a sense of alienation and therefore vulnerability. Nor can they be the primary way to facilitate integration and cohesion.'

The Muslim press and newspapers like *The Independent* and *The Guardian* are also an important forum for the airing of grievances and perceived persecutions. Media outlets which report complaints of harassment provide militant Islamist youth with a stake in society. But they are not enough on their own to absorb the growing demand for forums which provide British Muslims with an opportunity to rebut untested allegations which the state has made against them.

Imams and Islamic clerics who have spent their entire careers winning the respect of their Muslim communities must not be shut out of the debate. Britain's treatment of Abu Qatada, the Jordanian-born cleric who was accused of being a spiritual adviser to Osama bin Laden, should serve as a lesson in how not to handle community relations. He spent thirteen years in prison and under house arrest because the authorities feared the influence he had over British Muslims. But despite this he went out of his way to try to save Ken Bigley, beheaded by the forerunners of the Islamic State, and more recently Alan Henning, beheaded by the Islamic State itself. In 2014 he voluntarily returned to Jordan where he was acquitted of terrorism charges. Today he is one of IS's most outspoken and effective critics.

The Islamic State and al-Qaeda are no longer capable of being destroyed because they have become more than terrorist organizations. They are the expression of ideas about Muslim solidarity and a response to Muslim oppression. Many thousands of their membership have been and will be killed but the idea of a caliphate run under strict shari'a law will live on. There are today seventy-eight terrorist organizations, mostly located in the Middle East, which each want to establish an Islamic state. And it was reported in 2015 that the Islamic State itself attracts forty suicide bombers every month to replenish its ranks. The American, Russian and British bombing strategy has only made their fighters more difficult to find.

How many of the 2.7 million Muslims in Britain have sympathy or understanding for what they believe lies behind the actions of the Islamic State? A hundred? A thousand? The figure is probably closer to a hundred thousand. These are British citizens who don't want to go to Syria and will privately and publicly condemn the atrocities but can still in some way rationalize the Islamic State. The vast majority are not interested in terrorism or supporting terrorism. But they are equally not interested in assisting the police or helping the security services in spying on Muslim communities. If they see something suspicious, someone buying chemicals from a hardware shop or a young man talking about travelling to Syria, they may decide to turn a blind eye. After all, performing your civic duty now comes at a risk. The first question the police might ask is: how well do you know the person you are reporting on? Are you part of the same plot? The consequences can be very serious indeed. Courts have been known to take children from a family deemed to be extremist. With so much at risk, and with so much existing intrusion, it's hardly surprising if Muslims question why they should police their own communities.

Trust is at the heart of all healthy community relationships but trust between the security services and the Muslim community is in very short supply. Part of this concern is shared by the former head of MI6, Sir John Sawers, which he expressed in an interview on American television in 2015. He said that in order to 'fight the new dangers, intelligence services need to gain the trust of Muslim leaders in their home countries and sneak secret agents into overseas terror organizations.'[19]

Scotland Yard recognizes that there is a problem with trust but a senior counter-terrorism officer I spoke to believed it applied to only a very small section of the Muslim community. Yet the engagement gap between the Muslim community and the government and its security services is widening. Using the

Investigatory Powers Tribunal members of the public can bring complaints against the security services, including MI5. But in its fifteen-year history it has only once ruled against the security and intelligence services and that was a complaint brought in the wake of the disclosures made by US spy Edward Snowden.[20] It is a cumbersome and lengthy procedure that does not have the confidence of the Muslim community, whose members don't believe the tribunal is capable of finding MI5's treatment of individuals to be at fault. Once the security services have intervened in someone's life it is almost impossible to repair the damage. It is usually left to the local police to answer complaints about harassment while SO15 or MI5 are under no obligation to account for their actions.

The reason why so many young, desperate Muslim men came to me seeking help through publicity is because there is no credible grievance process which can hold the security services to account.[21] They were demonstrably not suitable for the Prevent programme as they had already rebuffed approaches from security services and were, by the time I met them, outwardly hostile to the state.

There is no such thing as a perfect counter-terrorism policy and I accept that it is inevitable that some innocent feathers will have to be ruffled while Britain faces such a serious terrorist threat. So I propose the creation of a 'surveillance ombudsman', someone who can command the trust of both the security services and the Muslim community, directly appointed by the prime minister, to help settle grievances. The post should have the power to informally investigate complaints and concerns raised by members of *both* communities. I don't see any need for this work to be done in public. But it would be a credible forum for grievances to be fully aired and taken seriously. The 'ombudsman' should not be without teeth and whoever has the job should be able to correct mistakes or issue warning notices.

Not only would such a system help people to understand why they have been targeted, but where mistakes have been made the damage could at least be limited. Since we now know that a raw grievance over perceived mistreatment, if left unattended, can play a part in radicalization this could provide a vital opportunity to break the chain. It would be a two-way process so the security services would be able to use the system to issue informal warnings about extremist behaviour or suspicious patterns of behaviour.

We will never know if Mohamed Aden, Mahdi Hashi or even Mohammed Emwazi would have benefited from such a process. Each of their paths to radicalization was as different as their characters. But I wonder: if any of these young Muslim men had been offered such an alternative, would we still be talking about them today?

The importance of finding ways to stop British men being drawn to terrorist organisations has never been more urgent. At the time of going to press Islamic State had already selected a British Muslim to replace Mohammed Emwazi as the face of its horrific propaganda campaign. In an execution video posted on 3 January 2016, the masked jihadist defiantly pointed a gun at Britain and threatened more atrocities to come. Mohammed Emwazi may have been killed, but Jihadi John can be replaced.

ACKNOWLEDGEMENTS

First and foremost to my family because no man is an island. Special gratitude to my editor Alex Christofi and Oneworld for backing the book. To Mike Harpley for his initial support. A huge thanks to everyone who so generously gave their time to this project. To name a few: Charles Farr; Raffaello Pantucci; Asim Qureshi; Sharhabeel Lone; Richard Barrett; Tam Hussein; Omar Emwazi; Dr Rizwaan Sabir; and members of the security services who can't be named but who I nevertheless wish to acknowledge. Also the brave journalists and aid workers who continue to represent the values of humanity working in inhumane parts of the world.

NOTES

Prologue

1. Rukmini Callimachi, 'The Horror before the Beheadings', *New York Times* [online], 25 October 2014 (http://www.nytimes.com/2014/10/26/world/middleeast/horror-before-the-beheadings-what-isis-hostages-endured-in-syria.html?_r=0) (accessed 18 November 2015).
2. Ibid.
3. Javier Espinosa, 'He Could Have Fled Isis Dungeon . . . but Refused to Leave His Friend', *The Times*, 16 March 2015.
4. Abu Mohammed, 'Raqqa Is Being Slaughtered Silently, During a Year (2)', Raqqa News [online], 14 April 2015 (http://www.raqqa-sl.com/en/?p=980) (accessed 18 November 2015).
5. Eliot Higgins, 'The Hills of Raqqa – Geolocating the James Foley Video', Bellingcat [online], 23 August 2014 (https://www.bellingcat.com/resources/case-studies/2014/08/23/the-hills-of-raqqa-geolocating-the-james-foley-video) (accessed 23 November 2015).

Chapter 1: Mohammed the Outsider

1. Author's interview with family friend, September 2015.
2. Author's interview with Emwazi family member, October 2015.
3. 'Country Information and Guidance: Kuwaiti Bidoon', Home Office, 3 February 2014 (https://www.gov.uk/government/uploads/system/uploads/attachment_data/file/311943/Kuwait_country_information_guidance_2014.pdf) (accessed 19 November 2015).
4. David Collins, 'Inside Jihadi John's Birthplace in Kuwait: The Grim Town that Bred a Monster', Mirror [online], 28 February 2015 (http://www.mirror.co.uk/news/uk-news/inside-jihadi-johns-birthplace-kuwait-5251430) (accessed 19 November 2015).
5. 'Country Information and Guidance: Kuwaiti Bidoon'.
6. Ibid.
7. Ibid.
8. Ibid.
9. Ibid.
10. Ibid.
11. Ibid.
12. Ibid.
13. Collins, 'Inside Jihadi John's Birthplace in Kuwait'.
14. Ibid.
15. Author's interview with family friend on 21 September 2015 and 6 October 2015.
16. Ibid.
17. Author's interview with Emwazi family member, 6 October 2015.
18. Author's interview with family friend.
19. Ibid.
20. Ibid.
21. Vanessa Allen, Paul Bentley and Lucy Osborne, 'Exclusive: First Picture of the Face of the Angelic Schoolboy Who Turned into Reviled ISIS Executioner', Mail Online, 27 February 2015 (http://www.dailymail.co.uk/news/article-2971104/Angelic-schoolboy-turned-reviled-executioner-Jihadi-John-s-descent-polite-west-London-pupil-bloodthirsty-killer-revels-brutality.html) (accessed 19 November 2015).

NOTES

22. Author's interview with Emwazi family friend.
23. Amelia Hill, 'Mohammed Emwazi: Yearbook Reveals Boy who Liked Chips and S Club 7',The Guardian [online], 27 February 2015 (http://www.theguardian.com/uk-news/2015/feb/27/mohammed-emwazi-yearbook-reveals-boy-who-liked-chips-and-s-club-7) (accessed 19 November 2015).
24. Ibid.
25. Ibid.
26. Ibid.
27. Ibid.
28. Allen, Bentley and Osborne,'Exclusive: First Picture'.
29. 'Jihadi John: First Video of Mohammed Emwazi Unmasked' Channel 4 News [online], 5 March 2015 (http://www.channel4.com/news/jihadi-john-mohammed-emwazi-video-unmasked-teenager-video) (accessed 19 November 2015).
30. '"I Went to School with Jihadi John": Remarkable Account', LBC [online], 27 February 2015 (http://www.lbc.co.uk/i-went-to-school-with-jihadi-john-remarkable-account-105601) (accessed 19 November 2015).
31. Martin Fricker, David Collins and Russell Myers, 'Mohammed Emwazi: Jihadi John's Schoolfriend Recognised Eyes of ISIS Butcher in Beheading Videos', Mirror [online], 27 February 2015 (http://www.mirror.co.uk/news/uk-news/mohammed-emwazi-jihadi-johns-schoolfriend-5245965) (accessed 19 November 2015).
32. Ibid.
33. Ibid.
34. 'Mohammed Emwazi Was a Loner, IS Defector Says', BBC News [online], 1 March 2015 (http://www.bbc.co.uk/news/uk-31688700) (accessed 19 November 2015).
35. Ibid.
36. 'Charities Withdraw Support for CAGE after Group's Comments on "Jihadi John"', ITV News [online], 2 March 2015 (http://www.itv.com/news/update/2015-03-02/inquiry-to-look-at-school-over-radicalisation-questions/) (accessed 19 November 2015).
37. Ibid.
38. 'Mohammed Emwazi Was a Loner'.
39. Ibid.

40. James Beal, 'Jihadi John's Drink and Drugs Binges', The Sun [online], 1 March 2015, (http://www.thesun.co.uk/sol/homepage/news/6350920/Jihadi-John-Mohammed-Emwazis-drink-drugs-binges-revealed-SEE-FORENSIC-ARTISTS-IMPRESSION-PIC.html) (accessed 19 November 2015).

41. Ibid.

42. Ibid.

43. Ibid.

44. Author's interview with family friend, September 2015.

45. Chris Woods, 'Parents of British Man Killed by US Drone Blame UK Government', Bureau of Investigative Journalism [online], 15 March 2013 (https://www.thebureauinvestigates.com/2013/03/15/parents-of-british-man-killed-by-us-drone-blame-uk-government/) (accessed 19 November 2015).

46. Secretary of State for the Home Department vs J1 [2011], and Secretary of State for the Home Department vs BX.

47. Ibid.

48. Ibid.

49. Ibid.

50. Secretary of State for the Home Department vs CE, QBD, Administrative Court [2011], EWHC 3159 (Admin), PTA/4/2011 (Transcript: Wordwave International Ltd (A Merrill Communications Company)), hearing dates: 24–31 October, 1–4 November, 21 December 2011.

51. 'First Photo of "Jihadi John" as Adult Revealed', Sky News [online], 28 February 2015 (http://news.sky.com/story/1435642/first-photo-of-jihadi-john-as-adult-revealed) (accessed 19 November 2015).

52. Author's interview with family friend, September 2015.

53. Ibid.

54. Robert Verkaik, 'Notorious Jihadi Rapper on the Run in Turkey', The Telegraph [online], 11 July 2015 (http://www.telegraph.co.uk/news/worldnews/islamic-state/11733538/Notorious-jihadi-rapper-on-the-run-in-Turkey.html) (accessed 19 November 2015).

55. Ibid.

56. Ibid.

Chapter 2: The Jihadi John Network

1. Chris Woods, 'Parents of British Man Killed by US Drone Blame UK Government', Bureau of Investigative Journalism [online], 15 March 2013 (https://www.thebureauinvestigates.com/2013/03/15/parents-of-british-man-killed-by-us-drone-blame-uk-government/) (accessed 19 November 2015).
2. Ibid.
3. CAGEprisoners interview with Bilal al-Berjawi, 2009.
4. Ibid.
5. Ibid.
6. Secretary of State for the Home Department vs K2, Special Immigration Appeals Commission [2014], Appeal No. SC/96/2010, SIAC (http://www.siac.tribunals.gov.uk/Documents/K2-april14.pdf) (accessed 19 November 2015), hearing dates: 1–4 April 2014, date of judgement: 18 December 2014.
7. Cedric Barnes and Harun Hassan, 'The Rise and Fall of Mogadishu's Islamic Courts', Chatham House, April 2007 (https://www.chathamhouse.org/sites/files/chathamhouse/public/Research/Africa/bpsomalia0407.pdf) (accessed 19 November 2015).
8. Mukoma wa Ngugi, 'How al-Shabaab Was Born', The Guardian [online], 4 October 2013 (http://www.theguardian.com/world/2013/oct/04/kenya-westgate-mall-attacks) (accessed 19 November 2015).
9. 'Somali Islamic State "Ruled Out"', BBC News [online], 7 June 2006 (http://news.bbc.co.uk/1/hi/world/africa/5051220.stm) (accessed 19 November 2015).
10. Mukoma, 'How al-Shabaab Was Born'.
11. Ibid.
12. Michael Bonner, *Jihad in Islamic History: Doctrines and Practice* (Princeton, NJ: Princeton University Press, 2006), p. 22.
13. Secretary of State for the Home Department vs CE, QBD, Administrative Court [2011], EWHC 3159 (Admin), PTA/4/2011, (Transcript: Wordwave International Ltd (A Merrill Communications Company), hearing dates: 24–31 October, 1–4 November, 21 December 2011.

14. Secretary of State for the Home Department *vs* J1, Special Immigration Appeals Commission [2011], Appeal No: SC/98/2010, SIAC (http://www.siac.tribunals.gov.uk/Documents/J1_SoRJudgment_11Jul2011.pdf) (accessed 19 November 2015), hearing dates: 14–17 June 2011, date of judgement: 11 July 2011.

15. Tam Hussein, 'The Inside Story of the British Suicide Bomber of Ramadi', Syria Comment [online], 21 July 2015 (http://www.joshualandis.com/blog/the-inside-story-of-the-british-suicide-bomber-of-ramadi-by-tam-hussein/) (accessed 19 November 2015); author's interview with Tam Hussein, August 2015.

16. Secretary of State for the Home Department *vs* CE [2011].

17. Author's interview, September 2015.

18. Secretary of State for the Home Department *vs* J1 [2011].

19. Ibid.

20. Ibid.

21. Ibid.

22. Ibid.

23. Ibid.

24. Woods, 'Parents of British Man'.

25. Raffaello Pantucci, 'Bilal al-Berjawi and the Shifting Fortunes of Foreign Fighters in Somalia', Combating Terrorism Center [online], 24 September 2013 (https://www.ctc.usma.edu/posts/bilal-al-berjawi-and-the-shifting-fortunes-of-foreign-fighters-in-somalia) (accessed 19 November 2015).

26. Ibid.

27. Bill Roggio, 'Shabaab Leader Recounts al Qaeda's Role in Somalia in the 1990s', Long War Journal [online], 31 December 2011 (http://www.longwarjournal.org/archives/2011/12/shabaab_leader_recou.php) (accessed 19 November 2015).

28. Ibid.

29. 'Fazul Abdullah Mohammed: Death Is "Blow" for al-Qaeda', BBC News, 11 June 2011 (http://www.bbc.co.uk/news/world-africa-13739567) (accessed 19 November 2015).

30. Paul Cruickshank and Nic Robertson, 'Before "Jihadi John", Mohammed Emwazi in London Terror Network', CNN [online], 5 March 2015 (http://edition.cnn.com/2015/03/05/world/jihadi-john-terror-network/) (accessed 19 November 2015).

31. Special Immigration Appeals Commission, 11 July 2011.

32. Secretary of State for the Home Department *vs* CE [2011].

33. 'Memorandum for Commander, United States Southern Command, 22 May 2007', WikiLeaks [online], 24 April 2011 (https://wikileaks.org/gitmo/prisoner/10025.html) (accessed 19 November 2015).

34. Ibid.

35. 'Torture Policy Grounds for Judicial Review', Reprieve (http://www.reprieve.org.uk/wp-content/uploads/2014/10/2010_02_23_PUB_Torture_Policy_Grounds_for_Judicial_Review.pdf) (accessed 25 November 2015).

36. Ibid.

37. Ibid.

38. Ibid.

39. Secretary of State for the Home Department *vs* CE [2011].

40. Ibid.

41. Ibid.

42. BX *v.* Secretary of State for the Home Department [2010], EWHC 990 (Admin Queen's Bench May 10 2010 England and Wales High Court (Administrative Court) Decisions, Case No: PTA/54/2009, 10 May 2010 (http://www.bailii.org/ew/cases/EWHC/Admin/2010/990.html) (accessed 19 November 2015).

43. Ibid.

44. Ibid.

45. Ibid.

46. Ibid.

47. Author's interview with Asim Qureshi, 2015.

48. Souad Mekhennet, Adam Goldman and Griff Witte, '"Jihadi John" is a Kuwaiti-Born Londoner Named Mohammed Emwazi', Washington Post [online], 26 February 2015 (https://www.washingtonpost.com/world/national-security/jihadi-john-is-a-kuwaiti-born-londoner-named-mohammed-emwazi/2015/02/26/c5a7373c-bdfd-11e4-bdfa-b8e8f594e6ee_story.html) (accessed 19 November 2015).

49. Kim Sengupta, 'Jihadi John: ISIS Executioner Mohammed Emwazi Wanted to Wage Jihad in Somalia until His Friends Were Betrayed and Killed by al-Shabaab', *The Independent*, 21 April 2015.

50. CAGEprisoners interview with Bilal al-Berjawi, 2009.

51. Ibid.

52. Ibid.

53. Ibid.

54. Woods, 'Parents of British Man.'

55. Ibid.

56. Ibid.

57. Ibid.

58. Author's interview with Emwazi family friend, September 2015.

59. Author's interview with Asim Qureshi, August 2015.

60. Author's interview with Emwazi family friend.

61. Robert Verkaik and Robert Mendick, 'Free to Walk London's Streets: The Extremist Preacher and "Mentor" of Jihadi John', *Sunday Telegraph*, 6 July 2015.

62. Jamie Doward, 'My Meeting with Mohammed Emwazi's Friend as They Sought a Radical Path', The Observer [online], 28 February 2015 (http://www.theguardian.com/world/2015/feb/28/encounter-mohammed-ezzouek-friend-mohammed-emwazi-isis) (accessed 19 November 2015).

63. Special Dispatch No. 932, MEMRI [online], 12 July 2005 (http://www.memri.org/report/en/0/0/0/0/0/0/1411.htm) (accessed 19 November 2015).

64. Ibid.

65. Doward, 'My Meeting with Mohammed Emwazi's Friend'.

66. Thomas Joscelyn, 'Al Qaeda Ally Calls for Statement on Islamic State's Caliphate', Long War Journal [online], 9 July 2014 (http://www.longwarjournal.org/archives/2014/07/al_qaeda_ally_calls.php) (accessed 19 November 2015).

67. Youseff *vs* Home Office [2004], EWHC 1884 (QB).

68. CJEU judgment of 21 March 2014 in Case T-306/10 Hani El Sayyed Elsebai Yusef *vs* European Commission.

69. Ibid.

70. Ibid.

71. Insight, 'War on Terrorism', Sunday Times [online], 11 November 2001 (accessed 2 June 2015).

72. 'Three Alleged International Terrorists Extradited from Great Britain', FBI press release, 6 October 2012 (https://www.fbi.gov/

newyork/press-releases/2012/three-alleged-international-terrorists-extradited-from-great-britain) (date accessed 6 June 2015).

73. Alison Pargeter, *The New Frontiers of Jihad: Radical Islam in Europe* (London: I. B. Tauris, 2008), p. 54.

74. Victoria Brittain, 'Life as the Spouse of a Suspected al-Qaeda Terrorist', The Guardian [online], 20 February 2013 (http://www.theguardian.com/world/2013/feb/20/wife-of-alqaida-terrorist-suspect) (accessed 19 November 2015).

75. Ibid.

76. Ibid.

77. 'Three Alleged International Terrorists'.

78. 'Fact Sheet on Extradition of 5 Terrorism Suspects to US: Information on Charges', Embassy of the United States, London [online], 5 October 2012 (http://london.usembassy.gov/gb197.html) (accessed 19 November 2015).

79. Pantucci, 'Bilal al-Berjawi and the Shifting Fortunes'.

80. Cahal Milmo, 'Mohamed Hamid: From Petty Criminal to Tutor of Terrorists', Independent [online], 30 May 2013 (http://www.independent.co.uk/news/people/profiles/mohamed-hamid-from-petty-criminal-to-tutor-of-terrorists-8638594.html) (accessed 19 November 2015).

81. Ibid.

82. Secretary of State for the Home Department *vs* CE [2011].

83. Ibid.

84. Ibid.

85. Ibid.

86. Ibid.

87. Duncan Gardham, 'The Al Qaeda Fanatic from Britain who Funded Jihad Trip to Syria by Mugging Londoners with a Taser' Mail Online, 30 November 2013 (http://www.dailymail.co.uk/news/article-2516137/The-Al-Qaeda-fanatic-Britain-funded-jihad-trip-Syria-mugging-Londoners-Taser.html) (accessed 19 November 2015).

88. Hussein, 'The Inside Story'.

89. Ibid.

Chapter 3: MI5 and the Horn of Africa

1. Rob Wise, 'Al Shabaab', Center for Strategic & International Studies, July 2011 (http://csis.org/files/publication/110715_Wise_AlShabaab_AQAM%20Futures%20Case%20Study_WEB.pdf) (accessed 19 November 2015).

2. Nick Hopkins and Jake Morris, 'Former Agent: I Was Abandoned by MI5 after Breakdown', BBC News [online], 15 July 2015 (http://www.bbc.co.uk/news/uk-33543352) (accessed 19 November 2015).

3. Robert Verkaik, 'Exclusive: How MI5 Blackmails British Muslims', Independent [online], 21 May 2009 (http://www.independent.co.uk/news/uk/home-news/exclusive-how-mi5-blackmails-british-muslims-1688618.html) (accessed 19 November 2015).

4. Ibid.

5. Ibid.

6. Ibid.

7. 'Case File: Mahdi Hashi', CAGE [online] (http://www.CAGEuk.org/case/4-mahdi-hashi) (accessed 20 November 2015).

8. 'Mohammed Emwazi "Deported for Being Drunk and Abusive"', BBC News [online], 8 March 2015 (http://www.bbc.co.uk/news/uk-31785166) (accessed 20 November 2015).

9. '"You're Going to Be Followed ... Life Will Be Harder for You": The Story of Mohammed Emwazi', CAGE [online], 26 February 2015 (http://www.CAGEuk.org/article/youre-going-be-followed-life-will-be-harder-you-story-mohammed-emwazi) (accessed 20 November 2015).

10. Ibid.

11. Ibid.

12. Ibid.

13. Ibid.

14. Ibid.

15. Ibid.

16. Ibid.

17. Ibid.

18. Ibid.

19. Ibid.

20. Ibid.

21. Ibid.

22. Ibid.

23. *The Horn of Africa Inquisition: The Latest Profile in the War on Terror* (London: Cageprisoners, 2010), p. 20.

24. 'The Emwazi Tapes: "9-11 Was Wrong"', CAGE [online], 3 March 2015 (http://www.CAGEuk.org/press-release/emwazi-tapes-9-11-was-wrong) (accessed 20 November 2015).

25. Ibid.

26. Ibid.

27. Ibid.

28. '"You're Going to Be Followed"'.

29. Ibid.

30. James Beal, 'Jihadi John's Drugs Binges', The Sun [online], 1 March 2015, (http://www.thesun.co.uk/sol/homepage/news/6350920/Jihadi-John-Mohammed-Emwazis-drink-drugs-binges-revealed-SEE-FORENSIC-ARTISTS-IMPRESSION-PIC.html) (accessed 19 November 2015).

31. *The Horn of Africa Inquisition*, p. 4.

32. Ibid.

33. Ibid., p. 22.

34. Ibid.

35. Ibid.

36. Ibid.

Chapter 4: Face to Face with Jihadi John

1. Chris Woods, 'Parents of British Man Killed by US Drone Blame UK Government', Bureau of Investigative Journalism [online], 15 March 2013 (https://www.thebureauinvestigates.com/2013/03/15/parents-of-british-man-killed-by-us-drone-blame-uk-government/) (accessed 19 November 2015).

2. *The Horn of Africa Inquisition: The Latest Profile in the War on Terror* (London: Cageprisoners, 2010).

3. Secretary of State for the Home Department *vs* K2, Special Immigration Appeals Commission [2014], Appeal No. SC/96/2010,

SIAC (http://www.siac.tribunals.gov.uk/Documents/K2-april14. pdf) (accessed 19 November 2015), hearing dates: 1–4 April 2014, date of judgement: 18 December 2014.

4. Ibid.
5. Ibid.
6. Woods, 'Parents of British Man'.
7. Ibid.
8. Ibid.
9. Author's interview with Asim Qureshi, August 2015.
10. Woods, 'Parents of British Man'.
11. Author's interview with Mohammed Emwazi, December 2010.
12. Ibid.
13. Ibid.
14. Ibid.
15. Ibid.
16. Ibid.
17. Ibid.
18. Author's interview with friend of Emwazi, August 2015.
19. Martin Chulov, '"The Best Employee We Ever Had": Mohammed Emwazi's Former Boss in Kuwait', The Guardian [online], 2 March 2015 (http://www.theguardian.com/world/2015/mar/01/mohammed -emwazi-best-employee-we-ever-had-former-boss-kuwaiti-it-firm) (accessed 20 November 2015).
20. Ibid.
21. Ibid.
22. Ibid.
23. Author's interview with friend of Emwazi, August 2015.
24. Ibid.
25. Chulov, '"The Best Employee We Ever Had"'.
26. Author's interview with friend of Emwazi, August 2015.
27. Ibid.
28. Ibid.
29. Ibid.
30. Ibid.
31. 'First Photo of "Jihadi John" as Adult Revealed', Sky News [online], 28 February 2015 (http://news.sky.com/story/1435642/first-photo- of-jihadi-john-as-adult-revealed) (accessed 19 November 2015).

32. Inal Ersan, 'Kuwait Says Foils Qaeda Plan to Bomb US Army Camp', Reuters [online], 11 August 2009 (http://uk.reuters.com/article/2009/08/11/us-kuwait-qaeda-idUSTRE57A35F20090811) (accessed 20 November 2015).

33. 'Kuwait: Terrorism Trial Continues', WikiLeaks, 3 February 2010 (https://www.wikileaks.org/plusd/cables/10KUWAIT99_a.html) (accessed 20 November 2015).

34. Kim Sengupta and Tom Brooks-Pollock, 'Muhsin al-Fadhli Dead: Leader of Shadowy al-Qaeda Offshoot Khorasan "Killed by US Airstrike in Syria"', Independent [online], 22 July 2015 (http://www.independent.co.uk/news/world/middle-east/muhsin-alfadhli – leader-of-shadowy-khorasan-group-alqaeda-offshoot – killed-by-us-air-strike-in-syria-10406341.html) (accessed 20 November 2015).

35. Robert Tait, 'Jihadi John Radicalised after Meeting al-Qaeda Chief, Kuwaiti Sources Say', The Telegraph [online], 1 March 2015 (http://www.telegraph.co.uk/news/11442904/Jihadi-John-radicalised-after-meeing-al-Qaeda-chief-Kuwaiti-sources-say.html) (accessed 20 November 2015).

36. 'The Emwazi Emails: CAGE Releases its Correspondences with Emwazi in Full', CAGE [online], 28 February 2015 (http://www.CAGEuk.org/article/emwazi-emails-CAGE-releases-its-correspondences-emwazi-full) (accessed 20 November 2015).

37. Author's interview with friend of Emwazi, August 2015.

38. 'The Emwazi Emails'.

39. Ibid.

40. Ibid.

41. Ibid.

42. Ibid.

43. Ibid.

44. Ibid.

45. Ibid.

46. Ibid.

47. Ibid.

48. Ibid.

49. Ibid.

50. Ibid.

51. Ibid.
52. Ibid.
53. Ibid.
54. Ibid.
55. Ibid.
56. Ibid.
57. Ibid.
58. Ibid.
59. Ibid.
60. Author's interview with Emwazi confirmed in emails sent to author.
61. Ibid.
62. Ibid.
63. Ibid.
64. Ibid.
65. Ibid.
66. Ibid.
67. Ibid.
68. Ibid.
69. Ibid.
70. Ibid.
71. Robert Verkaik, 'Guilty: Britain Admits Collusion, New Torture Claims Emerge', Independent [online], 1 March 2009 (http://www.independent.co.uk/news/uk/politics/guilty-britain-admits-collusion-new-torture-claims-emerge-1634735.html) (accessed 20 November 2015).
72. Author's interview with Emwazi, December 2010.
73. Ibid.
74. Ibid.
75. Ibid.
76. Ibid.
77. Ibid.
78. Author's interview with friend of Emwazi, August 2015.
79. Author's interview with Emwazi, December 2010.
80. Ibid.
81. Ibid.
82. Ibid.
83. Robert Verkaik, 'Exclusive: Caught in America's Legal Black Hole',

Independent [online], 9 August 2010 (http://www.independent.
co.uk/news/world/americas/exclusive-caught-in-americas-legal-
black-hole-2047307.html) (accessed 20 November 2015).

Chapter 5: Subject of Interest

1. Interview with Omar Emwazi, October 2015.
2. 'The Emwazi Emails: CAGE Releases its Correspondences with
   Emwazi in Full', CAGE [online], 28 February 2015 (http://www.
   CAGEuk.org/article/emwazi-emails-CAGE-releases-its-corre-
   spondences-emwazi-full) (accessed 20 November 2015).
3. Ibid.
4. Ibid.
5. Author's correspondence and telephone conversations with Emwazi,
   December 2010 – March 2011.
6. Ibid.
7. Ibid.
8. Ibid.
9. 'The Emwazi Emails'.
10. Author's correspondence and telephone conversations with Emwazi,
    December 2010–March 2011.
11. 'The Emwazi Emails'.
12. Ibid.
13. Author's interview with Emwazi's friend in Kuwait, September
    2015.
14. 'The Emwazi Emails'.
15. Ibid.
16. Mark Hookham and Dipesh Gadher, 'Harrods Sales Assistant
    Linked to Jihadi John', *Sunday Times*, 15 February 2015.
17. Ibid.
18. Ibid.
19. '"You're Going to Be Followed … Life Will Be Harder for You":
    The Story of Mohammed Emwazi', CAGE [online], 26 February
    2015 (http://www.CAGEuk.org/article/youre-going-be-follow-
    edlife-will-be-harder-you-story-mohammed-emwazi) (accessed
    20 November 2015).

20. Interview with Omar Emwazi, October 2015.
21. Raffaello Pantucci, 'Bilal al-Berjawi and the Shifting Fortunes of Foreign Fighters in Somalia', Combating Terrorism Center [online], 24 September 2013 (https://www.ctc.usma.edu/posts/bilal-al-berjawi-and-the-shifting-fortunes-of-foreign-fighters-in-somalia) (accessed 19 November 2015).
22. Ibid.
23. Bill Roggio, 'US Targets "Senior Leader" for Shabaab in Southern Somalia', Long War Journal [online], 29 December 2014 (http://www.longwarjournal.org/archives/2014/12/us_targets_senior_le.php) (accessed 23 November 2015).
24. Stephen Wright, David Williams and Keith Gladdis, 'SAS Seized Terror Suspect Three Years Ago: Michael Adebolajo Deemed So Significant, Special Forces Were Sent to Grab him in Kenya in 2010', Mail Online, 29 May 2013 (http://www.dailymail.co.uk/news/article-2333005/Michael-Adebolajo-deemed-significant-Special-Forces-sent-grab-Kenya-2010.html) (accessed 23 November 2015).
25. 'America's Deadly Drones Programme', Reprieve [online] (http://www.reprieve.org.uk/case-study/drone-strikes/) (accessed 23 November 2015).
26. Robert Verkaik, 'Britain's Secret Role in America's Drone War: Government Approves UK Defence Company to Supply Technology to the US', Mail Online, 20 April 2013 (http://www.dailymail.co.uk/news/article-2312201/Britains-secret-role-Americas-drone-war-Government-approves-UK-defence-company-supply-technology-U-S.html) (accessed 23 November 2015).
27. Robert Verkaik, 'US Drones Bombing Africa Operated from RAF Bases in the Heart of Lincolnshire Countryside', Mail Online, 9 March 2013 (http://www.dailymail.co.uk/news/article-2290842/US-Drones-bombing-Africa-operated-RAF-bases-heart-Lincolnshire-countryside.html) (accessed 23 November 2015).
28. Chris Woods, Alice K. Ross and Oliver Wright, 'British Terror Suspects Quietly Stripped of Citizenship ... then Killed by Drones', Independent [online], 28 February 2013 (http://www.independent.co.uk/news/uk/crime/british-terror-suspects-quietly-stripped-f-citizenship-then-killed-by-drones-8513858.html) (accessed 23 November 2015).

29. Author's interview with Asim Qureshi, August 2015.

30. Secretary of State for the Home Department *vs* CE, QBD, Administrative Court [2011], EWHC 3159 (Admin), PTA/4/2011 (Transcript: Wordwave International Ltd (A Merrill Communications Company)), hearing dates: 24–31 October, 1–4 November, 21 December 2011.

31. Ibid.

32. Ibid.

33. Ibid.

34. Ibid.

35. Ibid.

36. Ibid.

37. Ibid.

38. Ibid.

39. Robert Verkaik, 'British Man Who "Vanished" after Being Stripped of Citizenship Says He Was Tortured and Forced to Sign a Confession by the CIA', Mail Online, 19 January 2013 (http://www.dailymail.co.uk/news/article-2265185/British-man-vanished-stripped-citizenship-claims-tortured-forced-confess-CIA.html) (accessed 23 November 2015); author's subsequent interview with Mahdi Hashi's father Mohamed, May 2015.

40. Pantucci, 'Bilal al-Berjawi'.

41. 'Oversight of the Intelligence and Security Services', Tom Watson MP [online], 31 October 2013 (http://www.tom-watson.co.uk/2013/10/oversight-of-the-intelligence-and-security-services/) (accessed 23 November 2015).

42. Pantucci, 'Bilal al-Berjawi'.

43. Ibid.

44. Ibid.

45. Ibid.

46. Robert Verkaik, 'Theresa May Strips British Passport from Muslim Care Worker Who Refused to Join MI5 and May Now Be in African Prison', Mail Online, 27 October 2012 (http://www.dailymail.co.uk/news/article-2224155/Theresa-May-strips-British-passport-Muslim-care-worker-refused-join-MI5-African-prison.html) (accessed 23 November 2015).

47. Author's interview with Mahdi Hashi's father Mohamed, May 2015.

48. Ibid.
49. Verkaik, 'British Man Who "Vanished"'.
50. Ibid.
51. Ibid.
52. Ibid.
53. Ibid.
54. Ibid.
55. Ibid.
56. 'Three Supporters of Foreign Terrorist Organization al-Shabaab Charged in Brooklyn Federal Court, Face Life in Prison', Federal Bureau of Investigation [online], 21 December 2012 (https://www.fbi.gov/newyork/press-releases/2012/three-supporters-of-foreign-terrorist-organization-al-shabaab-charged-in-brooklyn-federal-court-face-life-in-prison) (accessed 23 November 2015).
57. Ibid.
58. Ibid.
59. Ibid.
60. Verkaik, 'British Man Who "Vanished"'.
61. Ibid.
62. Ibid.
63. 'Three Members of al-Shabaab Plead Guilty to Conspiring to Provide Material Support to the Terrorist Organization', Federal Bureau of Investigation [online], 12 May 2015 (https://www.fbi.gov/newyork/press-releases/2015/three-members-of-al-shabaab-plead-guilty-to-conspiring-to-provide-material-support-to-the-terrorist-organization) (accessed 23 November 2015).
64. Robert Verkaik, 'Mahdi Hashi: Guilty of Supporting al-Shabaab – but Was His Plea Coerced?', Independent [online], 15 May 2015 (http://www.independent.co.uk/news/world/americas/mahdi-hashi-guilty-of-supporting-al-shabaab-but-was-his-plea-coerced-10254530.html) (accessed 23 November 2015).
65. 'Three Members of al-Shabaab'.

Chapter 6: Road to Syria

1. Aaron Y. Zelin, 'Foreign Fighter Motivations', Washington Institute for Near East Policy, 2 February 2015 (https://www.washingtoninstitute.org/uploads/Documents/other/ZelinStatement20150202.pdf) (accessed 23 November 2015).

2. Thomas Hegghammer, 'Syria's Foreign Fighters', Foreign Policy [online], 9 December 2013 (http://foreignpolicy.com/2013/12/09/syrias-foreign-fighters/) (accessed 23 November 2015).

3. Ibid.

4. Hansard, HC Deb, 19 June 2014, vol. 582, col. 1285.

5. 'Commander Abu Musab's Weekly Address April 1 2013', YouTube, 1 April 2013 (https://www.youtube.com/watch?v=3wE0VWLgQnA&feature=youtu.be) (accessed 23 November 2015).

6. Robert Mendick, Robert Verkaik and Alastair Beach, 'British Jihadists Seen in "War Crime" Video', The Telegraph [online], 20 September 2014 (http://www.telegraph.co.uk/news/uknews/11111071/British-jihadists-seen-in-war-crime-video.html) (accessed 23 November 2015).

7. Richard Kerbaj and Malik al-Abdeh, 'Dead at 21: Britain's Veteran Jihadist', Sunday Times [online], 3 March 2013 (http://www.thesundaytimes.co.uk/sto/news/uk_news/National/jihadists/article1224370.ece) (accessed 23 November 2015).

8. 'David Cameron: Syria's President Assad "Appalling"', BBC News [online], 13 January 2012 (http://www.bbc.co.uk/news/world-middle-east-16556784) (accessed 23 November 2015).

9. 'Britons Fighting with Syria's Jihadi "Band of Brothers"', Channel 4 News [online], 14 June 2013 (http://www.channel4.com/news/syria-war-rebels-jihadi-ibrahim-al-mazwagi) (accessed 23 November 2015).

10. Ibid.

11. Ibid.

12. Author's interview, July 2015.

13. Ibid.

14. Tam Hussein, '"The Inside Story of the British Suicide Bomber of Ramadi,"' Syria Comment [online], 21 July 2015 (http://www.joshualandis.com/blog/the-inside-story-of-the-british-suicide-bomber-of-ramadi-by-tam-hussein/) (accessed 23 November 2015).

15. Ibid.
16. BX *vs* Secretary of State for the Home Department [2010], EWHC 990 (Admin Queen's Bench May 10 2010 England and Wales High Court (Administrative Court) Decisions, Case No: PTA/54/2009, 10 May 2010 (http://www.bailii.org/cgi-bin/markup.cgi?doc=/ew/cases/EWHC/Admin/2010/990.html&query=BX&method=boolean) (accessed 23 November 2015).
17. Tom McTague, 'Terror Suspect "Escaped from Police Surveillance by Jumping into Black Cab"', Mirror [online], 8 January 2013 (http://www.mirror.co.uk/news/uk-news/ibrahim-magag-missing-terror-suspect-1524543) (accessed 23 November 2015).
18. Interview with Omar Emwazi, October 2015.
19. 'Case File: Mohammed Emwazi', CAGE [online] (http://CAGEuk.org/case/mohammed-emwazi) (accessed 23 November 2015).
20. Ibid.
21. 'Commander Abu Musab's Weekly Address'.
22. Ibid.
23. Ibid.
24. 'Britons Fighting'.
25. Ibid.
26. Richard Spillett, Jenny Stanton and Tom Wyke, 'Is This Jihadi John's First Filmed Fanatical Rant? Masked Figure in 2013 Terror Video Praising Notorious ISIS Leader in Syria Could Be West London Killer, Experts Say', Mail Online, 2 March 2015 (http://www.dailymail.co.uk/news/article-2975602/Masked-figure-2013-terror-video-Jihadi-John-experts-say.html) (accessed 23 November 2015).
27. Ibid.
28. Paul Wood, '"Jihadi John": Mohammed Emwazi Was a Cold Loner, Ex-IS Fighter Says', BBC News [online], 1 March 2015 (http://www.bbc.co.uk/news/uk-31686582) (accessed 23 November 2015).
29. Ibid.
30. Ibid.
31. Author's interview with Tam Hussein, August 2015.
32. Author's interview with Emwazi family friend, September 2015.
33. 'Jihadi John: A Quiet Man Who Hated Britain and Was "Always Ready for War"', ITV News [online], 26 February 2015 (http://www.itv.

com/news/2015-02-26/jihadi-john-a-quiet-man-who-hated-brit-ain-and-was-always-ready-for-war/) (accessed 23 November 2015).

34. Ibid.
35. Ibid.
36. Ibid.
37. Ibid.
38. Interview with Asim Qureshi, corroborated by source from Kentish Town Community Centre.
39. Moazzam Begg, 'The Idea that I Endorse ISIS Is Unbelievably Ignorant. CAGE Fought to Save Alan Henning in the Face of the Government's Failings', Independent [online], 9 March 2015 (http://www.independent.co.uk/voices/comment/the-idea-that-i-endorse-isis-is-unbelievably-ignorant-CAGE-fought-to-save-alan-henning-in-the-face-10089091.html) (accessed 23 November 2015).
40. Ibid.
41. 'Treasury Designates Twelve Foreign Terrorist Fighter Facilitators', US Department of the Treasury [online], 24 September 2014 (http://www.treasury.gov/press-center/press-releases/Pages/jl2651.aspx) (accessed 23 November 2015).
42. Ibid.
43. Julie Hirschfeld Davis, 'Treasury Imposes Terrorism Sanctions', New York Times [online], 24 September 2014 (http://www.nytimes.com/2014/09/25/world/middleeast/treasury-imposes-terrorism-sanctions-on-those-linked-to-islamic-state.html?_r=1) (accessed 23 November 2015).
44. Ibid.
45. Ibid.
46. Ibid.
47. Robert Verkaik, 'Photographer Prison Hell at the Mercy of "Pinocchio" the British Torturer: ISIS Defector Says Hostage John Cantlie Was Waterboarded and Given Electric Shocks by Jihadi who Always Lied', Mail Online, 5 October 2014 (http://www.dailymail.co.uk/news/article-2780905/Photographer-prison-hell-mercy-Pinocchio-British-torturer-ISIS-defector-says-hostage-waterboarded-given-electric-shocks-jihadi-lied.html) (accessed 23 November 2015).
48. Javier Espinosa, 'ISIS Captive Could Have Fled Dungeon but Refused to Leave His Friend', The Times [online], 16 March 2015

(http://www.thetimes.co.uk/tto/news/world/middleeast/article4383011.ece) (accessed 23 November 2015).
49. Verkaik, 'Photographer Prison Hell'.
50. Espinosa, 'Isis Captive'.
51. Verkaik, 'Photographer Prison Hell'.
52. 'Treasury Designates'.

Chapter 7: Beheadings That Shocked the World

1. Rukmini Callimachi, 'The Horror before the Beheadings', New York Times [online], 25 October 2014 (http://www.nytimes.com/2014/10/26/world/middleeast/horror-before-the-beheadings-what-isis-hostages-endured-in-syria.html?_r=0) (accessed 24 November 2015).
2. Javier Espinosa, 'Isis Captive Could Have Fled Dungeon but Refused to Leave His Friend', The Times [online], 16 March 2015 (http://www.thetimes.co.uk/tto/news/world/middleeast/article4383011.ece) (accessed 24 November 2015).
3. Javier Espinosa, 'I Survived Jihadi John's Threats to Cut My Throat', Sunday Times [online], 15 March 2015 (http://www.thesundaytimes.co.uk/sto/news/uk_news/National/Terrorism/article1531324.ece) (accessed 24 November 2015).
4. Ibid.
5. Marc Marginedas, 'Con el yihadista John', El Periódico [online], 17 March 2015 (http://www.elperiodico.com/es/noticias/internacional/con-yihadista-john-4023143) (accessed 24 November 2015).
6. Ibid.
7. Ibid.
8. Ibid.
9. Tam Hussein, 'The Inside Story of the British Suicide Bomber of Ramadi', Syria Comment [online], 21 July 2015 (http://www.joshualandis.com/blog/the-inside-story-of-the-british-suicide-bomber-of-ramadi-by-tam-hussein/) (accessed 24 November 2015).
10. Ibid.
11. Marginedas, 'Con el yihadista John'.

12. Ibid.
13. Ibid.
14. Ibid.
15. Ibid.
16. Espinosa, 'I Survived'.
17. Ibid.
18. Ibid.
19. Nicholas Schmidle, 'Inside the Failed Raid to Save Foley and Sotloff', New Yorker [online], 5 September 2014, http://www.newyorker.com/news/news-desk/inside-failed-raid-free-foley-sotloff (accessed 24 November 2015).
20. James Harkin, *The Hunting Season: The Execution of James Foley, Islamic State, and the Real Story of the Kidnapping Campaign That Started a War* (London: Little, Brown, 2015).
21. Lizzie Dearden, 'Iraq Crisis: Islamic State's Message to America – 'We Will Drown You All in Blood', Independent [online], 19 August 2014 (http://www.independent.co.uk/news/world/middle-east/iraq-crisis-islamic-states-message-to-america-we-will-drown-you-all-in-blood-9677701.html) (accessed 24 November 2015).
22. 'Islamic State Beheads American Journalist James Foley', LeakSource [online], 19 August 2014 (http://leaksource.info/2014/08/19/graphic-video-islamic-state-beheads-american-journalist-james-foley/) (accessed 24 November 2015).
23. Clare Morgana Gillis, 'Our Jim: A Fellow Journalist Remembers James Foley', Vice News [online], 26 August 2014 (https://news.vice.com/article/our-jim-a-fellow-journalist-remembers-james-foley) (accessed 24 November 2015).
24. Brendan Conway, 'Man Held Captive in Libya Thanks Marquette University', WISN [online], 7 December 2011 (http://www.wisn.com/Man-Held-Captive-In-Libya-Thanks-Marquette-University/8043876) (accessed 24 November 2015).
25. Callimachi, 'The Horror'.
26. Heather Saul, 'James Foley Beheading Sparks International Manhunt for "John" the British Jihadist', Independent [online], 21 August 2014 (http://www.independent.co.uk/news/uk/james-foley-beheading-sparks-international-manhunt-for-john-the-british-jihadist-9682506.html) (accessed 24 November 2015).

27. Ibid.

28. Ibid.

29. Warren Strobel and John Irish, 'In Case of Slain Journalist, Negotiations, Silence, Then a Chilling Warning', Reuters [online], 22 August 2014 (http://uk.reuters.com/article/2014/08/22/uk-syria-crisis-beheading-foley-idUKKBN0GL02J20140822) (accessed 24 November 2015).

30. Lucy Williamson, 'Islamic State Ex-Hostage Henin: Asking for Pity Is Stupid', BBC News [online], 9 March 2015 (http://www.bbc.co.uk/news/world-europe-31806085) (accessed 24 November 2015).

31. Ibid.

32. Ibid.

33. 'James Foley Beheading Suspect Probably British, David Cameron Says', BBC News [online], 20 August 2014 (http://www.bbc.co.uk/news/uk-28873051) (accessed 24 November 2015).

34. Ibid.

35. Andrew Osborn, 'How a Young Conscript Became a Russian Saint', Independent [online], 24 November 2004 (http://www.independent.co.uk/news/world/europe/how-a-young-conscript-became-a-russian-saint-534373.html) (accessed 24 November 2015).

36. Pete Lentini and Muhammad Bakashmar, 'Jihadist Beheading: A Convergence of Technology, Theology, and Teleology?', *Studies in Conflict & Terrorism*, 30, 2007, pp. 303–25.

37. Timothy R. Furnish, 'Beheading in the Name of Islam', *Middle East Quarterly*, Spring 2005, pp. 51–7.

38. Adam Taylor, 'From Daniel Pearl to James Foley: The Modern Tactic of Islamist Beheadings', Washington Post [online], 20 August 2014 (https://www.washingtonpost.com/news/worldviews/wp/2014/08/20/from-daniel-pearl-to-james-foley-the-modern-tactic-of-islamist-beheadings/) (accessed 27 August 2015).

39. Jonathan Hayes, 'Second Opinion', New York [online], 31 May 2004 (http://nymag.com/nymetro/news/columns/witness/9183/) (accessed 24 November 2015).

40. Javier Espinosa, "We Were Taunted with Song about Hotel Osama', The Times [online], 17 March 2015 (http://www.thetimes.co.uk/tto/

news/world/middleeast/article4384038.ece) (accessed 24 November 2015).

41. 'IS Behead Steven Joel Sotloff, Threatens to Execute Briton David Cawthorne Haines', Site [online], 2 September 2014 (https://news.siteintelgroup.com/Jihadist-News/is-behead-steven-joel-sotloff-threatens-to-execute-briton-david-cawthorne-haines.html) (accessed 24 November 2015).

42. Ibid.

43. Ibid.

44. Heather Saul, 'Steven Sotloff's Mother Appeals to ISIS Leader Abu Bakr al-Baghdadi to Free Her Son in Video'. Independent [online], 28 August 2014 (http://www.independent.co.uk/news/world/middle-east/steven-sotloffs-mother-appeals-to-isis-leader-abu-bakr-al-baghdadi-to-free-her-son-in-video-9696041.html) (accessed 24 November 2015).

45. Ibid.

46. Ibid.

47. 'Profile of British Hostage David Haines', BBC News, 14 September 2014 (http://www.bbc.co.uk/news/uk-29086517) (accessed 24 November 2015).

48. Callimachi, 'The Horror'.

49. 'Islamic State Beheads British Aid Worker David Haines', LeakSource [online], 13 September 2014 (http://leaksource.info/2014/09/13/graphic-video-islamic-state-beheads-british-aid-worker-david-haines/) (accessed 24 November 2015).

50. 'The Emwazi Tapes: "9-11 Was Wrong"', CAGE [online], 3 March 2015 (http://www.CAGEuk.org/press-release/emwazi-tapes-9-11-was-wrong) (accessed 24 November 2015).

51. Moazzam Begg, 'The Idea that I Endorse ISIS Is Unbelievably Ignorant. CAGE Fought to Save Alan Henning in the Face of the Government's Failings', Independent [online], 9 March 2015 (http://www.independent.co.uk/voices/comment/the-idea-that-i-endorse-isis-is-unbelievably-ignorant-CAGE-fought-to-save-alan-henning-in-the-face-10089091.html) (accessed 24 November 2015).

52. David Williams, '"Show My Husband Mercy ... We Need Him Back Home": Taxi Driver Alan Henning's Wife Makes Tearful Plea

to his Islamic State Captors', Mail Online, 30 September 2014 (http://www.dailymail.co.uk/news/article-2775212/We-need-home-Wife-British-hostage-Alan-Henning-urges-ISIS-captors-release-moving-video.html) (accessed 24 November 2015).

53. 'Islamic State Beheads Alan Henning in Video', Site [online], 3 October 2014 (https://ent.siteintelgroup.com/Statements/islamic-state-beheads-alan-henning-in-video-public-and-edited.html) (accessed 24 November 2015).

54. Ibid.

55. 'Murder of Alan Henning: Government Response', Prime Minister's Office, Gov.uk, 4 October 2014 (https://www.gov.uk/government/news/murder-of-alan-henning-by-isil-government-response) (accessed 24 November 2015).

56. 'IS Beheads Peter Kassig, Challenges US to Send Ground Troops', Insite blog, 16 November 2014 (http://news.siteintelgroup.com/blog/index.php/categories/jihad/entry/313-is-beheads-peter-kassig,-challenges-u-s-to-send-ground-troops) (accessed 24 November 2015).

57. Ibid.

58. Ibid.

59. Heather Saul, 'Isis Japanese Hostages: Who Are Kenji Goto and Haruna Yukawa?', Independent [online], 20 January 2015 (http://www.independent.co.uk/news/world/middle-east/isis-japanese-hostages-who-are-kenji-goto-and-haruna-yukawa-9989946.html) (accessed 24 November 2015).

60. Ibid.

61. Ibid.

62. 'IS Threatens in Video to Behead Two Japanese Citizens Unless Paid $200m Ransom', Site [online], 20 January 2015 (https://news.siteintelgroup.com/Jihadist-News/is-threatens-in-video-to-behead-two-japanese-citizens-unless-paid-200m-ransom.html) (accessed 19 June 2015).

63. 'Japanese Hostage Kenji Goto Jogo Gives Final Message, Says He and the Captive Jordanian Pilot Will Be Killed in 24 Hours', Site [online], 27 January 2015 (https://news.siteintelgroup.com/Jihadist-News/japanese-hostage-kenji-goto-jogo-gives-final-message-says-he-and-the-captive-jordanan-pilot-will-be-killed-in-24-hours.html) (accessed 24 November 2015).

64. Adam Taylor, 'The Horrific Failure of Jordan's "Prisoner Swap" with the Islamic State', Washington Post [online], 3 February 2015 (https://www.washingtonpost.com/news/worldviews/wp/2015/02/03/the-horrific-failure-of-jordans-prisoner-swap-with-the-islamic-state/) (accessed 24 November 2015).

65. 'Analysis: The Islamic State Beheads Kenji Goto Jogo', Site [online], 1 February 2015 (https://news.siteintelgroup.com/blog/index.php?view=entry&id=353) (accessed 24 November 2015).

66. Ibid.

67. Levi Winchester, 'New Image Shows Jihadi John "Was at the Islamic State Execution of Jordanian Pilot"', Express [online], 27 February 2015 (http://www.express.co.uk/news/world/560862/Jihadi-John-new-image-execution-Jordanian-pilot) (accessed 24 November 2015).

Chapter 8: The Unmasking of Jihadi John

1. James Murray, 'Exclusive: Jihadi John Exposed by Web Error – Killer Downloaded Software Using Student ID', Express [online], 1 March 2015 (http://www.express.co.uk/news/uk/561135/Jihadi-John-Mohammed-Emwazi-identified-web-error-student-ID-Westminster-university) (accessed 24 November 2015).

2. Author's interview with BBC source, August 2015.

3. Ibid.

4. Souad Mekhennet and Adam Goldman, '"Jihadi John": Islamic State Killer is Identified as Londoner Mohammed Emwazi', Washington Post [online], 26 February 2015 (https://www.washingtonpost.com/world/national-security/jihadi-john-the-islamic-state-killer-behind-the-mask-is-a-young-londoner/2015/02/25/d6dbab16-bc43-11e4-bdfa-b8e8f594e6ee_story.html) (accessed 24 November 2015).

5. Adam Goldman, 'How the Post Identified "Jihadi John"', Washington Post [online], 26 February 2015 (http://www.washingtonpost.com/posttv/world/how-the-post-identified-jihadi-john/2015/02/26/ca8d4328-bded-11e4-9dfb-03366e719af8_video.html) (accessed 24 November 2015).

6. Mekhennet and Goldman, '"Jihadi John"'.

7. Author's interview with Asim Qureshi, 2015.
8. Heather Saul, '"Jihadi John": Mohammed Emwazi Was "Extremely Kind, Gentle, Beautiful Young Man," Says CAGE Director', Independent [online], 26 February 2015 (http://www.independent.co.uk/news/uk/home-news/jihadi-john-mohammed-emwazi-was-an-extremely-kind-gentle-beautiful-young-man-says-CAGE-director-10073338.html) (accessed 24 November 2015).
9. Heather Saul, '"Jihadi John": Mohammed Emwazi's Father "Condemned Son as Dog" and Hoped "He Would Be Killed" after He Fled to Syria', Independent [online], 4 March 2015 (http://www.independent.co.uk/news/world/middle-east/jihadi-john-mohammed-emwazis-father-condemned-son-as-dog-and-hoped-he-would-be-killed-after-he-fled-10082940.html) (accessed 24 November 2015).
10. William Turvill, 'Mother of "Jihadi John" Sues Telegraph and Times over Claims She Knew but Did Not Report Terrorist's Identity', Press Gazette [online], 10 September 2015 (http://www.pressgazette.co.uk/mother-jihadi-john-sues-telegraph-and-times-over-claims-she-knew-did-not-report-terrorists-identity) (accessed 24 November 2015).
11. Ibid.
12. Jerome Starkey, 'Terrorist Expelled from Tanzania after Binge: Killer Was Drunk and Disorderly', *The Times*, 7 March 2015.
13. Ed Thomas, 'Mohammed Emwazi "Deported for Being Drunk and Abusive"', BBC News [online], 8 March 2015, (http://www.bbc.co.uk/news/uk-31785166) (accessed 24 November 2015).
14. Ibid.
15. 'Mohammed Emwazi Went to Tanzania "to Commit Terrorism"', BBC News [online], 9 March 2015 (http://www.bbc.co.uk/news/uk-31799541) (accessed 24 November 2015).
16. 'Mohammed Emwazi: Tanzanian Officer Recalls Airport Arrest', BBC News [online], 8 March 2015 (http://www.bbc.co.uk/news/uk-31785820) (accessed 24 November 2015).
17. Author's interview with Asim Qureshi, 2015.
18. Author's interview with Richard Barrett, September 2015.
19. 'RAF/FBI Using Spy Plane over Britain in Search for "Jihadi John"

Associates', LeakSource [online], 23 September 2014 (http://leak-source.info/2014/09/23/raf-fbi-using-spy-plane-over-britain-in-search-for-jihadi-john-associates/) (accessed 24 November 2015).

20. Ben Tufft, 'Mohammed Emwazi: "Jihadi John" Apologises for Problems He Has Caused Family – but Not for Executing Isis Hostages', Independent [online], 8 March 2015 (http://www.independent.co.uk/news/uk/home-news/mohammed-emwazi-jihadi-john-apologises-for-problems-he-caused-his-family-but-not-for-executing-10093769.html) (accessed 24 November 2015).

21. Jürgen Todenhöfer, *Inside IS: 10 Tage im „Islamischen Staat"* (Munich: C. Bertelsmann, 2015).

22. Sharon Feinstein, '"I Came Face-to-Face with Jihadi John": ISIS Expert Rattles Killer in Restaurant Confrontation', Mirror [online], 12 July 2015 (http://www.mirror.co.uk/news/world-news/i-came-face-to-face-jihadi-john-6050331) (accessed 24 November 2015).

23. Omar Wahid, 'Jihadi John – "I Will Go Back to Britain . . . and Will Carry On Cutting Heads Off": In a Chilling New Video, Man Said to Be Hooded Butcher Vows to Return . . . and Murder All Unbelievers', Mail Online, 22 August 2015 (http://www.dailymail.co.uk/news/article-3207366/Jihadi-John-Britain-carry-cutting-heads-chilling-new-video-man-said-hooded-butcher-beheaded-two-British-hostages-vows-come-home-murder-unbelievers.html) (accessed 24 November 2015).

24. Hansard, HC Deb, 7 September 2015, vol. 599, cols 25–6.

25. Brendan Carlin and Robert Verkaik, 'PM: I'll Hunt Jihadi John . . . Even to Syria. Cameron Prepared to Send In SAS – and Won't Seek Approval of MPs', Mail Online, 27 September 2014 (http://www.dailymail.co.uk/news/article-2772171/PM-I-ll-hunt-Jihadi-John-Syria-Cameron-prepared-send-SAS-won-t-seek-approval-MPs.html) (accessed 24 November 2015).

Chapter 9: Who Are the Terrorists?

1. Kim Sengupta, 'MI5 Chief Andrew Parker: Edward Snowden's GCHQ Leaks Gave Terrorists "the Gift to Evade us and Strike at Will"',

Independent [online], 8 October 2013 (http://www.independent.co.uk/news/uk/politics/mi5-chief-andrew-parker-edward-snowdens-gchq-leaks-gave-terrorists-the-gift-to-evade-us-and-strike-8867399.html) (accessed 24 November 2015).

2. Author's interview with Charles Farr, London, 30 November 2015.
3. Steven Stalinsky and R. Sosnow, 'From al-Qaeda to the Islamic State (ISIS), Jihadi Groups Engage in Cyber Jihad: Beginning with 1980s Promotion of Use of "Electronic Technologies" up to Today's Embrace of Social Media to Attract a New Jihadi Generation', MEMRI (http://cjlab.memri.org/wp-content/uploads/2014/12/cyber-jihad-2.pdf) (accessed 25 November 2015).
4. Ibid.
5. 'Al-Qaeda Khorasan Cell in Syria Attack "Was Imminent"', BBC News [online], 23 September 2014 (http://www.bbc.co.uk/news/world-middle-east-29330395) (accessed 25 November 2015).
6. Author's interview with SO15 officer, November 2015.
7. 'Terror Arrests Reach Record Level, Says Metropolitan Police', BBC News [online], 14 May 2015 (http://www.bbc.co.uk/news/uk-32735484) (accessed 17 May 2015).
8. 'In the Matter of X (Children) and in the Matter of Y (Children) (No 2)', [2015] EWHC 2358 (Fam), High Court, 4 August 2015.
9. Elise Labott, 'Clinton Makes Unannounced Visit to Libya', CNN [online], 19 October 2011 (http://edition.cnn.com/2011/10/18/world/africa/libya-clinton/) (accessed 25 November 2015).
10. Robert Verkaik, 'MI5 Stops British Extremists Joining Syria War after Concerns They Will Return Home with Deadly Skills', Mail Online, 1 September 2012 (http://www.dailymail.co.uk/news/article-2196933/MI5-stops-British-extremists-joining-Syria-concerns-return-home-deadly-skills.html) (accessed 25 November 2015).
11. Ibid.
12. 'Guide to the Syrian Rebels', BBC News [online], 13 December 2013 (http://www.bbc.co.uk/news/world-middle-east-24403003) (accessed 25 November 2015).
13. Mehdi Hasan, 'What the Jihadists Who Bought "Islam for Dummies" on Amazon Tell Us about Radicalisation', Huffington Post [online], 21 August 2014 (http://www.huffingtonpost.co.uk/mehdi-hasan/

jihadist-radicalisation-islam-for-dummies_b_5697160.html) (accessed 25 November 2015).

14. Author's interview with Asim Qureshi, 2015.

15. Author's interview with north London community leader, 2015.

16. Author's interview with Richard Barrett, 2014/2015.

17. Raffaello Pantucci, 'Thick as Thieves: European Criminals to Take to Syria's Battlefield', RUSI [online], 31 March 2014 (https://rusi. org/commentary/thick-thieves-european-criminals-take-syria%E2%80%99s-battlefield) (accessed 25 November 2015).

18. 'Joint Terrorism Analysis Centre', Security Service MI5 [online] (https:// www.mi5.gov.uk/home/about-us/who-we-are/staff-and-management/joint-terrorism-analysis-centre.html) (accessed 25 November 2015).

19. 'The UK's Threat Level System', Security Service MI5 [online] (https://www.mi5.gov.uk/home/about-us/what-we-do/the-threats/terrorism/threat-levels/the-uks-threat-level-system.html) (accessed 25 November 2015).

20. Ben Brumfield, 'Former MI6 Chief John Sawyers: Terror Has Become Tougher to Stop', CNN [online], 13 September 2015 (http://edition.cnn.com/2015/09/13/us/terrorism-harder-to-stop-mi6-john-sawers/) (accessed 25 November 2015).

21. Ibid.

22. Faisal Hanif and Sean O'Neill, 'Signs of the Hostility That Sets Shia against Sunni , The Times, 14 August 2015.

Chapter 10: How to Beat the Terrorists

1. Author's interview with Rizwaan Sabir, July 2015.

2. Ibid.

3. Ibid.

4. Ibid.

5. Ibid.

6. Chris Osuh, 'Mersey Man Prosecuted for Sending Trainers to His Terrorist Brother', Liverpool Echo [online], 8 May 2015 (http://www.liverpoolecho.co.uk/news/liverpool-news/mersey-man-prosecuted-sending-trainers-9220647) (accessed 25 November 2015).

7. 'Terrorism arrests at record levels, figures show', BBC News [online], 10 December 2015 (http://www.bbc.co.uk/news/uk-35059860) (accessed 21 December 2015).

8. Steven Swinford, Martin Evans and Matthew Holehouse, 'Britons Who Go to Syria "Are Guilty until Proved Innocent", says Boris Johnson', The Telegraph [online], 24 August 2014 (http://www.telegraph.co.uk/news/uknews/terrorism-in-the-uk/11054372/Britons-who-go-to-Syria-are-guilty-until-proved-innocent-says-Boris-Johnson.html) (accessed 25 November 2015).

9. Richard Wheatstone, '"Self-Radicalised" Soldier Made Potentially Lethal Bomb Packed with Shrapnel while Glorifying EDL and Hitler', Manchester Evening News [online], 28 November 2014 (http://www.manchestereveningnews.co.uk/news/greater-manchester-news/self-radicalised-soldier-made-potentially-lethal-8191412) (accessed 25 November 2015).

10. Anthony Bond, 'ISIS: Young Mum Jailed after Trying to Send Cash to Jihadi Husband Fighting in Syria', Mirror [online], 13 November 2014 (http://www.mirror.co.uk/news/uk-news/isis-young-mum-jailed-after-4623042) (accessed 25 November 2015).

11. Jonathan Leader Maynard, 'The Government Doesn't Understand Terrorism – and It's Making Things Worse', Independent [online], 5 July 2015 (http://www.independent.co.uk/voices/comment/the-government-doesnt-understand-terrorism-and-its-making-things-worse-10367519.html) (accessed 25 November 2015).

12. Ibid.

13. Ibid.

14. Jamal Osman, 'I am a British Citizen – Not a Second-Class Citizen', The Guardian [online], 26 May 2014 (http://www.theguardian.com/commentisfree/2014/may/26/british-citizen-passport-control) (accessed 25 November 2015).

15. 'Working for Intelligence Services! #SuhoorReminders #Ramadan Reminders', YouTube, 3 July 2014 (https://www.youtube.com/watch?v=0tmHys7gPfo) (accessed 25 November 2015).

16. 'Charities Withdraw Support for CAGE after Group's Comments on "Jihadi John"', ITV News [online], 27 February 2015 (http://www.itv.com/news/update/2015-02-27/claim-mi5-is-responsible-for-jihadi-john-reprehensible/) (accessed 19 May 2015).

17. Aisha Gani, 'CAGE "Seeking Legal Advice" on Whether It Was Defamed by David Cameron', The Guardian [online], 22 July 2015 (http://www.theguardian.com/politics/2015/jul/22/CAGE-seeks-legal-advice-on-whether-it-was-defamed-by-david-cameron) (accessed 25 November 2015).

18. Alan Travis, 'MI5 Report Challenges Views on Terrorism in Britain', The Guardian [online], 20 August 2008 (http://www.theguardian.com/uk/2008/aug/20/uksecurity.terrorism1) (accessed 25 November 2015).

19. Ben Brumfield, 'Former MI6 Chief John Sawyers: Terror Has Become Tougher to Stop', CNN [online], 13 September 2015 (http://edition.cnn.com/2015/09/13/us/terrorism-harder-to-stop-mi6-john-sawers/) (accessed 25 November 2015).

20. Investigatory Powers Tribunal, (http://www.ipt-uk.com/) (accessed 12 September 2015).

21. 'Intelligence Services Commissioner', Security Service MI5 [online], (https://www.mi5.gov.uk/home/about-us/how-we-operate/how-mi5-is-governed/oversight/judicial-oversight/intelligence-services-commissioner.html) (accessed 25 November 2015).

INDEX

INDEX